Growing Up Literate

Heinemann Educational Books, Inc.
361 Hanover Street   Portsmouth, NH 03801
Offices and agents throughout the world

The following have generously given permission to use quotations from published works:

"Dream Deferred." Copyright 1951 by Langston Hughes. Reprinted from *The Panther and the Lash* by Langston Hughes by permission of Alfred A. Knopf, Inc.

Figure 2–47: Reprinted with permission of the publisher from AMIGOS Workbook (Level 7, Series r: Macmillan Reading Program)—1980 edition by Carl B. Smith and Ronald Wardhaugh, Senior Authors. Copyright © 1980 Macmillan Publishing Company.

LIBRARY OF CONGRESS
Library of Congress Cataloging-in-Publication Data

Taylor, Denny, 1947–
    Growing up literate : learning from inner-city families / Denny Taylor, Catherine Dorsey-Gaines.
        p.   cm.
    Bibliography: p.
    ISBN 0-435-08457-7
    1. City children—United States—Education—Language arts—Case studies.   2. Afro-American families—Case studies.   3. Urban poor—United States—Social conditions—Case studies.   4. Literacy—United States—Case studies.   I. Dorsey-Gaines, Catherine.
II. Title.
LC5131.T39 1988
370.19'346'0973—dc19   87-35270
                                                        CIP

Designed by Maria Szmauz.

Illustrations prepared by Marie McAdam.

Printed in the United States of America.

10   9   8   7   6   5   4   3

Growing Up Literate

Learning from Inner-City Families

Denny Taylor

Catherine Dorsey-Gaines

With a Foreword by
Rudine Sims Bishop

Heinemann
Portsmouth, New Hampshire

To the families

Their optimism about the future and their ability to imagine what life would be like if conditions were better seemed to keep them going, struggling and surviving, albeit precariously, against the odds and without the support of the society to which they belong.

Contents

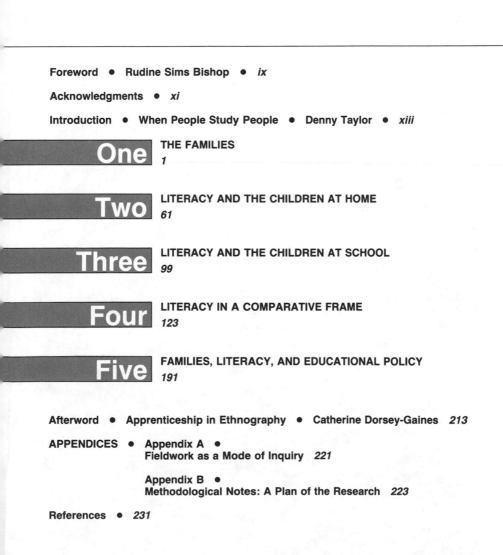

Foreword

Rudine Sims Bishop

Growing Up Literate is an important and powerful work; educators and social policymakers will find it both enlightening and disturbing. It looks at literacy and literacy learning in relation to the socio-political climate in which they occur. That climate, in the case of the Black urban poor families portrayed in this book, seems so overwhelmingly negative as to render mere survival a full-time occupation. That the six-year-olds in these families were successfully becoming literate is a testament to the strength of the families and the power of the printed word in this society.

Denny Taylor and Cathé Dorsey-Gaines were not detached, "objective" researchers, studying a number of "subjects." They were ethnographers, participating in as well as observing the lives of the families. Consequently, the nearly devastating portrait of the economic poverty of the families is balanced with a sense of their strengths and optimism, as well as the lack of significant help from the agencies and institutions that are supposed to serve their needs. Taylor and Dorsey-Gaines, unlike many researchers and policymakers, do not end up blaming poor people for their own problems. They show clearly that a person who is poor must certainly be "bright" as well as determined in order to survive in the face of potentially overpowering odds.

Though others have drawn the same conclusion, Taylor and Dorsey-Gaines' statement that sex, race, economic status, and setting cannot be used as significant correlates of literacy still seems revolutionary, since many educational researchers almost automatically use those variables in studies of school achievement. Furthermore, school policymakers, administrators, and teachers often tend to base their expectations of whole classrooms and schools full of children on those very criteria. If Taylor and Dorsey-Gaines are correct, then the onus is on educators to look elsewhere for the causes for our failures.

There are lessons to be learned from these families about schools and schooling and how they can be so disconnected from and even potentially destructive of the lives of the children they are supposed to be educating. The description of a child's day at school is heartbreaking. We see, among other things, how the reduction of literacy to a set of empty "skills" simply renders it senseless. We are reminded forcefully that "a mind *is* a terrible thing to waste."

This book also reinforces the idea that ours is indeed a literate society, and that even many of the poorest among us (next to the street dwellers, and my guess is that literacy plays important roles in their lives, too) are literate. It calls into question the definition of functional literacy and leaves us to wonder about the statistics that cite so many millions of "functional illiterates," many of whom are purportedly the urban poor. It may be that we just have not taken the time and effort to learn how and why literacy functions in the lives of poor Black families living in large cities. Taylor and Dorsey-Gaines have taken the time, made the effort, and created for us an honest, yet hopeful, portrait of a few such families.

This book could make a difference. James Baldwin, in an interview in the *New York Times Book Review* (September 23, 1979), stated that:

The bottom line is this: You write in order to change the world, knowing perfectly well that you probably can't.... In some way, your aspirations and concern for a single man in fact do begin to change the world. The world changes according to the way people see it, and if you alter, even by a millimeter, the way a person or people look at reality, then you can change it.

I hope the readers of *Growing Up Literate* will include educators at all levels as well as people who make and carry out social policy. The obvious concern that Denny Taylor and Cathé Dorsey-Gaines have for the Shay Avenue families, as manifested in this book, should most certainly change the way readers view the reality of growing up poor and Black in an urban environment and still growing up literate. It's a start.

Acknowledgments

We would like to thank the many people whose support and encouragement have helped us both individually and collectively during the research and writing of *Growing Up Literate*. We are especially grateful to Rudine Sims Bishop, David Bloome, Judith Green, Shirley Brice Heath, Jerome Harste, Angela Jaggar, Trika Smith-Burke, Elizabeth Sulzby, and William Teale, all of whom helped us in significant ways during the six years of the study.

Our special thanks go to Charles Harrington, the Director of the Institute of Urban and Minority Education at Teachers College, Columbia University; to Dorothy Strickland, the Institute's Associate Director for Research and Academic Programs; and to Paula Russell, who is the Institute's Administrative Associate.

At Heinemann Educational Books, we are especially grateful to Philippa Stratton, Editor-in-Chief, and to Donna Bouvier, Manager of Editing and Production, for their constant encouragement and assistance.

We also want to thank the International Reading Association for their recognition of the research project and for the support we received through the Elva Knight Research Fund. The money that we received from the International Reading Association enabled us to provide the families with stipends for their participation in the research.

Finally, we both want to thank our families—our parents, Liz and Harry Coles and Burnell and Joseph Dorsey; our husbands, David and Jim; and our children, Louise, Ben, Jimmy, and Jeffrey. We have all grown together over the years, and our lives are blessed by the family stories that we share.

Introduction
When People Study People

Denny Taylor

These resonances between the personal and the professional are the source of both insight and error. You avoid mistakes and distortions not so much by trying to build a wall between the observer and the observed as by observing the observer—observing yourself—as well, and bringing the personal issues into consciousness. You can do some of that at the time of the work and more in retrospect. You dream, you imagine, you superimpose and compare images, you allow yourself to feel and then try to put what you feel into words. Then you look at the record to understand the way in which observation and interpretation have been affected by personal factors. . . .

Mary Catherine Bateson

There is always much more to be said than can be written on the page. There is the inevitable mass of ethnographic data that must be taken, piece by piece, and fitted together in some sensible fashion so that others can study the fieldwork without reading all the fieldnotes, listening to the audiotapes, and examining the photographs and artifacts. That job is done. The text is written, except for this introduction. It is easy to write about the beginning of the study and of the ways in which we have presented it in the text, but it is not so easy to write about the human element of the research. Cathé and I work well together. We enjoy each other's company, and our families are friends. Friendship has made the research possible. It has enabled us to be professionally demanding, to push each other, to explore ideas that make us uncomfortable. Because we are friends we can talk of our own frustrations and self-doubts, and of the despair that we sometimes experienced when we realized how little we could do to help the families that we visited. Similarly, because we are friends we can enjoy the warmth and humor that is a part of this research and we can laugh together at some of the things that have happened to us during the course of the study.

Cathé speaks of sharing philosophies, of learning from one another, and of teaching each other to see the world a little differently. In a working paper that we wrote during the first year of the study (Taylor and Dorsey-Gaines 1982) there was a section entitled "The Place: Learning to Recognize Our Own Ethnocentrism and Mental 'Baggage.'" The section began:

In his book *School Power*, Comer (1980) quotes a mayor who talks of his visits after a long absence to the poor areas of the town in which he was campaigning. The mayor states:

> I came out from one of these homes on Oak Street, and I sat on the curb and I was as sick as a puppy. Why? The smell of this building; it had no electricity, it had no gas, it had kerosene lamps. Light had never seen the corridors in generations. The smells . . . It was just awful and I got sick. (p. 44)

This is an apt description of the way an outsider might respond to an initial visit to the neighborhood in which the present study takes place, for no previous experience is sufficient preparation for the sight and smells of inner-city slums.

In this section on the environment we will share with you some of our own initial reactions to the place in which we are working. And we will try to make visible our increasing awareness of our own ethnocentricism as the collection of ethnographic data heightened our awareness of the suppositional depiction of inner-city environments and the people who are poor and live in them.

Coming into the neighborhood of Shay Avenue for the first time brought immediate questions into our minds that reverberated back and forth in a disquieting fashion. We found ourselves asking, "Why aren't these people in their homes? Why are they staring?" "The temperature is twenty degrees Fahrenheit—how can that old man just sit on the steps in this cold weather?"

It seemed an ugly environment with its old houses and apartment buildings. The burned-out, razed, and decaying buildings all added up to such desolate surroundings, and the empty spaces between the structures only seemed to magnify the desolation. The garbage, broken glass, graffiti, boarded-up windows, and peeling paint all helped to set our minds in a negative frame. There were no trees. Nothing seemed to be growing.

Like other outsiders, we came upon the scene with images from the mass media in our minds. We were apprehensive and did not know what to expect. Even though both of us had experienced similar environments, and one of us had lived in a town in which there was a comparable neighborhood, it was still difficult to penetrate the hidden mental baggage of our own ethnocentric assumptions.

But as time passed, we began to realize that *the place is just the setting, and it is within this setting of societal and economic neglect that the families actively create their own contexts of everyday life* (see Billingsley 1968). We made frequent visits in which some strangers became friends, and the neighborhood became warm and alive. The old houses that we had seen during our initial visits were not just ugly buildings but old Victorian-style homes, and among the many dilapidated and boarded-up houses we began to see a few neat, freshly painted one- and two-family homes. And, as the months went by, out of the empty spaces of the razed buildings came signs of rebirth. People stopped to talk to us about their patches of garden, which they had cleared from the rubble, and in the summer heads of cabbage, stalks of collard greens, green and red peppers, and tomato vines all became a part of the inner-city scene. . . .

More and more we became aware of the ways in which societal images impinged upon what we saw. Each visit heightened our awareness of further assumptions that we had initially made. We were surprised by the number of young men that we saw coming in and out of houses, going places and staying home. We are told in the social science literature that the Black male is absent from the family, and yet we find that men are ever present. We see them in the street talking to their friends and watching the children who play on the sidewalk and spill out onto the road. Many meet their sons and daughters or sisters and brothers from school. At a nearby day-care center we have watched how these men help the children with their coats before taking their hands and walking home with them in the late afternoon. (pp. 5–7)

It is almost four years since this account was written. This book itself gives some indication of how far we have come since then, but we still have to deal on a daily basis with our own ethnocentrism and mental baggage. Reflection and introspection are continuous processes that have taken place throughout the course of the study. Georges and Jones (1980) state, "Field-workers channel their efforts to achieve goals that demand amassing of information about the behavior of other human beings. Therefore, the frequency and intensity of reflection and introspection tend to be greater during periods of fieldwork than is the case at other times" (p. 109). This has certainly been our experience. For Cathé it has been the sharing of familiar places that has made them strange. Ethnographic fieldwork provided her with opportunities to look anew at inner-city families, to look closely at their lives, and to see them a little differently than she did in her daily life. For me it has been more a matter of teaching myself to see what I had learned not to see, but it is only in the last few weeks that I came to realize that it was not just a lack of experience that dimmed my eyes. In 1986, Tom Gralish photographed the homeless of Philadelphia; some of the photographs were published in the *Philadelphia Inquirer*. One of the photographs, of a man sheltering himself in a cardboard box, was republished in *The New York Times*. The caption under the picture read, "Now you see him," and the text began, "Most people don't. To many people Walter is invisible. They've trained themselves not to see him. They look the other way when Walter and other street people come into view." In retrospect I think this has been my experience. My working-class upbringing was rarely touched by poverty. There was caring and compassion, but I was shielded from the experiences of my parents, who had both grown up in Welsh coal-mining villages during the Depression. In adult life my family, research, and writing left little time for "social issues." It is easy to fill up time with important events, a child learning to walk, a deadline for a manuscript.

Cathé, through her insistence on the importance of a previous study of mine, made me look at lives that I had never thought to see. She would pass me in the corridor at Kean College and tell me that she knew of some families that she wanted me to meet. She had read my dissertation about white middle-class families in which there were children successfully learning to read and write, and she wanted me to do another ethnographic study, this time of inner-city families with children who were similarly successful in learning to read and write. Teaching new courses and taking care of my family left little time for anything else and, although I listened to Cathé when she talked about the life of one young woman who was living in an abandoned apartment house with her two young children, I was not eager to begin another long-term project. But as the weeks went by, Cathé and I continued to talk, imagining and speculating. Then Cathé brought Queenie, one of the children, to the college and left her in my office. I think that was the first day of the study for me. In some notes of that time (Taylor 1982a), of Cathé and the beginning of the research, I wrote:

Cathé's office is full of people. Students stand around waiting to talk with her, the cleaning woman stops for a chat, and professors call in or wave as they pass by. Cathé has time for everyone. The telephone rings and she carries on a three-way conversation as she tells the person in her office about the person on the phone. Sometimes, when I've been in her office she has given the telephone voice to me while she talks to a student who is on her way to her next class. It is chaotic and friendly. Cathé laughs and no one is left out. Occasionally she closes her door to talk with a student who has a problem, and the others wait outside knowing that she won't hurry. Many of her students are first-generation college, and they are working their way and doing it on their own. Cathé talks with them about student teaching and advises them about their programs; she evaluates their transcripts and discusses tuition. Students tell her that their families do not understand why they want to teach. They talk about their friends who are making money, and they say their families ask them why they are not studying some technological trade. Outside the closed door students talk with each other, filling the quiet corridors with their noise, and conversations get louder as one on top of the other they vie to speak. Cathé opens her door, smiling greetings to those who wait, and the comings and goings begin again. After a while Cathé looks at her watch, gasps, and grabs for some papers as she sticks an arm in her coat and reaches for her bag. Another meeting. Students follow her down the corridor, and an empty quiet is left behind. A few students remain, waiting outside other doors, but the merriment and confusion fades. It will not return until Cathé is back.

On December 20, 1981, the bustle of Cathé's office was more intense than usual as grade-anxious students swelled the numbers of those who gathered by her door, and the telephone rang constantly as colleagues and students mixed business calls with holiday pleasure. In the midst of these festivities Cathé received a call from a city hospital about a young woman whom she had been trying to help. The young woman had been brought into the intensive-care unit and was asking for her. Cathé had told me of the young woman, who was living in an abandoned building with her two young children, and she had told me how well the six-year-old was doing in school. We had discussed the possibility of visiting this family as I had visited families in my earlier study of family literacy. Cathé was nervous about the idea of doing fieldwork, and I was concerned about working with Black families. I told Cathé that I could teach her to do fieldwork and she talked about working as Black and White together. Nothing was decided, but we were both interested in the idea, and we agreed to go and visit the young woman after the holiday rush. In the meantime I suggested to Cathé that she keep notes of any visits that she made to the young woman during the Christmas holidays. Cathé made some notes on the day that she received the phone call from the hospital, so that day marks the beginning of the research that we've shared. Cathé asked her sons, who were home from college for Christmas, to visit the young woman (whom we have called Tanya in the study). Jimmy and Jeffrey told her they'd let her know what was going on. Cathé continued working on her end-of-semester chores, grading papers and projects, and talking to students who had last-minute difficulties with their class assignments. Then Jimmy called back. Tanya was suffering from an acute asthmatic attack. He and Jeffrey had been to see her, and she had told them to "get the kids." They had got the kids. Jimmy told his mom that the house had been "a shambles" and that there was only a young girl there to take care of the children. He said that Queenie and Gary had been scared and had cried when they carried them out of the building and put them in the car. Jimmy said that they had been worried that the police would think that they were kidnapping the children and added that "it was a bad scene." They had taken the kids to Cathé's house and given them peanut butter sandwiches, and Jeff had gone to the hospital to tell Tanya that they were O.K. Queenie and Gary stayed with Cathé and her family, and Cathé brought them to the college. One afternoon Queenie stayed with me in my office, and while I talked with students about their grades she copied an L. L. Bean label from a box filled with papers that was squeezed into a space at the bottom of my bookshelves. Queenie seemed quite content to sit there drawing the letters and coloring the paper blue. She didn't seem to be worried that she had been left with someone that she didn't know. It was hard for me to imagine this bright-eyed six-year-old living in an abandoned building with her mother and her four-year-old brother. Cathé told me of the tales that the children told, and she tried to tell me about the house in the inner-city neighborhood where they had been living. Usually her descriptions of the building ended abruptly as she grimaced and shuddered. She couldn't tell me what it was like, and if she had I probably wouldn't have believed her. There is only so much that you can imagine, and it seemed inconceivable to me that it could be as bad as all that.

Tanya was released from the hospital on December 24 and spent Christmas with her children and Cathé's family. She returned to her home after New Year's, and on January 12 Cathé and I went to see her.

In the months that followed we visited the first of the families to participate in the research, and we began to formulate a theoretical rationale for the study. The version that follows was written in the spring of 1983.

The present study of family literacy focuses upon Black children living in urban poverty who are perceived by their parents to be successfully learning to read and write. Currently there are few descriptive studies that seek to develop sensitivities to and understandings of the meanings and functions of the familial contexts in which young Black children living in urban poverty develop written language skills. We know very little of the ways in which the personal biographies and educative styles of families shape the literate experiences of children, or of how the children themselves initiate, absorb, and synthesize the educational influences in their lives. And yet there is a considerable body of literature that emphasizes that literacy develops best in rational contexts that are meaningful to the young child. Thus we need to know more of the learning styles, coping strategies, and social support systems of young children living in poverty if reading and writing instruction in school is to become a meaningful complement to their everyday lives. The present study is one attempt towards this aim, and we believe that the research is especially important since it focuses upon children who are *successfully* learning to read and write despite the extraordinary economic hardships of their lives. We hope that the research will have a positive effect in providing new images of the *strengths* of the family as educator, and that it will provide practical ways in which we can build relational contexts that bring the strengths of home learning into the classrooms of the children that we study and teach. (Taylor and Dorsey-Gaines, in press)

Organizing questions were also formulated to give focus and direction (Taylor and Dorsey-Gaines 1983b). Originally, there were twelve questions; many others evolved during the course of the study. However, it is interesting to note that the four questions that we eventually pose in chapter 5, "Families, Literacy, and Educational Policy," are not far from the twelve questions that we asked in the early stages of the study. The four questions are perhaps a little more balanced in that they focus as much on family as on literacy, but a response to each of the original twelve questions may be found in our discussion of the four questions that we finally decided to present:

1. What have we learned from the Shay Avenue families?
2. How have the families helped us understand the social, political, and economic forces that shape their lives?
3. What have the families taught us about literacy?
4. How can we (as researchers, educators, and policymakers) use the information we have gained from the Shay Avenue families to enhance the learning opportunities of young children so that they can develop the literacy behaviors they will need to survive, prosper, and become productive members of American society?

As mentioned above, these questions are dealt with in chapter 5. The main body of the text is comprised of ethnographic descriptions of the families and increasingly abstract arrangements of data as the focus shifts from literacy at home and at school towards literacy in a comparative frame. Although I was responsible for the actual writing of the chapters, the text is presented in a shared voice to reflect the ways in which Cathé and I worked together in collecting the data. There is little of ourselves in it—just enough for the reader to gain some understanding of our participation in the lives of the families, but not enough to detract from their stories. In the afterword, "Apprenticeship in Ethnography," Cathé has written a personal commentary on the research.

There are a few final comments to be made on the human element of fieldwork that I think may be helpful. Georges and Jones (1980) state:

The fieldworker must explain his or her presence and purpose to others, gain their confidence and cooperation, and develop and maintain mutually acceptable relationships. These requirements create dilemmas, produce confrontations, demand clarifications and compromises, and evoke reflection and introspection that one can neither fully appreciate nor prepare for in advance. (p. 2)

Neither experience nor lack of experience prepared Cathé and me for the confusion (and sometimes grief) that we felt at times when critical incidents in the lives of the families spilled over into our own lives (see Hansen 1981). On one occasion at a conference I was asked over lunch if I always ended my presentations with pathos. It was a sharp comment, but justified given the turn my talk had taken before we sat down to eat. Writing an ethnographic study is to experience many times events that have taken place during the course of the research. The death of a father occurs over and over again as a taped conversation is played and replayed so that the writer can write what the father said, share his comments, give him credit for trying, and sometimes shout at the reader through his transcribed words. In the middle of the transcription and writing of the text I had, in effect, shouted at the participants of a conference that I had taken time out to attend. I was frustrated by the levels of abstraction in the presentations that were made, and of the use of "context" as some analytic category instead of as a metaphor for the lives that we live and the lives of those whom we study in our research. But anger serves little purpose except, perhaps, that there are times when being angry helps you move beyond frustration so that you can see the situation a little differently—to hope and, for Cathé, to pray.

Henry, in Tom Stoppard's play, *The Real Thing*, holds up a coffee cup and says:

There is, I suppose, a world of objects which have a certain form, like this coffee mug. I turn it, and it has no handle. I tilt it, and it has no cavity. But there is something real here which is always a mug with a handle. I suppose. But politics, justice, patriotism—they aren't like coffee mugs. There's nothing real there separate from our perception of them. So if you try to change them as though there were something there to change, you'll get frustrated, and frustration will finally make you violent. If you know this and proceed with humility, you may perhaps alter peoples' perceptions so that they behave a little differently at that axis of behaviour where we locate politics or justice. (pp. 53–54)

Stoppard, through Henry, goes on to speak of words. He says, "If you get the right ones in the right order, you can nudge the world a little." This is the most a writer can expect. Cathé, through her daily life, makes a difference in the lives of others. She is a member of the president's task force on minority enrollment and director of minority enrollment at Kean College. She meets regularly with people in the communities surrounding the college campus. She visits schools and talks with the Urban League as she works to encourage the enrollment of Black students in college programs. She is involved in day-care centers and Head Start programs, and she is active in the state and local library associations. She is a member of the board of education of her local Baptist church, and she is organist and director of a women's choir at the nearby Presbyterian church. Working on the manuscript for this book, living quietly and writing daily, is a selfish life in comparison. But what if the writing gets read and gives someone a nudge or changes some "popular" perception? In responding to the question "What have we learned from the Shay Avenue families?" in chapter 5, we state:

The families spent time together, ... there was a rhythm to their lives, and ... they enjoyed each other's company. Friends visited. Children played. People helped one another. Sometimes there was sadness and grief, at other times there was anger and resentment, but there was always a quiet determination in the way in which they approached the difficulties that confronted them. Their optimism about the future and their ability to imagine what life would be like if conditions were better seemed to keep them going, struggling and surviving, albeit precariously, against the odds and without the support of the society to which they belong.

If we remember this, if we can change our perceptions of families with children living in poverty so that we behave a little differently at that axis of behavior where we locate politics and justice, if we can convince ourselves that the myths and stereotypes that create images of specific groups (inner-city families, teenage mothers and their children) have no relevance when we stop counting and start observing and working with people, then we will have nudged the world a little. And if we can persuade others that sex, race, economic status, and setting cannot be used as significant correlates of literacy, the writing will have been worthwhile.

In chapter 1 we present ethnographic descriptions of the families. These are followed by descriptions of the literate lives of the children, both at home and at school. From these accounts we then shift towards the more abstract and tentative arrangements of data that are presented when we discuss literacy in a comparative frame. This chapter is followed by our presentation of some of the interpretive explanations that we have developed during the course of the research. In the afterword, Cathé writes of ethnography and returns the discussion to when people study people.

One
The Families

What happens to a dream deferred?

Does it dry up
like a raisin in the sun?
Or fester like a sore—
And then run?
Does it stink like rotten meat?
Or crust and sugar over
like a syrupy sweet?

Maybe it just sags
like a heavy load.

Or does it explode?

Langston Hughes

Tanya, Queenie, and Gary

When Tanya was eleven years of age she went to work for a thirty-six-year-old man who lived in her neighborhood.* Every Saturday she did his housework and sometimes, if there was not enough money for Tanya to buy food, he paid her extra money to have sex with him. Tanya never told anyone. At the end of eighth grade she gave birth to a little girl, whom she named Queenie. After her six-week postpartum checkup she returned to school, and her mother took care of the baby. Tanya says, "My mother did everything that needed to be done for her. I did my homework. School was a breeze for me. I always liked school. I never cut. I went to my classes. I listened." In eleventh grade Tanya gave birth to a baby boy, Gary, and again she returned to school after her six-week checkup. In 1979 Tanya graduated from high school.

---

*The names of the family members and the names of the streets have been changed.

Tanya managed to get a job working as a cashier in one of the cafeterias at the airport, and her mother continued to take care of her children. Then in 1980 her mother died. She was thirty-eight years old and Tanya was nineteen. Tanya spent what money she had on her mother's funeral and continued working at the airport. She had made friends with a young woman called Brenda, who came from Georgia and had no family living in the area. Tanya invited Brenda to live with her in the apartment that she had once shared with her mother. For a while the two young women continued to work at the airport, staggering their shifts so they could share the responsibility of Tanya's young children. However, the arrangements were complicated by bus schedules and time changes in their shifts, so Tanya took a job working at the local pool hall and Brenda stayed home to take care of the children and the apartment. Tanya spoke of the friendship working well and of them living quietly, cooking special meals, listening to music in the evenings, and taking the children to a nearby park on weekends. She said that it didn't matter what was happening around them; they were happy together.

But the arrangement abruptly came to an end when the city took over the building (when the owner failed to pay the taxes) and families received notices to leave. People moved out. Tanya and Brenda stayed on for a while, living in the third-floor apartment of the emptying house. Then Brenda's uncle arrived and, seeing the surroundings in which Brenda was living, took her home. Tanya was left alone with her two small children. Brenda had gone, and the last of the families had moved out. She had nowhere to go, so she remained in the building, ignoring the notices that the city sent telling her to relocate.

In January 1982, the weather was bitterly cold and television news focused on the plight of families living without heat. There was no heat in the building in which Tanya lived; no lights, except in their third-floor apartment; and no water, except for what Tanya, Queenie, and Gary collected in buckets and carried from a cold-water tap in the basement of the house. The freezing temperatures finally drove Tanya out. It was at this time that we began the study. We spent our first visit trying to find Tanya and her children. Jeffrey, Cathé's son, was home from college and he went with us. The house seemed to be empty, but Jeffrey managed to open the front door and we made our way up the stairs to the third-floor apartment. Another young woman, Sharon, was living in Tanya's apartment. Sharon was seventeen. When we arrived we found her sitting in front of the gas stove trying to keep warm. In the next room a small oil heater was placed next to the bed directing heat towards her baby, who was sucking on an empty bottle while he slept. Sharon told us that Tanya had moved out the night before because she could not stand the cold. She said that all she knew was that Tanya had said she was going to stay with a friend.

Sharon closed the door of the apartment, and we were left in the dimly lit corridor. There was a smell of cats and a more ominous smell of gas. A boarded-up window at the top of the stairs gave us some light as we climbed down but it had faded by the time we reached the second floor. We held onto the bannister and felt our way down the stairs to the ground floor. It was with considerable relief that we managed to open the front door. For one moment we could see the crumbling flakes of old brown and green paint that covered the scraps of linoleum that were scattered on the floor. Then we were outside wondering where to find Tanya.

We visited the school that Queenie attended and asked to speak with her, but no one knew who we were so they refused to tell us anything. Then we visited the pool hall and asked the owner if he knew where we could find Tanya. He told us to ask the mother of one of her friends and gave us directions to the street on which the mother lived. The directions were straightforward, and we soon stopped the car outside the house where we had been told to inquire. Jeffrey spoke to an old man who was sitting on a short pillar at the bottom of the steps, and a woman above opened a window and called down. Jeff spoke to her and went into the house. A few minutes later he got into the car and told us he knew where to find Tanya. He drove back past the pool hall, turned down another road, and stopped the car outside a large apartment building. We went inside. The grey concrete walls made the place seem empty and cold, and the place echoed as we spoke quietly to one another. The elevator wasn't working, so we climbed the stone stairs to the fourth floor. We went to apartment 4B and knocked.

Tanya opened the door. We told her that we had been looking for her, and she smiled and moved back for us to step inside. Tanya's friend Jean was frying eggs and sausages, and she greeted us as we passed through a small bright kitchen into the living room. The curtains were drawn and the room was dark but very warm. We sat down and Tanya pulled up a chair and sat close to us. She was a small young woman, and she seemed sickly and frail. Her face was partly covered by a blue woolen ski hat that she had pulled down over her forehead, and she was wearing a navy sweatshirt with a vest over it, dark blue pants, and worn sneakers. She had on glasses that slipped down her nose as she spoke, and every so often she would push them up with her left hand as it moved in time to her speaking. We asked her about Gary, who was then four years old, and she told us that he was asleep in the next room. She got up quietly and went to get him. A few minutes later Gary followed her into the room, and as she sat down he came around in front of her and put his head in her lap so that his back was to us and his face was hidden.

Tanya talked about the cold weather and of the problems she was facing with the lack of heat in her apartment. She said she had tried to get someone to fix the heating system and that she had got an old man to look at it. She told us that he did get it going but that it went off again just after he left. Tanya explained that this had happened before and that she had tried to get the man to stay but he said he couldn't. "Couldn't or *wouldn't*," she cried.

Tears fell and her voice rose until she was almost shouting. Gary moved his head and looked up at her and she talked quietly again, shifting the conversation to her fears about living in an empty building and of her attempts to find another place to live. She rubbed Gary's back as she spoke and he put his head back in her lap. Tanya went on, "They want too much money," and she explained that even the worst of apartments would cost more per month than she had to live on. She told us that her friend's apartment was subsidized and that she would like to live in her building. She could pay the rent and the place had heat. Tanya smiled and for a moment she looked hopeful as she told us that there was an apartment for rent and that she was going to try and get it. She said that she knew someone who worked in the building and that she was going to give him $100 to help.

Tanya stayed with Jean for one night. Nothing came of the "help" she paid for, and she continued to live in the abandoned house that had once been her mother's home. In the weeks that followed we often spent time looking for her, but she was never far away. Sometimes she was out getting Gary from school and occasionally she was visiting a friend, but most of the time she was in her third-floor apartment at the back of the house. The bell didn't work so there was no way of reaching her except by banging on the door or calling up from the street below. Sometimes when we arrived Jack would be outside fixing his car. Jack was a retired merchant seaman who had once lived in the house, and he told us that he tried to help Tanya when he could. Jack told us that he would have liked to have taken Tanya and her children to live in his house when he had moved out of his Shay Avenue home. Later Tanya laughed, "What does he care?" She told us that the third floor of his house was still unoccupied and added that he had never tried to help her. She said that just after he had moved out she had heard a noise downstairs and had gone down and found him taking the back door. Tanya began to shout that she had told him that she needed that door and that if he took it anyone could get inside.

Tanya often talked about safety and of being alone in the house. She told us that she had asked Sharon to live with her so that they could take care of the place together. She said that they never went out at the same time and that one of them was always there to make sure no one broke in. Often when she talked to us she would drop her head and tears would fall, but her voice never faltered as she talked of her life, and sometimes she would see humor in the things that troubled her. She told us that while she was at the welfare office she had met two people who told her that she could get an energy check. Tanya grinned and said they had given her a number to phone and that as soon as she dialed they pestered her to find out about their energy checks. "All they wanted was to use my dime!" she said. "They just wanted me to phone for them."

Then, hopeful again, she said she had heard about some apartments that were being renovated and that she was going to find out about them. The housing office was several bus rides away and would take most of the day but she said she would walk if she had to. Tanya held out her arm and showed us the hospital bracelet that was around her wrist. She was severely asthmatic and was given the bracelet a few weeks earlier, when she was admitted to the hospital just before Christmas. She said she hoped the bracelet would help at the housing office. She explained that she was going to say that she had just got out of the hospital and had nowhere to go. When we saw her the following week, Tanya told us that there was a long waiting list for the apartments and that it would be a year before the renovations would be completed.

During these early visits Tanya nearly always talked about Queenie and Gary as she told us about her struggle to find somewhere to live. On one occasion she said, "My kids have been so good through all of this. All the cold and the problems they know I've been having and they just stuck it here with me. All at one time I want to get all this mess out of our lives. But they handle it quite well.... They've been good kids. They see what I have to go through. We have to go downstairs to get water. We all go downstairs and we get water together. We get our buckets and we go downstairs. We all do that together. I think that it's important. I don't want them to be away from me now at this time of my life. I want them to see what I'm going through. I want us to go through it together as a family."

Tanya began to cry. "All coming on, that's all I want." She brushed away the tears and shifted the conversation away from her fear of losing her children. "I'm interested in how Gary is going to do," she said. "I think he's going to be like me. He's going to do well at school. I give Queenie's books to him now and I have him name things and that type of thing.... He gets Queenie's books himself and fumbles through them, and if there's something there that I think he should know then I bring that into the conversation and we talk about that for a while." Again Tanya cried. "People tell me all I can do is hope for the best. I think if I give it my go I think that my kids will turn out fine. I'm hopeful. Hopefully ... there's no reason why my child should be standing out there on the corner. I'm not going to have it. Not what I went through."

For a while Tanya's strength and determination seemed to keep the family going. She was working in the pool hall, and Sharon took care of her children. Tanya talked about overcoming her problems. She said she was lucky because she knew she was going to make it. During this time she talked a lot about Queenie and Gary and of the things she did to ensure that they would do well in school. She said that when Queenie was in a preschool program she was told that "Queenie had a problem cutting paper." Tanya grinned and said that at that time she was still at school herself so she had taken some scissors from the art room and brought them home so that Queenie could "practice cutting paper at home." She laughed as she told us, "I just let her cut." She talked about Queenie learning to read. She said, "The other day she read almost a whole book. She wanted to read it." Again Tanya laughed, "I didn't really want to hear it but I just let her read until she got tired. She wanted to try so I let her try. . . . She's interested. She wants to know how to read and to write." Tanya grinned. "She has a lot of things she wants to do, I guess." Then, more seriously, she continued, "I have some cue cards with sentences and words that I thought she should know in kindergarten. . . . I bought them at the store. And, um, we go over them. I try maybe a half hour a day to spend some time with her going over them. . . . That was more so in kindergarten and in first grade. Now she's starting to read." Tanya found some of the cards to show us and she explained how she used them. "I pronounce the word for her. I have her pronounce it after me and say each letter, and I have her do it herself once, and then we go to the next one. . . . She should know all of these." Tanya also talked about Queenie writing, and she told us how difficult it was for her to keep paper away from her. She complained that every time she tried to write a letter Queenie had written on all the pages of her writing pad.

The weather changed and Tanya had a short respite from the bitter cold of winter. But her situation did not improve. We arrived one day to find Sharon sitting on the steps outside the house. We said hi and asked how she was doing. She smiled. "Bad," she said, "and when I say bad, I mean bad." She had been sitting with her elbows on her knees and her chin in her hands, but as she spoke she moved her arms away. Her sweatshirt was stretched tight across her stomach and for the first time we realized that Sharon was going to have another baby. She told us that she thought she was about six months pregnant. We asked her if she had seen a doctor. She told us that she hadn't. The front door was open, so we went inside. There was more trash and litter inside, and the stairs were in complete darkness. The smell of gas was overpowering. As we felt our way up the stairs the half-boarded-up windows of the third floor provided enough light for us to see the bucket of muddy water that had collected after a night of rain and the cat feces that filled the corners of the third-floor hallway. The door to the rooms in which Tanya was living was open, and we called to her as we went inside. Queenie and Gary had been out playing. We heard them laughing with their friends as they came up the stairs behind us. Jean was in the kitchen and Tanya was sitting on one of the beds in the next room. She had on navy blue sweats and a T-shirt. She was wiping her face with a towel. Her forehead was hot. We asked her if she was all right. She told us she had a lot on her mind. She was perspiring, and it was difficult to understand her when she spoke. For a while Tanya did not speak, and Jean talked to us about her children and her job at a nearby day-care center. Then Tanya told us that she was depressed because of a fight with Sharon. Tanya said she had been bringing in her friends—"riff-raff," Tanya called them—and they had tried to take over the apartment. Tanya said she finally asked them all to leave. She said she didn't know where Sharon was staying, that most of the time she seemed to just sit on the steps outside of the house. Tanya lapsed into silence. Tears rolled down her cheeks and every so often she would wipe them away with her towel.

Queenie and her friends were dancing to disco music and she stopped to show us her report card. She said she had eight A's and that the rest of her grades were B's. Both of us read the report and gave her a hug, then she went back to dance with her friends. In the middle of all this, Gary sat on a bed "reading" a prayer book, seemingly untouched by both the laughter and the despair. We asked him to read the book for us and he did, turning over chunks of pages from left to right until he came to a picture of Jesus. Gary pointed at the picture and he said "Je-sus," as if reading the word.

On our next visit Tanya met us as we were climbing up the stairs. She began to cry. She said that someone had broken into the house and stolen her stereo equipment and the tape recorder that we had given her to tape the stories that she read with Queenie and Gary. As we reached the second floor we saw that the door to one of the apartments had been knocked off its hinges. It lay amidst the piles of trash that filled the empty room. The cat's mess had been cleaned up on the third floor. There was nothing to hide the smell of gas, which filled Tanya's rooms. Tanya told us that she had swept all three flights of stairs on Wednesday and that the robbery had taken place on Thursday. We sat in the kitchen. Tanya was bent forward, her arms resting on her knees. Every so often she would lean back in her chair and push her fingers through her hair, then wipe her eyes as she returned to the hunched position. Queenie asked Tanya if she could go and play with a friend, but her mother said no and Queenie began to cry. Gary was coughing and had a fever, but he also wanted to go and play. He started to cry and hit Tanya. Tanya shouted at them, but she too was in tears. All three of them were crying. Tanya looked at us and smiled. We cut up apples for the children and they went in the other room to watch TV.

Tanya told us about the robbery. She said that she had been out and that Queenie had been in the apartment alone. Gary had been visiting a friend. She began to cry again as she told us of her fears. She said that Queenie could have been beaten or raped, and she told us how easy it had been for the robbers to get into the house. She said she could no longer leave her children. She talked again about Sharon and said that even when Sharon had been living with them Tanya did not want to leave the children with Sharon. She said that Sharon did not feed them, and that she had often seen Sharon give her baby bottles of water when she didn't have any money to buy him milk. Tanya said that a worker from the Division of Youth and Family Service had been to the house and inquired about Sharon because someone had reported her for not taking care of her baby. For a moment Tanya smiled. She said that the worker had asked questions about Sharon, but she didn't seem to care about the conditions in which Tanya was living with her two children. She kept telling us that it wasn't safe anymore. The two men who had broken into the house told Queenie that her mother had sent them to take the stereo equipment to be repaired. She said they had threatened to hurt Queenie if she didn't let them in. Later Queenie, who was just seven, told us that they had said they would "put their fists through her lips" if she told anyone about them. Tanya called the police and said that she went with them to "the projects" to see if they could find out who had taken the equipment, but nothing had come of it.

That week, on a TV program called "Town Meeting in New Jersey," we listened as concern was expressed over the housing shortage. It was stated that there were 800,000 substandard or nonexistent units in the state. Our own vain attempts to help Tanya find a place to live made these impersonal, abstract statistics come alive. We seemed unable to help. We spoke to a lawyer in the Housing Law Unit of a nearby law school and were told that in the city in which Tanya lived about a hundred houses had been taken over that winter by the city because of nonpayment of taxes. The lawyer stated that the city wanted the people out and was unwilling to offer any support. He said the city accepted no responsibility for the people who were living in the buildings and just wanted to board them up. He went on to say that the woman that we were trying to help must have known for over a year that the building was going to be taken over, so why hadn't she found somewhere else to live? He was impatient and said there was plenty of housing. Why didn't she go to a realtor? He did give us the name of a person to reach at the local Tenants Association.

The woman that we phoned seemed concerned but explained that there was very little that she could do. She said she didn't know of any housing at the present time. She told us that there were hundreds of families in the city without homes, that many who did have somewhere to live did not have heat and that many, like Tanya, were warming themselves by gas stoves. She said, "Don't give up. Try any agency that you can." We made many phone calls, but all that followed was confusion. A member of one city agency told us that there was a signed consent from a judge for the sheriff to lock the family out. Later we were told that this was incorrect, that the building was not listed to be padlocked, and that there was nothing in the sheriff's records. During another telephone conversation we were told that the building was unfit for human habitation and that it would be publicly advertised and publicly bidded upon. None of this seemed to be of much help. We tried the Department of Health and Welfare, the Bureau of Code Enforcement, the City Real Estate Department, and then the state senator's office and the office of the local assemblyman. It seemed that nothing could be done. No housing was available for someone who lived on so little money.

When we next visited Tanya, she met us at the front door. We followed her into the house. She told us not to try to shut the door behind us, as the lock had been broken during the break-in. We went up the stairs and we could see that the door to the apartment on the second floor had been replaced. It leaned precariously in the hole that was the doorway, but we could still see past it to the trash inside. On the third floor the smell of gas was as strong as ever. Tanya showed us the valve that was leaking and she turned the faucetlike handle around and around without meeting any resistance. The corridor was still littered with papers and cat feces, but once we were inside the kitchen it was clear that things were better. Tanya was smiling. She had tidied up. The floor was swept and the table was cleaned. Gary was no longer congested and, although thin and pale, he was bright-eyed and mischievous. We sat down, and Tanya told us that she had asked Sharon to come back to help her protect her things. We told Tanya about our attempts to help her find a place to live. We talked about the housing shortage, of the tales we had been told of the many families without homes, and of the families living without heat. Tanya said that it had been a bad winter for everybody and added that she was one of the lucky ones. With that, she got up and went into the bedroom and came back with some of the schoolwork that Queenie had brought home. She said she'd been saving it for us. On one sheet of lined paper Queenie had written in careful upper- and lowercase letters, "We give thanks for food, homes, family, and clothes."

Queenie and Gary were playing with a little girl named Tasmika. We had met Tasmika once before; she had read a book to us. Tanya went to get a photograph album and said that she wanted to show us some photos of Queenie and Gary. Queenie picked up the school papers that Tanya had placed on the table and took them into the next room. She sat on one of the beds next to Tasmika and together they looked through the papers. Tanya came back with the album and we looked at the photographs. Queenie came back into the room with a ditto that she had found among the papers. She put it on the table beside Tanya and waited for her mother to help her fill in the items on the sheet. Tanya helped her, balancing her conversation with us about the photographs with the assistance that she was giving her daughter. Tanya supplied the words that Queenie did not know and checked her daughter's answers.

The conversation returned to the dilemma of finding an apartment and we suggested to Tanya that she visit the Urban League. We arranged to go with her. Then it was time for us to leave. Before we left we went into the adjoining room to say good-bye to the children. There, almost hidden from view, was a stereo that looked like the one that had been stolen. Seeing our surprise, Tanya laughed. "It's new," she said. She told us that she had made a good down payment and that she had got a good deal. Still laughing she added, "I've gotta have somethin'." Tanya's spirit was infectious, and we left feeling better than we had when we arrived.

A few days later we telephoned Jean and asked her to tell Tanya that we would drive by to get her at ten o'clock the following morning to go with her to the Urban League. Tanya was watching for us when we arrived and called down to us. "Just a minute!" she shouted. She must have run down the stairs because the door quickly opened and Tanya came outside. She was wearing turquoise pants and navy canvas shoes, a yellow T-shirt and a madras check shirt, and a navy blue jacket. Tanya got into the car. She said she'd been up all night with a fever but that she felt much better this morning. We asked her if she knew how to get to the Urban League. She said she thought she could find it, although she wasn't sure. Tanya explained that although she had lived in the city all her life she really didn't know it very well. She said that it was difficult to get around because she had never had a car. No one spoke as we drove through Tanya's neighborhood. We just watched as we drove by vacant lots filled with garbage and dilapidated houses that looked ready to collapse. Many of the houses that we passed seemed to be in a worse state than the one in which Tanya was living, and yet they too were occupied. But then we started to talk again. We were passing a vacant lot that had been cleared. It was newly tilled and ready for planting. Three young men were at work putting in seedlings and getting rid of the last of the stones. We slowed down to watch and one of them smiled and waved as we drove by.

We made our way into the center of town and around the complicated one-way system. Tanya told us that she had never been in this part of the city, so we drove slowly, looking at the numbers on the fronts of the buildings as we tried to locate the office of the Urban League. The neighborhood in which it was situated was similar to the one in which Tanya lived, except for the stores, which seemed to be filled with people. It took us a few minutes to find a parking space, but we did eventually find one down a side street. Nearby, an old woman had set up a rack of second-hand clothes, which she stood beside as she watched the people who passed her on the street.

Inside the storefront offices of the Urban League we met Mrs. Deignan. She greeted us kindly and gave Tanya some forms to fill in; then she went back into her office. Later Mrs. Deignan (who was white) told us that she had four grown-up children and that she had gone back to college and had found herself in her present job as much by chance as by planning. Tanya sat down and filled in the forms. She wrote quickly and didn't seem to have any difficulty providing the necessary information. Once the forms were completed we sat and waited for Mrs. Deignan to return. We talked about our children. Tanya told us how independent Queenie was and how she was glad that she had a son as well as a daughter.

Mrs. Deignan came back into the room. She took the forms from Tanya and asked us to follow her into her office. The room was well furnished and comfortable except for the chairs, which were placed against a wall far away from Mrs. Deignan's desk. We sat down with Tanya and waited while Mrs. Deignan read the information that Tanya had written on the forms. Then Mrs. Deignan looked up and asked Tanya how much money she had to live on per annum. Tanya told her that she had $3,600 and added that she also received $120 of food stamps every month. Mrs. Deignan then asked her if she had managed to save any money. Tanya said, "$500." Mrs. Deignan nodded and said, "Good, that will help." The next question was about Tanya's age. Tanya said that she was twenty-one. Mrs. Deignan looked down at the form and after a quiet moment she looked up and said, "You're twenty-one and you have a seven-year-old and a four-year-old?" Tanya just smiled. Mrs. Deignan continued by saying that Tanya had not had time to be a young girl; later she commented that Tanya was twenty-one going on forty-five. Mrs. Deignan then wanted to know about Tanya's mother. Tanya told her that her mother was dead. The phone rang and we waited.

When Mrs. Deignan had finished the phone call she talked with Tanya about the house in which she was living. She began by asking if there were any other people in the building, and she explained that she always began by advising people to stay together. "Fight, not flight," she said. Tanya told Mrs. Deignan that she was the only one left in the house. Mrs. Deignan wanted to know if the city had "passed off" the building, and Tanya said that she was sure that they had not. She told Mrs. Deignan that she read the local papers regularly and that she always looked to see if the house was listed by the city. There had been no notices of an impending auction. Tanya said that she knew that the city had taken over the building because someone had come to see her in the fall. She said she was told she would be receiving some papers but they had never arrived. Mrs. Deignan shook her head and told Tanya that the city would regard her as a squatter. She explained that the city would have expected her to go to the appropriate office to get the papers and fill in the necessary forms. Tanya sat quietly and her eyes filled with tears.

Mrs. Deignan moved on as if the worst was over. She smiled at Tanya and told her that despite the difficulties of her situation it was important to establish that Tanya was a responsible tenant. She told her to collect together all the old rent receipts that she could find and any other receipts of bills that she had paid. Mrs. Deignan continued by saying that she would need a letter of recommendation from a former landlord. Tanya said she could get a letter from a woman who had rented an apartment to her mother. Mrs. Deignan said that would be fine and she told Tanya that it wouldn't matter if the receipts were in her mother's name. Then she went on to say what should be written in the letter. She said it should state that Tanya was responsible and quiet, that her children were good, that the family was an asset to the community, and that Tanya had always paid her rent on time and that she would make a good tenant. Mrs. Deignan said, "If you've got it, flaunt it!"

Then Mrs. Deignan focused on Tanya. She looked stern. She told Tanya not to give any money to anyone unless she had a firm lease agreement. Tanya gave a small smile and said that she had already lost $60. She said she had answered an ad in the paper, but all she had received was a list of phone numbers of apartments that she had seen advertised in the papers. Mrs. Deignan said that many of her clients had similar experiences and that part of her job was to help people gain the consumer skills that they needed so that others could not take advantage of their situation. Mrs. Deignan explained to Tanya that it was important that when she went to look at an apartment that she not act as if her situation was desperate. She told her to be a good consumer, to try all the light switches, to flush the toilets, to ask about the schools and about the neighborhood. Then she emphasized that a landlord could not discriminate against her because of her race or sex, nor could a landlord ask her about her source of income. Mrs. Deignan spoke firmly to Tanya: "Poverty does not mean that you don't have dignity," she said.

Mrs. Deignan told Tanya that she would start looking for an apartment and that Tanya should also continue to try to find a place. She wanted a telephone number so that she could reach Tanya if she managed to find any apartments that Tanya could go and see. She also asked Tanya to phone in once a week. Tanya said she would phone and added that she had seen one apartment that she had liked and that she had filled in an application. Mrs. Deignan knew the apartment building of which Tanya spoke and said she thought it would be a good place for her live. She picked up the telephone directory that was on her desk, found the telephone number of the apartment building, and phoned the manager. Mrs. Deignan said she was calling for Tanya Yates. She said that she had interviewed Tanya and that she was a fine young woman who would be an asset to his apartment building. After a few minutes Mrs. Deignan put down the phone and said that the manager was going to "look into" her application.

As we left Mrs. Deignan's office she said that she thought we ought to be able to find Tanya somewhere to live. She pointed out of her window at the bustle below and told us that although the neighborhood looked really seedy it was not. The storekeepers would give credit, she said, and they often gave the local children free oranges. Mrs. Deignan said that there was a community organization and that the neighbors helped each other. She said there were similar "pockets" all over the city.

On the way back to Tanya's house we stopped and had hot dogs at a tiny cafe. Tanya talked about her brother, who was in prison. She said that he was not a bad kid and she told us that she often wrote to him. She added that things would have been better if he had been there to help her. Then she talked about herself. She said she had promised herself one degree. She explained that her mother had always told her that it was important for her to get a high school diploma but that Tanya wanted her own children to get degrees. "I'm not goin' to have them saying that they don't want to go to college because I didn't," she said. Tanya went on to say that she wanted to go herself for them.

Nothing much came of the visit to the Urban League. Mrs. Deignan did provide Tanya with the addresses of two apartments, but Tanya said that they were almost as bad as the one she was living in. Tanya read the papers and kept looking for a place to live. She had the lock repaired and stayed on in her third-floor rooms. By then, the weather was getting warmer, so she opened up the door to the room at the front of the apartment and the children played in there. Sharon moved out. A few weeks later we heard that she had given birth to another baby boy, but we did not know where she was living. One day when we went to visit, there was another young woman in the apartment. Her name was Donna. Tanya told us that she had been living with her brothers but that they had told her to leave. Tanya had offered her a home, and Donna had moved in with her three daughters. Tanya told us, "I'm helping a needy person, that's all. She had no place to go, so she moved in." The young woman was tall and thin and she seemed to be distracted most of the time.

Conditions in the apartment continued to deteriorate. Donna brought her friends in, and Tanya told us that she could no longer take care of the place. But she did continue to take care of her children. Whatever else happened, Queenie kept up with her homework, and Donna's children would join Queenie working at the kitchen table. Tanya and Donna would both be in the kitchen, too, and Tanya said, "We helped them if they needed it." Speaking of homework she said, "They have to if they ever expect to be anybody, to be able to hold their head high and walk down the street."

A few weeks later there was a second robbery. The apartment was torn apart and all of Tanya's clothes were taken. "They stole my clothes," she said. "Stole all my clothes." Nothing was left. There were no pieces left for Tanya to pick up. Tanya, Queenie, and Gary went home with Cathé. Tanya's building was boarded up and eventually torn down. Sharon remained on the streets; her children were taken away from her. Donna was sent to prison for shop-lifting, and her children went to live with an aunt. Tanya said that Donna stole "anything that she could sell. Out on the street. Clothes. That's because she didn't have any money."

Several months later Tanya sat at the kitchen table in Cathé's house talking to us about those last days in the apartment. She said, "It was just a bad phase of my life. This is the good part. What can I say? . . . I survived. With a lot of heartaches and pain. But I made it." Tanya began to cry. "It almost took me down to the ground." Shouting, she continued as if back in her old house, "Boy! What's happening to me?" and then quietly, her voice trembling as she remembered, "I was out of control. First time. But that's not going to happen to me again. Might have been worse. It didn't take me long to realize that I had to change things. Because from the way that it used to be before my [first] roommate left. I can show you pictures of the house. . . . It was livable." Tanya was quiet and then she said, "I want to be somebody. That's all. I want to find what I'm good at and go and do it."

Postscript: July 1987. Tanya and her children lived with Cathé for almost a year. Then the young family moved into their own apartment. They did not return to the Shay Avenue neighborhood. In 1986 they moved again. "The environment isn't so hot," Tanya says, "but I like the apartment. We have more room. We *all* have bedrooms." Tanya has had several jobs and is now working in a day-care center. The ages of the children at the center range from two to eight. Tanya works mostly with the older children. She speaks of how much she enjoys working with them and of her hopes to become an early childhood teacher. "Right now I'm working as a teacher's aide," she explains. Then she adds that aides do not make much money. Tanya laughs and says that she is still hard on herself. She still wants to get a college education.

As of the summer of 1987, Tanya is at home with her children. She will return to work in September. Gary, who is now nine, is attending summer camp, enjoying the arts-and-crafts programs, and going on field trips. When he is at home Gary is often out with his friends playing basketball or swimming in the local pool. Tanya is not happy with Gary's progress in school, but she emphasizes that he has not been left back. She says that Queenie is at home with her this summer. Queenie, she says, stays in the apartment and will not go outside. "She doesn't like the environment," Tanya explains. Queenie is now twelve and as tall as her mother. Tanya smiles when she speaks of Queenie growing up. "She's wearing *my* clothes," she says, "and I can wear *her* clothes." At school Queenie continues to do well. Tanya says her report card is still filled with A's and B's. "She's still just a good student," Tanya says. "I never get any complaints out of the teachers. They always have good things to say."

Pauline, Shauna, and Family

We met Pauline early one morning in the spring of 1982 when we were standing outside Tanya's place waiting to go with her to the welfare office. When we arrived Tanya came out to the sidewalk to greet us and at that moment Pauline, a friend of Tanya's, walked by. Tanya introduced us, and while she went inside to get her coat we stood and talked with Pauline. She had on navy slacks and a white blouse, and she seemed to be about the same age as Tanya. We asked her if she had any younger brothers and sisters. Pauline said that she had two younger brothers and three younger sisters. We asked if any of them were in first grade. Pauline said, "No." She looked curious at our question, so we explained that we were studying families in which there was a first-grade child who was successfully learning to read and write. Pauline smiled at us and told us that her daughter was in first grade and that she was "top of the class." We asked Pauline if we could visit and talk with her about her daughter. Without any hesitation she said, "Sure."

Pauline came with us to the welfare office, and we spent the morning talking as we waited for Tanya's caseworker to call her name. Tanya had not received any food stamps for several months, and she was trying to find out what had happened to them. Tanya gave her name to the woman behind the desk and was asked the name of her caseworker. The woman told Tanya to write her name and number on a piece of paper and put it in the box. Pauline told us that the caseworker would take the papers out and call names. Both young women knew their numbers. Tanya tried to find out if her caseworker was in the office, but the woman behind the desk ignored her question. Pauline told us that she rarely came to the welfare office, as her caseworker was a friend. She said if there was a problem she phoned him. After Tanya had given her name, we sat down. We looked around the room and Pauline said, "It ain't pretty," and smiled. Tanya pulled a face, saying, "They're goin' to be on welfare for the rest of their lives." Later she said, "I know there's better. I'm not going to settle for less." Tanya told us that one day she had been waiting at the desk when a woman collapsed on the floor behind her. Tanya shook her head. "The woman said she was dying!" Tanya looked up and, still shaking her head, she continued, "I thought 'Why me?' I don't need that. I've got enough to put up with." She then told us that the woman was faking and that she was just trying to get someone to notice her.

Pauline and Tanya had not seen each other for several months, and they talked about their friends. They shared stories with each other and filled in the details for us as they went along. Every so often their talk would cease and we would sit quietly watching the people who were waiting to get help. Two Spanish-speaking women were carrying on an energetic conversation. One of them was constantly spitting in a trash container. Pauline watched them and commented, "Puerto Ricans bring interpreters." An old Black woman was standing beside a young woman. The young woman was trying to take care of her two little children. Both children were fretful. They wanted to leave. The old woman bent forward and lifted her arm as if she might hit one of them. Pauline smiled and spoke quietly, "I love to see grandmothers try to hit kids. They're kiddin'." The grandmother picked up one of her grand-children and took the other by the hand. Together they walked around the room, keeping each other company during the long wait.

Tanya decided she would try to telephone her caseworker, who was presumably upstairs in her office. "Somebody will answer if it rings long enough," she said. She went over to the telephone and dialed the number. She stood for a while but nobody upstairs lifted the receiver of the ringing phone. Tanya went over to the desk. This time the woman answered her question about her caseworker. She told Tanya that she had gone to lunch. Tanya came back to where we were sitting and she told us that her caseworker had gone to lunch. "Let's go eat," she said. Pauline agreed and told us that the worker would not return for hours.

We found a small place to eat, and Pauline talked about her plans to become a computer programmer. She talked of applying for college that spring. Tanya talked about attending a business school to become a paralegal secretary. It seemed that Trisha, one of Pauline's sisters, was hoping to do the same. Time passed quickly, and we returned to the welfare office. The office was filled with the same people. The two Puerto Rican women were sitting quietly. One of them had her arms around a sleeping child, and the other was talking quietly with another small child who was standing beside her. Tanya phoned upstairs and this time someone answered. She came back to where we were sitting and said that her caseworker had not returned. Then she went to check the box in which she had deposited the piece of paper with her name on it. The paper was gone. She wrote her name and number and again she placed the paper in the box. Tanya came back and sat beside us. She nodded her head towards the people who filled the room and with quiet resignation she commented that she would probably have to stay there for the rest of the day. The doors kept opening and more people came into the office: a pregnant woman in bright red overalls and whitened tennis shoes, a man in a flat cap and a white shirt, and a young woman with a small baby in a pretty pink dress. It seemed that there were many more people waiting inside. The seats were all taken. Mothers stood in small groups talking among themselves, while others waited outside on the sidewalk. We stayed for a while but eventually we had to leave. Tanya remained. Pauline came with us and we gave her a ride to the house in which her sister was living. She wrote her address and telephone number on a piece of paper, and we arranged to visit her family the following week.

Pauline was twenty years old when we began to visit her, and her daughter Shauna was seven. They lived with Pauline's mother, Cora, and four of her brothers and sisters. Trevor was sixteen, Gina was fourteen, Megan was ten, and Joe-Joe was eight. A few weeks after we began to visit the family Trisha, Pauline's nineteen-year-old sister, and her four-year-old son, Sherran, moved in with the family. This meant that there were nine family members living in the five rooms of the second-floor apartment that was their home. Sometimes Trevor went to stay with his father and Mike, the oldest son, who lived in a nearby town, but most of the time he was with his mother and his brothers and sisters. Joe-Joe went south one year and lived with his paternal grandmother. Then he, too, returned.

Cora held her family together. Her home was invariably busy and always friendly. Cora had time for her children, and they had time for one another. During one of our early visits to her home, Cora talked to us about her family. She said, "Part of my life is just watching them grow up and to try and help guide them in the right way. You can't tell them not to do some such thing ... you can tell them not to do it. But, you know—'Mommy or grandma told me not to, I think I'll go out there and try it anyhow.' So the only thing I can do is advise them to the best of my ability and hope everything turns out to be the best." Cora talked about her children's hopes to finish school and Pauline's interest in becoming a computer programmer. Cora said, "Even when she got pregnant with Shauna. She told me she wanted to finish school, and she said she had to find a baby-sitter. I said, 'Find a baby-sitter,' I said, 'when I'm here?' ... If she wants to finish high school I said, 'O.K. That's a good idea.' I said I was glad to hear her say she wanted to finish school. I said, 'I will be here to take care of the baby for you while you're in school.' I said, 'But. When school is out you come home.' And I said, 'And then the baby be your re-sponsibility because you have to learn the responsibility of your own family, since you have a family now.' And the same thing with Trisha. I told her the same thing too." Cora continued, " 'Cause like with some parents I see, the daughter have a child and they sit and they just keep that baby for them while the daughter just keep running out, and before you know it they come back with another baby again. It's not that I think Pauline would do that, but I don't know what they're going to do when they go out. I mean, they're grown now and everything else but when they were younger they could probably be more persuaded then. So I sit here and try and tell them, 'You have a responsibility to come home, do your homework, attend to your baby.' This way they didn't have too much time. If they want to go out, 'O.K., you can go out,' but yet I was still trying to teach them that they had a responsibility of a child or son here at home. It's like I did when I was raising them. I mean, I went out sometimes, but yet I knew I had a responsibility of children at home, and they came first. . . . People say, considering I'm an only parent in the household it seems like I done a pretty good job. Two girls made mistakes having a baby, but, I mean, that's everyday thing. That's life. But otherwise, like being picked up by the cops or run down into the court or somewhere, I don't have any problem with that."

While Cora was talking to us about her children, we asked her why she thought Shauna was doing so well in school. She answered quickly, "I think because there are so many older children in the house. Everybody just takes time out for her. All the younger children get their attention. . . . They're just growing together."

The house in which Cora and her children and grandchildren live stands in a row of similar old houses. Some of the houses are boarded up and stand precariously next to others that are bright with fresh paint. The house to one side of Cora's has been pulled down, and the man who lives on the ground floor of Cora's building uses the lot to grow vegetables. The empty space brings light into the crowded rooms, and in the summer a welcome breeze cools the heat. During our early visits to the family, we would ring the bell and then shout up the stairs, "Pauline. It's Denny and Cathé." Then the door would open and Pauline would look over the bannister and tell us, "Come on up." Or Sherran would come down the stairs and, after telling us, "Pauline's washing her hair," or, "Pauline's getting dressed," he would climb the stairs before us and take us into the apartment. Sometimes we'd wait a few minutes, and then Pauline would come out of the bathroom with her hair wrapped in a towel, or from her bedroom, fixing her clothes as she entered the room. At other times when we would not get any answer to our calls we would climb the wooden stairs and knock on the apartment door. Then we would find Pauline sitting in her favorite place at one end of a couch. But however we entered, Pauline would be smiling and welcoming. During our visits she often asked us questions about our families and the research that we were doing.

Sometimes she looked at us as if our visits amused her. Once she said that instead of writing about them we should write about ourselves. She said, "The way you two work together would make a best-seller," and then, laughing, she said, "I'll settle for 2 percent of the profits."

On June 9, 1982, it was 80 degrees Fahrenheit and the first sunny day after three weeks of clouds. When we arrived at the house in which Pauline and her daughter Shauna live with their family, we rang the bell and waited. A large woman opened the door of the ground-floor apartment and we knew immediately that we had rung the wrong bell. We apologized and told her we had come to visit Pauline. The woman smiled at us and pushed the other bell. Pauline's four-year-old nephew, Sherran, came down the stairs, and the woman asked him who was upstairs in the apartment. Sherran told her that Pauline was there and so was his grandmother. The woman told him to take us up.

Cora was cleaning up. There was a soda cup under the couch, and the top was on the floor near the window. The green outer layer from a chewing-gum wrapper was also on the floor along with various papers that looked like receipts. A child's picture was on the chair, and several of Shauna's school assignments were on the couch. Pauline came out of her bedroom combing her hair, and she sat on the couch. The stereo filled the room with music, and we talked above the beat. Mike arrived. During our last visit he had come in and asked his mother for $5. This time he wanted $10. He talked to Cora and to Pauline. He told them he needed new sneakers and cleats for baseball. Cora sat down on a chair opposite Pauline, and Mike moved between them. They talked quickly in a good-humored banter, with Mike persisting and the women resisting. It was difficult to hear what they were saying. The music drowned out most of their words, and they were too in tune with one another for us to understand the family talk that they shared.

The banter stopped, and Mike talked to us about his baseball team and told us we should come and see him play. He asked if anyone wanted anything from the store. Pauline asked for a bean pie, and Cora said that she'd like a Coke. We also asked for Cokes and Mike left. Pauline talked about the baseball team that Mike plays for. She told us that he was a good player. A few minutes later he returned with a bean pie for Pauline and Cokes for Cora and for us. Mike refused to let us pay for the sodas and resumed the discussion that he had been having with his sister and mother. Again he moved between them as he tried to convince them that he needed the money. There was much laughter and the three of them seemed to be enjoying the game. Then it ended abruptly. Mike left. "Did he get the money?" we asked. Cora grinned: "He left, didn't he?"

The talk went on around us. There was never an occasion when we visited Pauline that we weren't aware of the closeness of her family. Our summer visits were spent talking with Pauline, Cora, and Trisha, who was then living at home with her mother. The days were impossibly hot, and we would sit near the windows to catch the breeze. Music played and trucks rumbled by. Sometimes a dog climbed out of a window onto the flat roof of the house across the street and we would watch as he passed back and forth panting in the summer heat. There were many occasions when we would arrive to find Cora, who worked as a waitress in an all-night diner, sleeping in a bedroom that opened into the living room. There was no partition between the rooms, but the noise of the family did not seem to disturb Cora, who slept on a mattress under a thin cover.

It was at this time that Shauna became our "mythical" child, for we rarely saw her. Before the summer break we were often there when she came home from school, but now when we visited she always seemed to be out playing or with older members of her family, roller skating or at the movies. Sometimes when we were there Shauna would arrive with Megan or Gina, her sisters, and we would hear young feet running up the wooden stairs. Then they'd burst into the room filling the tiny space with the exuberance of their play and with the vitality of their talk. Shauna would invariably go over to her mother and sit beside her on the arm of the couch. Sometimes Shauna would offer Pauline a piece of candy or a bite of cookie. Then Pauline would smile at her as she shared the food and talked with Shauna about the things she had done while she was out with her family or friends. Then, within minutes, Shauna would be gone, back out to play or off to visit friends. We asked Pauline if she worried about her, and she smiled and said that everybody knew Shauna and that she was safe as long as she stayed in the neighborhood.

Much of the time we talked with Pauline about school. She had taken the college entrance verbal and quantitative exams and was waiting to receive the results. Pauline told us that she was a good student, and she spent much time talking about her own experiences in school. She told us that she had lived with her grandmother "down south" for a year and that she had started school a few months later than most of her friends. Then she told us about kindergarten: "I remember the teacher name: Miss L——. She was nice. . . . She was real tall with blond hair. I don't remember doing any work, I just remember how she looked. That's it. . . . She was O.K. They weren't allowed to hit anybody then." We then asked Pauline if she remembered learning to read. "Yes," she said, "first grade. Miss W——. . . . She had freckles. Red hair. She was nice, she was real nice." Pauline went on to say that learning to read "was easy." Then she added, "No problem. Like they had the classes separated then on the basis of reading. And so I wasn't in the highest, I was in the next to highest." Pauline said that there were four groups and she was in the second group. "Then there was Miss P——. Oh, she was very big but she was nice. I had all these teachers with these unusual names." Pauline told us that she moved to the city when she was in fifth grade. She said, "I had my first man teacher here. Mr. P——. He didn't give no work. All we did was have parties. . . . Yeah, Mr. P——. We had this big old Christmas party. . . . I don't remember doing any work. . . . Everybody wanted to be in our class. My brother used to come to the class. They used to sit there. They used to like him. He never taught us anything." Pauline paused and then added, "Probably did but we were having so much fun." Pauline continued, "In sixth grade, that's when I got my first black teacher. She was something. I think she was the best one. Miss A——. She was little but they better listen. Seventh grade I had Mr. J——. Nothing unusual about him. . . . Then we had Mr. M——. That's the eighth-grade teacher. He taught everybody that they weren't going to be nothing because we always thought we knew everything." Pauline laughed, "We did. We was obnoxious." Then Pauline told us that all her friends who had been in school with her were back in school. She said some of them had dropped out, but that all of them were trying to continue their education.

At the beginning of September in 1982 Pauline was preparing to return to school to become a computer programmer. Pauline told us that she would have to get up early, as she had to be at the college by eight-thirty in the morning and that Shauna would have to be up at about the same time to get ready for school. She told us that during the summer months Shauna usually stayed up until one or two in the morning, and she talked pleasurably of the way in which the family spent the long evenings outside, sitting on the steps or standing on the sidewalk, talking, listening to music, and enjoying a respite from the humidity and heat. Pauline explained that in the summer their mornings were spent sleeping but in the fall that changed. She told us that Trisha was an early riser and that they were going to rely on her to wake them up. Pauline said that she would help Shauna get ready for school and then she would prepare for her own day of classes. We visited the family on many occasions during the fall of that year, and Pauline always seemed confident in her own abilities and focused upon the career she had chosen as a computer programmer.

In January 1983 we arranged to meet Pauline in the cafeteria of the college that she was attending. The cafeteria was an immense multilevel place. The tables were filled with students, and there were many more waiting for seats. Young men and women with precariously balanced trays moved between the tables looking for a place to sit and eat. Others lined up and waited to reach the counter to choose the food that they would eat. We walked around looking for Pauline but did not find her. Then we sat down to wait, hoping that Pauline was looking for us and figuring that she would be more likely to find us if we stayed in one place. We talked to a young woman who told us she was a nursing major. While we were talking, Pauline came over to where we were sitting. She smiled and said that she had walked around for a while and that as she couldnd't find us she had gone to the library with a friend. We said we had wondered if she had forgotten; she said that she had wondered if we had done the same. Pauline sat down. We talked with the young nursing student for a few minutes, and then she got up and left. We talked with Pauline about her studies. She told us that it was a two-year program but that she hoped to get a job in the summer using her skills as a computer programmer.

She said that she had been told that there were plenty of jobs and that she ought to be able to find a summer job without any difficulty. Pauline continued by telling us that she had heard that some computer programmers earned as much as $60,000 a year.

The conversation shifted to classes and assignments, and Pauline asked us about writing. She told us that she had two friends who were really good at writing but that most people in her classes couldn't write. Then she talked about oral reports and told us about a student who had tried that morning to present an essay to the class. Pauline said, "It was bad," and she explained that he had just stood there shaking. She wanted to know how we made presentations, and we told her of the ways we prepared for such occasions. She told us about her teachers and her assignments and of the students in her classes. Then we talked about her family and especially of Trisha, who we had noticed had seemed to have become so sad. Pauline explained that Trisha wanted to become a lawyer and that she was hoping that by working as a paralegal secretary she would be able to pay for her college education. Even then she would need assistance. Pauline told us that Trisha had applied for financial aid to study for an undergraduate degree and had been told that she would have to be a full-time student to be eligible for support. That would have meant taking daytime courses, but Trisha could only go to school at night. Pauline told us that she thought Trisha would take a course at the college that she was attending during the spring semester and that she would try to become a full-time student in the fall.

We left the college and drove home with Pauline. Our conversation continued. Pauline told us that she eventually wanted to own a condo and have her own car, and again she talked about becoming a computer programmer. The time passed quickly and we soon found ourselves driving down the street where she lived. We asked her about the houses that we used to see occupied and that now stood empty, their windows smashed and the doors gone. Pauline pointed at one of them and told us that the city owned the house and the people had moved across the street. We parked in front of Pauline's house and went inside to visit her family. Trisha was sitting on the arm of a chair talking on the telephone. On the seat of the chair was a piece of paper on which she had written Sherran's name with a red pen. She had written it many times and the careful script filled the page. Trevor told us that she had been writing while she was talking on the telephone.

The stereo was on. Sherran was sitting on his grandmother's bed watching T.V., and Megan was sitting beside him, playing with an electronic game. Shauna had been sitting with them, but as her mother entered the room she got up and came into the living room. Neither of them spoke. It was a quiet moment, a shared smile and a gentle hug. Then Pauline picked up *Sports Illustrated* from a small table near the window, went over to her favorite spot on the couch, and sat down. Trisha continued to talk on the telephone, and we watched Megan as she played the electronic game. We asked her if it was hers and she said, "No. It belongs to the family." Pauline looked up from the magazine that she was reading and called to us above the noise of the stereo and the T.V. that Megan was very good at the game and often scored in the 700s. Megan said that she had once scored 1200 and then shouted, "750!" Pauline smiled and looked at us as if to say, "What did I tell you?" Shauna went over to where her mother was sitting and sat beside her on the couch. She had been looking at a song sheet that was contained in a record album, and she showed it to her mother. They talked quietly together and as the music was loud we heard very little of their conversation, except to notice that they were reading the words of the songs.

On the day that we met Pauline at college we talked for a while about transportation. Pauline told us that although the college was not far from her home she had to take two buses to get there. Transportation to essential services often came up in the conversations of family members, and we became aware that although the family lived in an inner-city neighborhood, that did not mean that they were close to the services they needed in their daily lives. On one occasion we asked Pauline and Trisha to show us the location of essential services on a map that Pauline drew of her neighborhood. We asked Pauline and Trisha where they bought food. Pauline showed us on the map and then, when we asked her about the stores, she told us that one of them was not a store. She explained that a woman who lived across the road sold food out of her apartment. Pauline commented, "If you can call it that." Trisha added, "We ought to report her to Consumer's." Pauline laughed. We asked what the woman sold and Trisha quickly replied, "High-priced food!" Pauline continued to laugh. "It's higher than if you went into a supermarket?" we asked. Pauline said, "Mmm-mmmm!" and Trisha added an emphatic, "Anywhere!" We then asked about the nearest supermarket. "You gotta drive," Pauline told us. "Get in your car," Trisha said. The two women discussed the location of the various supermarkets, and then we asked what people did if they didn't have a car. "Tough!" Trisha said, and again Pauline laughed. Trisha told us that people would "catch a cab," and she went on to talk about some of the small stores that were within walking distance of the street on which they lived. She explained, "Those are just like little stores where you spend more money than if you went to a supermarket. There's not really a supermarket around here, you know, like Pathmark or something like that. . . . They should build one around here somewhere, a supermarket instead of building all these car lots and putting cars there." Speaking of the local stores, Pauline told us that they had to pay approximately 15 percent more on items than they would if they bought them at a supermarket. Trisha said that some items were double the supermarket price. Before we left the question of supermarkets and food, we asked if it was possible to walk to the nearest supermarket. The question got an immediate response. Pauline began by saying, "It's a nice walk!" Trisha said, "You know where downtown is? It's a long way." Pauline said, "You can walk." Trisha spoke quickly: "I wouldn't want to walk if it's cold. If it's nice and if you ain't got nothing else to do and not in a hurry, then you walk." Pauline echoed her, "Then you walk," and Trisha finished by commenting, "But that's anywhere, right?"

We asked about other necessities. What if they wanted to buy some socks for Shauna? "Go downtown," Trisha said. "What about a prescription?" Pauline and Trisha told us that there was a pharmacy within walking distance but that the prices were high and the drugstore did not stock many items. "How about the movies?" "Downtown or New York." Trisha laughed and told us we were in the wrong part of town. She continued laughing as she told us about the movie house: "They got rats and everything!" Shauna, who was listening to the conversation, quickly added, "And roaches!" We laughed for a while and then continued by asking what the family did if they needed to see a doctor. Pauline told us that the children's doctor was nearby but that she visited a doctor in another town. Pauline said it was a thirty-minute bus ride. We asked about churches, and Trisha, who went to church, told us that it was too far to walk. Similarly, the welfare office was "downtown" and a bus ride away. "Where is the nearest hospital?" "You gotta take a bus," Trisha said. Pauline nodded and agreed, "You gotta take a bus." "Or cab," Trisha added, "Or start walkin'."

We visited Pauline and Shauna through the remaining months of that academic year. Their lives seemed to move along smoothly. We often saw Shauna doing her homework as she sat beside her mother, and Pauline told us that they frequently worked together. Pauline explained that she wrote out math problems for Shauna to work on while she studied her class assignments. Trisha was also back at school studying to be a legal secretary. Then the summer came and Pauline looked for a job in which she could use the skills she had learned in her year of training as a computer programmer. There were no jobs within reach of her home. There had been one prospective position, but it was in a town many miles away. Pauline would have had to change buses several times, and she would have spent between three and four hours a day getting to and from work. Pauline decided to stay home. Shauna, Sherran, Megan, and Joe-Joe went south for the summer. We took a six-week break from the research project.

In September we visited Pauline. She told us she was not going back to college until after Christmas. When we asked her why she shrugged her shoulders and said that she didn't want to go. Trisha was at home during that visit and she told us that she would finish her course to become a legal secretary that semester. She said that she still hoped to take an undergraduate degree so that she could go on to law school. Several weeks later Trisha told us that she had switched one of her courses. She said it was a lot of reading, and she showed us the books that she was reading for the course. Later in the year Trisha moved out of her mother's apartment and into an apartment of her own. She finished the courses that she was taking and got a job as a secretary in a real estate office. Pauline continued to live at home. She did not return to school after Christmas. In the summer of 1984 she began to work in the same office as her sister and in 1985 returned to college to study real estate and get a license as a realtor.

Postscript: July 1987.   When we spoke with Pauline in July 1987, she was hoping to move into her own apartment with Shauna. She says that she wants to be on her own and that she has found a place in a nearby town. Pauline has studied for a real estate license. She has passed the necessary exams and is now working for a real estate and investment company. Shauna, who is now twelve, continues to do well at school. Pauline says, "She's in everything." She goes on to explain that Shauna is in the Beta Club, which is an honors society. She plays the flute in the band and she is in the Fashion Club. Pauline smiles as she speaks of Shauna and her accomplishments. She has been told by the school that Shauna is a gifted child.

Pauline's mother and her brothers and sisters are all well. Her mother continues to work. Pauline says, "She's still the same. She doesn't change." Gina and Megan are both living at home. Trevor has moved out of the apartment and is living with his girlfriend. Trisha is still working and living in her own apartment. Sherran spends his time with her and with his grandmother. He is nine years old and doing well in school.

Jerry, Jemma, Tasmika, and Jamaine

We met Tasmika one afternoon when we were visiting Tanya and her children. Tasmika was playing with Queenie. She was a small child with quick dark eyes and long braids of hair that reached her waist. There was nothing shy about Tasmika. She was happy and brash. She smiled and tossed her braids as she talked, and she seemed to fill the room with her exuberance. Tanya told us that Tasmika lived on the next street with her mother and father. She added with a smile that Tasmika was also in first grade and that she was a good reader. That was all Tasmika needed to hear. She had come straight from school, and she had her book bag with her. She opened it up, took out a basal, and flipped through the pages. Then she began to read. Occasionally she stumbled, but for the most part she read with the intensity with which she played.

Several months later we began to visit Tasmika and her family. Jemma, her mother, was then in her early thirties. She is a small woman and looks much younger than her years. Their apartment was a sharp contrast to the rooms in the abandoned building in which Tanya was living. Jemma told us that Jerry, her husband, had painted the living room. She told us that he was an artist and that he repainted the rooms whenever he could. The walls of the living room were painted in soft apricots, and Jerry had decorated them with a geometric design in muted browns. We learned that Jemma also focused her energies on creating the special ambiance of the home in which the family lived. The curtains that covered the first-floor windows were also soft apricot, and the couches, which they had found in a nearby suburban town during clean-up week, were covered in brown and beige fabric. Everything in the living room seemed to be carefully positioned, and new placements were constantly made. Each time we visited the family there would be another arrangement—tables moved, couches turned, and pictures and paintings replaced. But there was nothing artificial about this movement of things. The apartment was always comfortable and contrasted sharply with the drabness of the outside street.

In the summer of 1982 Jemma spent her days taking care of Tasmika and her little brother, Jamaine. Jerry was working in a silk-screen factory, so we rarely saw him when we visited the family at home. On one of our visits in July of that year we arrived early in the day. It was, as always, a chance visit. Jemma was on her way to the basement with a pile of laundry. She greeted us warmly and asked us to wait while she loaded the washing machine with the family's dirty clothes. When she had finished we went with her into the apartment and she told us to sit down while she helped the children get dressed so that they could go out to play. One of Tasmika's friends had stayed the night, and the two girls were peeping around the corner and giggling at us. Jemma told them to go and bathe. They giggled some more and ran down the corridor. A friend had also arrived to play with Jamaine. He was waiting for Jamaine to get dressed.

Jamaine came into the room and hid behind a couch. He was wrapped in a towel, and he held onto it tightly as he headed for the back of the couch. Safe, he stood there smiling at us as he waited for his mother to help him dress. Tasmika and her friend had crept back and were peeping around the corner again. Jemma took Jamaine's hand and together they made their way to the couch. Jemma sat down and Jamaine stood in front of her and waited. Jemma called to Tasmika and told her to bring Jamaine's clothes. She told Tasmika that she had put them on his bed. Tasmika squealed as she ran down the corridor with her friend and then reappeared with the neat pile of folded clothes. She placed them on her mother's back as she leaned forward to put talcum powder on Jamaine. Jemma pulled a face and then she thanked her daughter for bringing the clothes and again told her to go and bathe. Tasmika left and soon we could hear the water running in the bathroom. Jamaine stood still. Jemma dusted his front and back with the talc, and she lifted his chin and gently rubbed the powder into the soft folds of his neck. Then she helped him on with his clothes, shorts first, T-shirt last. Jamaine stood quietly. His mother looked at him. He smiled. She reached for some pomade, and she bent forward and rubbed it onto his legs. Again she sat back and looked at him. He stood straight in front of her for the inspection, as if he knew that she would want to make sure that he looked O.K. before she began to brush his hair. Satisfied, Jemma brushed Jamaine's long brown curls and then let him go. Jamaine ran around the room as if enjoying the moment when he was set free. Then he found some cars and began to shoot them across the uncarpeted section of the tiled floor. His young friend joined in the game, and the two of them waited until the girls were ready to go out to play.

Jemma began again, this time with the two girls. She dusted them with talcum powder and waited while they dressed; then she rubbed their legs with pomade and again made her inspection. Tasmika's friend had elaborate braids, so Jemma just brushed her bangs. Then Tasmika sat on the floor with her back to her mother, and Jemma held her still with her knees as she began the difficult task of brushing her waist-long hair. Tasmika wriggled and Jemma scolded her. Tasmika made herself comfortable as Jemma continued to brush. Jemma parted her hair into three sections, then took one section and brushed it until the tangles were removed. Once this was done she braided the ends together. This process was repeated with the two other sections of hair; then the three braided ends she braided together and fastened with a barrette. Tasmika turned around to show us how her mother had braided her hair. Then she left. The other children followed.

Jemma sat back on the couch and closed her eyes. Then she told us it had been a difficult night. She said that they had made a bed for Jamaine on the couch because Tasmika's friend had slept over, and they didn't want him sleeping with the girls. But in the middle of the night he had awakened and asked if he could sleep in his parents' bed. Jemma said that she spent the rest of the night with her nose against the wall. At that moment Tasmika called from outside. Jemma went to the kitchen window and spoke to Tasmika. She told her not to shout unless someone was chasing her with a knife. We heard Tasmika laugh. Jemma shut the window, came back into the living room, and sat down. She told us she had to take Tasmika to the dentist later in the day and that she was also going to visit the WIC office. Jemma explained that WIC stood for Women, Infants, and Children and that she receives vouchers from this program with which she can buy milk, cheese, eggs, and other essential foods. She talked about the program and of how she relied on it to ensure that her children were well fed. Her face clouded over as she spoke of how it looked as if Jerry would be out of work within a few weeks, as the factory where he worked was going to be closed down. She said she was worried about Jerry as he looked ill. She said the chemicals in the plant were making him sick. He was finding it difficult to breathe and sometimes coughed up blood. Then the shadow passed as she talked about Jerry and the children. She told us that the children enjoyed being with their dad and that the other day Jamaine had asked Jerry if he would stay home from work. She said that Jerry had asked him why and Jamaine had answered, "So we can get a soda together."

Jemma talked again about the visit the family was making to the dentist, and we got ready to leave. Jemma walked outside with us and for a moment or two we stood and watched the children play. Tasmika was pushing a baby in a stroller up and down the street. Jemma explained that the baby belonged to a young woman who lived in her apartment building. She told us that Tasmika, who was then six, often took care of the baby.

Tasmika and Jamaine were often outside playing with the other children who lived on the street. Sometimes the children were about the same age as Tasmika, but very often they were younger. Tasmika would greet us when we arrived and introduce us to her cousins. Jemma would laugh when we went into the apartment and ask her about the children. She would say, "Tasmika says everybody's her cousin." Most of the visits that we made were unannounced. The family did not have a phone, and there was no way for us to let them know that we were coming. Sometimes when we arrived Jemma was cleaning—sweeping the floors, rearranging furniture, washing clothes. We would call to her and she would invite us in. Then we'd sit and talk to her while she finished cleaning. At other times Jemma would be watching her favorite soap opera, and we would sit and wait until the story was over. Jemma watched with almost total concentration. Only her children coming into the apartment could bring her out of the story and back into the room. She spoke to Tasmika and Jamaine whenever they came inside. On one occasion Tasmika came in with a friend and headed for her bedroom to play. Jemma told her that it was a sunny day and to play outside. On another occasion Jamaine wanted a drink, so she went into the kitchen and poured him a glass of water.

When the show was over the T.V. was turned off. People visited—neighbors from upstairs, mothers with young children, family. Jemma welcomed them all. The apartment was comfortable. People came and relaxed. They would lean back on a chair, smoke a cigarette, talk to Tasmika, watch Jamaine, and listen to Jemma. Very often someone would ask Jemma if they could borrow something—vaseline, detergent. On one occasion Jemma's brother was visiting and asked if he could have some meat to take home for his dinner. Jemma took some meat from her freezer and gave it to him. During these visits Jemma would talk about Jerry, but he was never home. Jemma told us that she was worried about him. He was so tired. The fumes at the silk-screening factory were making him nauseous, and he was having difficulty eating and sleeping.

It was October when we finally met Jerry. When we arrived at the apartment building the front door was closed. During the summer it had always been open, and we would step inside and knock on the apartment door or push it open if Jemma had left it ajar. But by October the weather was turning and there was a nip in the air. We looked at the buzzers and tried to figure out which one we should press. The apartment was on the ground floor, so we decided it had to be A or B. We tried A. A small man came to the door. He opened it a crack and looked at us sharply. We told him we were looking for Jemma. He said that she was not at home and abruptly closed the door. Cathé shouted, "Are you Jerry?" The door opened. We told Jerry who we

were. He relaxed a little and told us that Jemma had talked about us. Then
he added that the apartment was "pulled apart." We said that it didn't matter.
Jerry said it mattered to him, but he stepped back and opened the door to
let us go inside.

The living room had become a studio where Jerry was working. He showed
us a sign for a vegetable store that he was painting. Then he pointed at a
portrait that was half completed, perched on top of a cupboard. A man with
a hat on was sitting at the table drawing. Jerry said he was sorry that Jemma
was not at home, and as he spoke he went over to where the man was sitting
and picked up a piece of paper. It was a note from Jemma. In it she said,
"Dear Jerry, I've gone to the hospital to see [a friend]. It's 2:30." The note
continued by instructing Jerry to get some tuna fish from the store for their
dinner. It ended "with love." We talked to Jerry for a few minutes and then,
as he was working, began to leave. It was then that Jerry told us to sit down,
and he sat down with us. For a few minutes we talked about his children. As
Jerry began to talk to us we asked if we could record the conversation. Jerry
laughed and said, "Sure." We placed the tape recorder on the table in front
of him and then sat quietly listening to Jerry. We didn't ask him questions;
none were necessary.

Jerry began by telling us that he was born in Maryland and that he moved
to the city in 1944. He said that he was the oldest of three sons. He said, "This
is where I began to learn to lie, to cheat, and everything. And this is where I
first got beat up. You know what I mean? On Clancey Street in 1944. I had a
very good father. He was a worker. A shoe repair man. You know, by trade,
that he had learned. Money was small then, but then so was everything
else—you know, the living, the expenses and everything else was very small,
but he always provided for us. But he always provided for us. He was an
individual who was very quick-tempered. And I was not able, me nor my
brothers or anybody, to come home with bad marks, D's or F's, because you
got a beatin'—you got an ass whippin' then. . . . My mother was more lenient.
She was more on the other side. You know, the tolerant side. But he didn't
tolerate anything. Plus he was a hustler and a gambler. So we always did have
something. Even a little more. We were the first to get television. . . ."

Jerry was quiet for a moment, as if reflecting on his childhood. Then he
continued by telling us about his own children. "My children. I raised them."
Jerry paused. "I don't believe in whippings. I really don't believe in whippings.
Not that I've never spanked any of them, but never hurt them like I've been
hurt. I mean whelps on my butt. I don't do that. I can howl at them and make
them jump if there's cause but since Tasmika can talk . . . [I say] 'Well, what's
the problem? Explain it to me. Why did you do this? Why did you do that?
Don't hunch your shoulders, that doesn't mean anything.'" Jerry laughed,
hunched his shoulders, and explained, "I used to do this. You know what I
mean?" And then he was back to his conversations with Tasmika: " 'Tell me.
Try and explain it to me. If you really can't explain it, well, listen and I'll

explain it to you....' You see what I'm saying? I try to explain every little thing to her. Every little detail. 'You want to learn how to paint? This is how Daddy do it. This is how I do it. Come on, here's a little paint set for you. Here, take a little bit of this paint. Here's a brush. Now see how I do this?' " Jerry looked at us and continued, "And I try and show her how to make a letter. How to make something. How not to do this. How not to do that. And in turn she goes right and shows her baby brother." Again Jerry laughed. He continued to chuckle as he told us that Tasmika was bossy. He said, "She's a little bossy like I am in the household. Oh, you should hear sometimes. 'Jamaine, get out of here with that noise. I'm looking at my program.' She's bossy—you know what I mean?—but this is because she is the big sister. I run the house. Jemma runs them, and she [Tasmika] runs him." Jerry is laughing. "You know what I mean. It goes right down the ladder. But it's never that much physical conflict.... If they have something to say, they have something to express, or anything else, I listen. I'm right here."

Jerry sat back in his seat and began a story about Tasmika. "I took her fishing one time. I was going fishing and I'll never forget.... Tasmika always loved water ... so we were out in the park ... it wasn't summer, it was autumn and this couple of guys were out fishing. You know they ain't catching nothing but sunfish. So I'm watching one and he says, 'I got one,' so he's pullin' the little fish in, and I look and I hear something—'Pshh, pshh, pshh' —I turn round and look and Tasmika has done and run out into the water. I had to run out and get her, so both of us was wet." Jerry is laughing and we are laughing with him. The lilt of his voice and the sparkle of his eyes help us see Tasmika in the water and her father as he runs out to pick her up and bring her safely back to the water's edge. Jerry continued, enjoying the story, "I picks her up and I carries her right back over to my mother-in-law's house, which is across from the park ... and the next time I took her out there we really went fishing. I got her a little line and I had the worms. She said, 'Daddy, I can do it.' So she watched me put the worm on the hook, and she picked the worm up and tried to put it on the hook like I did. She had him on there a little bit and, you know, I helped her because I didn't want her to hook her finger on that hook, you know, but she was interested. She's very fast. She catches on very fast."

Jerry looked tired. The light in his eyes was gone and he returned to his own story. "And this is what I've always been able to do is catch on fast. I quit school when I was sixteen. I quit high school. You know, during those days you're tough, you hanging out, you know. I'm trying to get me a little car, and my father had bought a shoe repair shop up on Summerhill Avenue. Shoe repair, shoe shine and hat cleaning, and everything.... Arthur's Shoe Repair, that was my father's place. And he had a couple of tractor trailers, him and one of his partners. So he brought me up there. I went to work for him when I quit school, and he taught me how to repair shoes and how to make them, and he left me in charge of the shop, and I had three people working for me—the hat cleaner, another shoe repair man, and the shoe-shine guy. . . . Oh, we did a good business." Jerry paused and looked at us as if he wanted to make sure we were ready for the connections that he was making. "But I learned," he said, emphasizing the words as he looked from one to the other of us. Then he dropped his voice and almost in a whisper he continued, "I learned it like that. I learned how to run the shops. Keep receipts. To pay off people. You know." Gradually his voice regained its tenor. "From there I went on. I learned other things, you know. I learned how to draw and paint. I used to go to Arts high during the summer vacation. I would go there for sculpture. Just to do something, you know. . . . You learn." Jerry's voice became strained. "You have pressures on you. I have pressures on me at times, you know. I'm in an area right now that is very depressive. I was livin' in ——— before. I didn't have enough room, and the rent that they wanted to charge me for five rooms, after Jemma was expecting another baby, at that particular time, knowing what I was making, I couldn't afford it. So Jemma started looking around. She ends up with this, but we's upstairs with another three-room apartment when we were supposed to get four rooms because we were already in a three-room apartment up there. So, you know, I came down. The area was all right at first. We's waiting for our four room. It took time but we finally did get it—down here." It became difficult for Jerry to speak: "I'm very displeased. It's very depressive. She's depressive. I get depressive. But at the same time I keep tryin' to, hey, we have to maneuver. I said, 'Everything is out of control right now.' It's not like, you know, O.K. I'm working, but do you know how much it takes to get a really good place? I've been tryin' to move into ——— for so long. I can't even get up there. I made a mistake. I could be up there right now in the new ones that they built. So-called low income but they went up 50 percent on their rents, you know. I'd be payin' $500 and some dollars a month just for rent for five rooms, room for my daughter, room for my son, bedroom for us. You know. It's rough out there." Jerry's voice grew stronger, and he spoke slowly and deliberately, "But. You cannot take it out on the children. You cannot do it."

Jerry smiled, and the light was back in his eyes. "I come home in the evening and it surprises me." He sat forward and was back to his children with another story to tell. "Last Friday I gave Tasmika a dollar. I gave my son a dollar." Jerry chuckled, "Kids can't use quarters no more." Jerry explained that Tasmika and Jamaine usually go to the store together, but on this occasion he couldn't find Jamaine. "Don't know where he's at. He's three years old. He crossed the street and went to Gino's and got him a hamburger—er, a cheese-burger with lettuce and tomatoes." Jerry continued, "I gave him some money yesterday . . . he wanted some french fries. I said, 'Well, here's the money.' I gave him fifty cents. Fifty-some cents. Right. So I watched him. He went up to the door by himself. I'm standing right out here, you know. Up the street . . . and he waited until a lady was coming out. He said, 'Thank you,' and she looked down at him and let him in. Now she doesn't see me. Right? And I'm looking. He stays in there because he can't open the other door to get in after he's inside [the first door]. A man sees him and comes over and I'm watching and he goes on in. Now he stays so long I'm lookin', so here he comes out. Somebody open the door for him coming out because he's not strong enough to push it open himself. And he's coming out the other door, and I look and he has his french fries and everything with extra ketchup." Jerry looked from one to the other as if he is not sure that we understand the importance of his story. "But do you understand what I'm saying?" Then he continued quickly driving home his meaning: "Little as he is, Gino's is serving him"—voice rising—"only because he has the money. 'Whose child is this?' 'Where does he come from?' None of that. No interest."

Jerry's voice was quiet, and he continued with the light gone out of his weary eyes. "There's no interest in a lot of these children around here. And you come out here at nighttime. You come out here at eleven, twelve o'clock at night and see them running around on the corners. Shaking poles down and doing this and that. It's really bad. You see, as long as my children live under my roof, if it's summertime . . . nine or ten o'clock and they're not going to school and somebody is out there, you know, watching them. 'O.K. Sit out there. But you're not going to be outside no eleven, twelve, or one o'clock.' " Jerry is looking at us again. His eyes are sharp and he speaks with conviction, "That don't get it, you know. This is just the beginning for you. You got a lot to go through. And even at my age I have a lot to go through. My son is three years old, that's my youngest one. I got another fifteen or twenty years to go to see him out there properly on his own." Jerry is hoarse. "I hope that I can do it. I can't do anything for myself. I can't buy a new car. If I didn't have them I could. You know, they are an expense and a burden." He smiles and his voice lightens, "But I love them. And I'm willing to sacrifice and everything else to see that we have something. We don't have everything, and I want more." Jerry chuckled, "We always want more you know." And then seriously, "But I do make the time to try and teach them, to play with them and everything. Last night he got a new car . . . and we was out here just playing with it." Jerry closed his eyes and smiled, "Just playin' with it."

Jerry moved on from the new car to Tasmika's new book bag. "Tasmika wanted a new book bag. She got two book bags and had to go downtown yesterday with the money I gave her and her mother and buy a new book bag to match her jacket." Jerry began to laugh and we laughed with him. "Red—a red book bag. Red. I watched her put it on today. I don't know how many books she has in it, but I said, 'Tasmika, you can't even lift that. Look at you.' " Jerry pointed towards Tasmika's room. "It's in there. I'm not kidding. Watch this." Jerry left and came back with the bag. He sat down in between us and showed us the books that were packed tightly inside. Cathé called it a "super sack" and we continued to enjoy the moment. But Jerry had not lost the purpose of his story. He continued by telling us about the hairstyling dolls that Tasmika liked to play with. He said, "Tasmika is very interested in hair styling.... She loves to hair style, so I want to get her another head. You know. An assortment of hair colors ... various colors where she can do what she wants to do." Again Jerry looked at us as if assessing whether we were capable of making the leap to comprehend his story. "You understand," he said, looking first at one and then the other. "Then I want to get her into this school. Possibly this month. Because she's interested in ballet. And it's a pretty good school. You know what I mean. I would like to get her in there for Saturday classes in ballet or if they see that she, er—" Jerry paused. "I want her in a school where if they see you excel in something—" Again he paused. It seemed that he was waiting to see if we understood. Cathé said, "They'll push?" Jerry nodded and smiled, "They'll push."

Jerry returned to his own education. He seemed to use it as a rationale for his belief in providing opportunities for his children to excel in the areas in which they were interested and showed ability. "In the schools I went to, I excelled with my hands. English, when it came to English, literature, music, this and that, I did not excel ... but I never failed ... I was always average. But I excelled in machine shop and various other things with my hands. But they never pushed. They never pushed any of us in them days." He searched our faces. "You know what I mean?" A nod was enough and he continued. "I took advantage of it later on. After I quit school I went back and got my GED and I went to college. I learned art, you know ... and I've been successful."

Jerry went on to tell us that he had taken courses in psychology and sociology and that he took a correspondence course with the Chicago Technical College in practical drafting and electrical drafting. Then he added, "And I also took a correspondence course with ICS in the fine arts." Jerry's voice was quiet. "I've been very busy and I'm tired. I'm tired and I'm old." Jerry laughed and clapped his hands, and when he spoke his voice was strong, "But I have to keep pushing." Then more quietly: "I am tired but I have to keep pushing. You know. My house looks like a junkyard. I need a house and it just seems that I can't get it. Every time things look a little good or fairly decent, then here comes taxes or this and that.... I'm saying 'Jesus Christ' every time I think I'm ahead I move two steps forward and I take three backwards. I remain where I'm at. You know. Now that piece of wood right there—" Jerry pointed across to where the man in the hat was sitting and drawing. On the floor beside him was a wooden frame. "This is a silk-screen outfit that I'm building for printing T-shirts and various other things, you know what I mean ... and I've got to cut some of the wood off there. I found that rather than buy it."

We talked for a moment of his need for a place for his silk-screening business, and Jerry agreed that what he really needed was a loft. But again he talked of the financial difficulties that he faced. "But there is so much expense involved. I had a store, but I lost that because I had no salesman. I can't stay in there and work and wait for people to come and get stuff from me. I have to have somebody out there bringing business to me. You know.

So I have a new thing going now and I have a guy who's going to be my salesman. So far it looks like—yeah—about next year I'll be into it. I'll have a registered business." We offered encouragement to Jerry and he quickly continued. "I'm tired of being a so-called supervisor, which I'm not. I'm just a working foreman, and I've been up here too long and it's time to do something for myself. It's time to really do something for myself. My wife has the capabilities and the qualifications, you know, to be a secretary for me and to keep books and keep records and this and that. That's what I want."

Jerry's voice had become a hoarse whisper, but once again his voice grew stronger as he made the connection between his own life and the lives of his children. "And whatever my children show interest in, this is what I want to push them in. I don't want to try and pull them into what I'm into. I want to push—to push them into what they want to go into. You know, so far my son, all he shows interest in is really those cars, trucks, and all that stuff. . . . But I've got a car down here. I do body and fender work. You know how I mean. And I swear I used to work for the service station over here. I have many trades. I can take a piece of metal and make anything out of it." Jerry spoke loudly, "And it's nothing but art. That's all body and fender work is— art. You know how to spray a little bit." Jerry drew in his breath and then released it to make the sound of a spray. "You know. My television stayed broke for a month. I fixed it. Because I can't afford to have nobody come in here and try and fix that T.V." He chuckled. "You know. You challenge things. You look up the basics. You've done some reading and this and that, then you get into it. You try."

We talked for a while about Tasmika in school, and of how she helped her friends and made us comfortable when we came to visit. Jerry talked of her independence and of the way she helped at home. "She washes dishes," he said. "She has got up and fried Jemma an egg and made her some coffee." Jerry laughed, "Jemma said she didn't like the coffee." Then he was serious again, "She knows how to do it. But the thing is, the school complains about it. 'Tasmika talks too much.' 'Tasmika, she does her work and then she gets up to help one of her friends, which she shouldn't do.' You know what I mean. 'Please talk with her on this.' 'Please discipline her on this.' You know. Before I would discipline her I would try and get her in somewhere but it's too expensive for me right now to put her in a private school. You know. But I'd rather have her in a private school because I want her to be her. I don't know what she will be, but it's my child, my seed, and whatever she will be I want to be right there. You know. 'Daddy, I need this or I want to do that,' and if it is reasonable I want to help her."

Jerry went on to tell us about his oldest son, who was then 22 years old. He talked about his graduating from school with honors and of his service in the Marine Corps. Jerry told us that his son was training at the local police academy and he pointed to a painting. "That's a portrait when he was young." He smiled and raised his eyebrows, "I love my children. I just love them." He paused and then went on, "I don't just love mine. I love all children." He made a quick chuckle, "But there is some I can deal with and some I can't deal with. You know." Again his voice was strained. "You cannot chastise all the children aroud here if you see them doing something wrong because some parents, you cannot tell them that their children do wrong. If you see my child doing something wrong, come and tell me. Because when I was young and coming up here in this city we couldn't do nothing wrong—we couldn't do nothing wrong. We did not disrespect grown-ups ... let me tell you. They didn't lie on you. You may have a couple that would lie on you—maybe. You know. You have some old people. Some old cranks in the neighborhood, but in the majority you did something wrong. Hey. I've got my little butt spanked many a time from next door or across the street or something and then when they told I got another one. But I had that respect, and right today I go to certain people, 'How you doin', Miss Flo?' 'How you doin', Mr. So-and-So?' I don't have to say that I'm 41 years old, I be 42 this month. I don't have to say 'Mr.' and 'Mrs.' because I'm a man. But it's that respect—which these kids don't have. Many of them don't have. Not all of them. Many of them don't have because they don't learn it. Their parents don't have time to teach it to 'em. Their parents are doing things that they see them doin'. I drink, but you know very seldom have my children ever seen me drink." Jerry was quiet and we waited for him to continue. "I may go on that corner and—this is between us. I may go on that corner and drink with them guys down there. Right? But I'll go around the corner—around the corner away from my children so that nobody can say 'Your daddy is a winey. You're daddy's a drinker.' Or anything else. They can't say that. Because I try and stay out of the way of them."

Jerry made another connection. "I can just as easy go right down there and buy myself something to drink and pour my little drinks and this and that while they out playin'. But there's a reason that I go down there because I'm living in a very aggressive area, and 'less I show them that there is aggression about me, and there is, because I'm also a very good fighter." Jerry chuckled, "You know what I mean. I done did it. You know what I mean. And I done and broke a couple of jaws around in the five years that I've been around here. So—if I don't do that, then the next thing I can look for is that my just being a man will be a sign of weakness." Jerry's voice became strained. "And I'm afraid to go out and take my wife and kids to dinner or anything else because when I come back somebody been and come in here, and my television is gone and everything else. I had that happen once. And it's a hurtin' thing when you come in and see your stuff gone, and you don't have any insurance and you got to start all over. So liker—er—" Jerry's voice had become small, but then he joked and we laughed. "That's a bad habit," he said. "Liker—er. That's one of those things." He continued to laugh for a moment and then was quiet as he tied the pieces together and came back to his children.

"There is communication between us," Jerry said. "There's communication between Tasmika and myself, Jamaine and myself, and Jemma and myself." He smiled, "And Jamaine—Jamaine questions me more than anybody else. You know." Jerry's voice was soft. "He's a very evil little guy at times. You know. Like he'll just fold up on you if he can't do something or have his way. But I deal with that also. 'No. You can't have it because you ate already or you're going to eat later.' Or this or that. Or whatever. 'You want some money later. You can't just keep getting money, money, money.' See. 'You don't even have a job.' You know what I mean. I mess with him. I play things out. You know. And then I read to them at night sometimes. Help them. Show them how to spell words or make letters. You know." Jerry smiles and there is a soft look in his eyes. "But I love 'em because they're a lot of fun. Then I sit back and watch them at times."

The soft look turned to pride as Jerry told us of how his children took care of each other. He explained, "You know how kids argue, kids fight, and this and that. No one can touch Jamaine—Jamaine out on that street. If they do, Tasmika is coming. She came in here and took my bat one time. She will fight over her brother. You know. And he will fight over her." Jerry was back to himself and his own struggle to take care of his family. He talked about tenants in the building who turned the building into "a transit house." He explained, "Oh man, ringing the bell, ringing my bell at two, three, and four o'clock in the morning. . . . My daughter's bedroom is there. You understand. I'd be so fired up." Jerry's voice cracked, and he shifted his place in the conversation. "Then somebody came one night and I don't know if they didn't know which building they were coming in because they be down there drinking and they beat people. So somebody came and busted my window. I was sittin' here looking at television. I jumped up. I thought a shotgun had come through the window. Scared me to death. I hit the floor. Then I ran outside because I wanted to see who it was if they were going to shoot again. I didn't know. But, like I said, I'm military orientated." Jerry recovered for a moment and laughed. "Somebody after me, you come on and get me, but you ain't goin' to hurt my family now." He was serious again. "It keeps me on edge. It keeps me very tense. You know. I don't sleep that much. I'm up four o'clock every morning, if I sleep at all, because I watch 'Groucho' and all of them. I'm always up." Jerry nodded with his head toward his friend who was quietly drawing on the table. "And like I was telling Dave there, I'm tired now. I'm tired. I need a rest. I don't—what's going on. I'm tired. I'm physically exhausted. I'm tired. But I gotta keep on going. I gotta keep goin', you know. I've got to see them get on their way like my other son is." Jerry's voice had faded away. Then it came back strong. "But it's going to work. Everything is going to work. I'm not a quitter." Jerry repeated, "I am not a quitter," pronouncing each word slowly and emphasizing the individual letters in "quitter."

Jerry talked of his plans for the future and of leaving his present job in the silk-screen factory. The tension in his voice returned. "I've gotta leave because the smell, the fumes of that vinyl ink and everything. It's a cancer-causing agent and it keeps me just—" Jerry paused. "When you get off you gotta drink, because if you drink water you taste the fumes. Jemma wanted me to have my own special laundry bag because the fumes get all over the house. You eat something you don't even feel like eatin' because it tastes like the thinners and everything." Jerry got up and went over to a cupboard and came back with a folder. He took out a decal and showed it to us. He explained, "They go in children's windows, and that particular ink that goes on is murderous. It is something else to stand the smell of that stuff for eight hours, and they been shippin' those things over the entire nation. I forgot what insurance company is involved in that, but one of them. You know, and they are effective. You put it in your children's room in case of a fire. The firemen come up, 'That's a child's room, get in there first.' This is the purpose of them. 'Tot Finders. Alert All.' " Jerry paused. "I been through a lot, and I want to be into my own business, which I hope we will be into," he paused again, then added, "next year."

Jerry spoke of "living in tough times" and of preserving food, and we talked of canning and pickling, of chutney and relish, and family traditions of saving foods. Jerry then told us about his belief in providing his children with a balanced diet. He told us of an experiment that he had read about in a psychology course that he had taken and of the effect of food on school achievement. "It is very important," he said, "because if you eat you have the energy and this and that. It really affects your thinking and everything else." He talked on about food and about "eating at an appropriate time." Jerry explained, "I don't believe in them late dinners now because if you eat too late you have bad dreams and everything else because the fluids in the body aren't working right." Jerry explained, "All the waters on the face of the planet work with the tides as they ebb and flow and that also goes for the human individual." We talked for a while about this possibility and we both must have looked skeptical, so Jerry pursued his argument and tried to convince us. "Our digestive juices and acids are able to work better during these particular hours. This is why you generally eat between four and five or somewhere around there. You go to nibbling eight or nine o'clock at night," Jerry chuckled and wrinkled his brow, "the tides done went, ain't nothin' workin', and your organs just a-cryin', 'Oh God! I don't know why she did this shit here.' " We were all laughing. "You know what I mean. You're a little miserable. You're tossin' and turnin'." We continued to laugh as Jerry talked of gum "trickin' your stomach." Then we got ready to leave. We stood up and Jerry, still chuckling, said, "I took enough of you all's time. But I try to impart a lot of these little jewels even on children."

Jerry talked on. "I have a lot of fun," he said, still chuckling. We thanked him for spending so much time talking to us. "You all come on back," he said, smiling and continuing to laugh, "because I won't be working much longer. I think next week will be my last week. The man's gone bankrupt."

Jerry began to really laugh. "This is the second time," he said, and his laughter faded. "He hasn't paid the government. He hasn't paid anybody. He hasn't paid anybody social security. One guy he laid off went to get his and they said, 'We ain't got no record of where you ever worked.'" The conversation had become serious again. We stood for a while. Then Jerry sat back down, and we returned to our seats and listened again as Jerry continued to tell us about his life and the life of his family. There were some books on the table, and our questions about them led him back to the beginning of our conversation when he had told us about his education and training as an artist. He went into his bedroom and came back with a vinyl briefcase. He sat down and shuffled through the papers inside until he found the piece of paper that he was trying to find. On one side of the paper he had typed "Books I Have Read" and on the other "Books I Want to Read." Jerry pulled out more paper, sketches for portraits he had promised to do for friends, his diploma from the Chicago Technical College, more papers, and press clippings. Jerry smiled and said, "I was also incarcerated at one time." He went on to tell us of the paintings he had done when he was in prison and of the works that he had displayed in art galleries. He showed us the cover of a book he had designed and a picture of himself with Rubin "Hurricane" Carter. Bumper stickers. Designs for a magazine produced by prisoners. Jerry explained, "I never been in any other trouble. But the point is I took advantage of everything. I took complete advantage of every moment." Jerry showed us designs he was doing for silk screens for T-shirts. He continued to talk about his time in prison and of the way he used his talents as an artist to support his first son. He talked of the portraits he had done of the warden's children and of the money that they sent to his mother in payment for the paintings. Jerry talked of the books that he had filled while in prison. He said that anything that interested him he typed and kept. He showed us one of the files, and we spent some time looking at the poems, quotations, and notes about particular laws that he had studied to try and help some of the men who were incarcerated with him. He told us of his attempts to learn Arabic and explained to us some of the rudimentary principles of the language. He joked about never meeting an Arabic woman and, laughing, he said, "I should have went and spoke Spanish."

We were all laughing, but Jerry continued and our merriment faded as he added, "I should have learned Spanish because it would help me with these jobs that I have as far as functioning as a foreman and supervisor." He told us that he had books on Spanish conversation but that he hadn't really had the time to get into them. We talked for a few more minutes about languages, but the joking had passed. He talked about religion and of there being only one God. "There is only one God. Jehovah. They can be the 144,000 they want to be, the Catholics can be what they want to be, the Muslims what they want to be. They don't know who God is. There is only one supreme being, and we don't know, we just believe. We believe in him, and we believe in ourselves." Jerry's voice was quiet. "And we try to do the best we can for each other. And if we all had that respect this would be a beautiful world. Instead, everybody wantin' to be, like I said, Santa Claus. Just greedy for everything." Jerry talked about a murder that had occurred the week before in his neighborhood. "You can't walk the street at night. Ten o'clock I don't come out. I don't come out on the streets." For a while he returned to his time in prison, and he talked again of the notebooks that he filled with poetry. "This was stuff I loved," he said. "This was my money. You may want money, I can sit back and read some of this." Jerry turned a page and began to read a poem to us. "These things they really meant a lot to me and I made a lot of friends in there and I've helped quite a few people in there. I've taught people how to read and write. Some people they even went to school with me and I couldn't believe that they couldn't read or write. . . . And I'm still the same way right around here. I put that sign up. I had the guys help me. I put signs up on stores. I have them help me even if they ain't got nothin' to do but hold a ladder. You know. But—I'm still right here in this poor-ass area, and I should have a home somewhere. You know. This is what I feel. But maybe I'm just destined to be one of them type of people that will stay here. You know and whatever." Jerry turned a page in his notebook. "Quotations —I love them. I love quotations," and he began to read, " 'Ability is of little account without opportunity.' 'Any fool can criticize, condemn, and complain, and most fools do.' " Then suddenly the twinkle was there again. " 'Here lies the body of William Jay / Who died maintaining his right of way. / He was right, dead right as he sped along / But he's just as dead as if he was wrong.' " We laughed. Jerry laughed.

He talked some more of prison and then of living in the neighborhood of Shay Avenue. "I want my daughter in a good school. I want my kids in a good school. I want this. I want that. But at the same time the jobs that I get and everything I do." Jerry's eyes filled with tears. "I'm being exploited. I'm really being exploited. Anytime I gotta get up at five o'clock in the morning. Wash up. Make me some coffee and everything and get up there and open that place up at seven-thirty in the morning. Catch two buses. This and that. You know. Now I'm a little better off because I have my bus card. I can catch my bus here and go and get my other bus and this and that. But I'm still paying. And I'm saying, 'Damn, I did a job over here.' " He pointed towards the trailers parked on the vacant lot on which he had painted the logo and the name of the construction company. And he explained that his boss at the silk-screen factory would not let him take the time off to pick up the check for the work he had done in his spare time. "I got fired. I got fired Monday. My boss wouldn't let me come and pick it up. Didn't want me to come and pick it up. I needed two hours. Because he's uptight. And he's a thirty-one-year-old junkie. A thirty-one-year-old Italian junkie. I said, 'Well, I'm goin' anyway, man. I'm goin'— I'm goin' to get mine. I know what the thing is here.' I said, 'You can't give me that consideration for runnin' this place?' He comes in eleven, twelve o'clock, often drunk and high an everythin', and I'm runnin' that place, man, for the last six or seven months. No. No. No way. I say, 'You goin' to put my money in my social security account.' I'll collect my unemployment, $140 every week. You understand what I'm sayin'? . . . I may not even collect because I'm goin' to make money. You see what I'm saying?" Jerry's eyes were bloodshot and his face was gray. "I got pictures. I got portraits. Man, I got all that shit. I got to do all this for people. I don't feel like it when I come home. After smellin' all that stuff, I eat and I go to sleep—for a few hours. Then I'm up for a few hours. Then I'm up watching the two-thirty, three o'clock movie. Groucho Marx and the rest of them. I go get her the paper and I'm gone again. Like a zombie. You know. I'm goin' to get my own thing together and you know who'll be my secretary? My wife is goin' to be my secretary, and I already told her today. I sat down. We started figuring that shit out. I say, 'You goin' to get $5 an hour.' . . . We goin' to work together. . . . I gotta do something for myself, and I got one person that will help me and he's helpin' me." Jerry looked over at the man who was sitting at the table. He had stopped drawing and he nodded at Jerry. "It's rough out here. It's rough out here, and we have to work together. You know. I took my kids downtown and got their things for them—what they wanted. You can see that. See all the book bags and she got another one. But I can't argue. I couldn't say nothin'. Women is women, and she's a little woman. Now I wasn't that pleased with it but I don't argue with her. You know what she told me this morning. She want pancakes. I made pancakes and sausage, and I cooked some eggs for me. You know, and we all ate."

Jerry was reaching the end of his story. He talked of working hard and earning money. "Then," he said, "I got lost somewhere along the way and I don't have it. I keep us eatin' and a roof over our head. You know, I maintain that, you know. But I don't have what I should have. You know. And sometimes I question whether I should stay here. I do. You're asking me how I feel. You want to know really how I feel. . . . I am a bona fide artist." He spoke quietly, "I'm a money maker. Or I'm a producer. I can produce. I'm not the one to get out there and do things, but at the same time I don't have no help nowhere. I'm not a salesman, and I know this. So I don't have the help. You understand? . . . Ain't nobody helpin' me, and I'm losin'. I can't even buy the paint this week to paint this little face up." Jerry began to cry. "The kids want a Christmas tree and everything, man. Christmas is here. You know, like she's lookin' like it ain't nowhere, you know, but it's here. This is October. Right. November. December. That's nothin'. That's a week. Ain't nobody helpin' me do shit. Ain't nobody helpin' me make no money." Jerry wiped the tears off his face with the back of his hand. "You all gotta excuse me, man, because this shit is serious out here." Jerry took a moment. "I can't keep the food, get the money to spend on little bullshit. You know. Ice creams and this and that and other junk. I can't keep doin' that. I'm gettin' tired. I'm gettin' old. This is makin' me old. Because I don't have the help that I need, and I've been needin' the help sometime. Because I can do. But I don't have it, and it's hard finding people who will really help you without exploitin' you. Without really exploitin' you and using you. And I'm tired of being used. I'm tired of it." Jerry got up. "I'm sorry. Book is closed. I'm sorry. The book is closed."

We said good-bye to the man sitting at the table and walked outside with Jerry. He looked sad but was smiling. He thanked us for taking the time to listen, and then he added, "Most people don't want to know." Two men passed us on the street and Jerry spoke to them, and then as they moved on along the street, he told us that the men were brothers and that they did everything together. "If one turns his head, so does the other," Jerry said. Then he laughed and we laughed with him.

We continued to visit Jemma and Jerry. A few weeks later, when we arrived, Jamaine was asleep on the couch and Tasmika was watching television. Jerry was just leaving with a friend, but he said he'd be back before we left. Then, as he was going through the door, he turned and nodded directing our gaze across the room towards the Christmas tree that was leaning against the wall. "Found it," he said, and left, calling to his friends who were already out of the building and waiting outside. We talked with Jemma after Jerry had left. She apologized for "the mess." Some of the furniture had been pushed to one side of the room, and there were paint cans on newspaper. Jemma said they were decorating. She took us to see the kitchen, which Jerry had painted a pretty shade of pale yellow. We asked her how things were going for Jerry, and she said, "Slow." Jemma said that he kept busy. He was painting some signs and had began working on some silk-screen designs that he was going to use on T-shirts. Tasmika stopped watching T.V. when we arrived. She showed us her phonics workbook and the page that she had done for homework. Jemma smiled at Tasmika and told us that she had just received Tasmika's report card. "All A's and B's," Jemma said. Tasmika giggled and said that she had all D's. We asked her what a D meant and she laughed. "Disgusting!" she said, laughing some more. Jemma laughed with her. "She didn't get any D's," she said as she went to get the report card. Jerry came back home and said he had something to show us. He went down the corridor to his bedroom, and a few minutes later he returned with a painting. It was of E.T. He had drawn the outline of the extraterrestrial on black velvet, and the face was completely painted. Jerry laughed as we admired his work and he said, "Me and E.T., we got feelings." He smiled, perhaps remembering our last visit.

It was bitterly cold when we next saw the family. Jemma was cleaning the apartment, and she told us that Jerry was asleep in the bedroom. He had not managed to find another job, and there were few signs to paint in the winter. In the middle of the floor, standing on newspaper, was an old tin cupboard. Jemma pulled a face that seemed to be of affectionate exasperation. She told us that Jerry had found the cupboard in some trash by the side of the road and that he was going to clean it up and paint it. Jemma moved on. She had something else to tell us. Tasmika was taking ballet. She went and got her ballet shoes from the bedroom and showed us how tiny they were. Jemma said that she had managed to get them for $15 even though they were $20 in most stores. While we were still admiring the shoes and reading the brochure about the ballet program, Tasmika arrived home from school with her red book bag on her back. She burst in, full of energy and nonstop talk. She asked us if we liked her shoes and then, without prompting, showed us the ballet positions that she had learned at her first class. When she had finished she returned to her book bag, which she had dropped on the couch, and took out her second-grade basal reader. She talked about the stories in her book and chose one to read. She read one page and then got out a piece of lined paper and said she was going to write. She wrote her name at the top of the paper and the numbers one through ten down the left-hand side. Next to number one she wrote, "I like to go to school." Then, by number two, "I do my work good." Tasmika put down the paper and left the living room. She returned quickly with a copy of *Babar*. She told us her mother sometimes read a whole book while at other times she would read part of a book and come back to it later. Tasmika settled in with her book and, except for several excursions to the kitchen to break pieces off a bean pie, she read until it was time for us to leave. She then returned to the sentences that she had been assigned as homework and asked us to remain until she had finished writing them. We apologized and told her that we both had to go. Tasmika wrote, "I like it," and held up her paper and waved it at us as we waved good-bye.

Early in 1983 there was a shooting on Shay Avenue. We arrived to see Jerry and Tasmika walking hand in hand along the street to their apartment building, but by the time we reached their door they had already gone inside. We rang the bell. Tasmika's voice said, "Who is it?" Cathé said, "Cathé and Denny." Jerry opened the door to the building, but quickly went back into his apartment and closed the door. We stood in the corridor and waited. On the wall there was a large message that we noticed for the first time. It announced, "THIS BUILDING WILL BE EXTERMINATED THE SECOND WEEK OF EVERY MONTH." Below the notice someone had written with a felt-tip pen, "Adolph Hitler." The door opened and an old man with a brown bag of bottles nodded at us and quickly left. Jerry opened the door wide and told us to come inside. Tasmika greeted us with a hug and then returned to the T.V. program that she was watching. Some of Jerry's friends were sitting in the room, and one of them stood up for a moment as we entered. Jerry introduced us and then began talking about the shooting. His eyes were tired and his voice strained. He told us that the kid who had been shot was a "seventeen-year-old punk" and that "he deserved it." Then he explained that it was because of kids like him that he had taken his friends with him when he had gone to get his unemployment check. He added that they had stayed for a drink.

After a while the men left, and Jemma arrived home with Jamaine. Jerry walked outside with his friends. Jemma looked ill. Her face was swollen and her eyes heavy. She had taken some tranquilizers, and her speech was slurred. Jemma talked for a while about how difficult it was for them to manage when Jerry was not working. She said that they were unable to pay the bills that were piling up and that Jerry was becoming increasingly despondent. She said she was going to visit a friend in the hospital who had cancer of the uterus. "She's only twenty-five," she said. Jerry returned and said he would take care of the children while she went to the hospital. We went outside with Jemma, and as we walked along she told us that Jerry had applied to a nearby college but had been told that he was not elegible for financial aid. Jemma looked at us in disbelief. "He makes $145 a week unemployment," she said. "How can that be too much?" It was late in the afternoon and the streets were busy with people coming home after work. Jemma left us and headed into the evening rush. It would take two bus rides for her to reach the hospital to see her friend, and with a bit of luck she would make it in time for the evening visiting hours.

In the spring of 1983 we again spent much of our time listening to Jerry as he talked about life in the city, welfare, and racism. It was late on a Saturday afternoon and unusually warm. After the cold of winter, people were glad to get outside. Jerry took the opportunity to walk with us through the neighborhood and he introduced us to his friends as we passed by. Jerry gave a continual commentary. "Those that don't have, get less," he said, and he spoke of the rough times at the beginning of every month when people went to collect their unemployment money, and then again at the end of the month when they collect their food stamps. He talked of gangs from other parts of the city and sometimes from out of town coming to rob people of their benefits. Again he talked of taking friends with him when he went to collect his money, and of buying them a drink to show his appreciation. As we walked along Jerry saw a tall, thin man across the street. He called to him and we dodged through the traffic as Jerry sped ahead to greet his friend. The man's name was Harry. Jerry told us he had just been released from the hospital. Harry said that he was out for the weekend only because it was his birthday. He told us that he had been in the hospital for about three months and had to return for further surgery. Harry went on to explain that the doctors were trying to piece his stomach back together. He said that he had been shot in the stomach with a sawed-off shotgun. Jerry added that he had just collected his unemployment benefits. The two men talked for a while. Harry told Jerry about the amount of weight he had lost and his inability to eat solid food. Then Jerry tried to encourage Harry not to give up. Harry smiled as if grateful for Jerry's concern. Then he said good-bye and went on down the street. Jerry turned and watched him go. He told us that Harry had been a big man. He was well over six feet tall and had weighed about two hundred pounds. Jerry said, still looking at Harry, that he must have lost about seventy pounds.

Jerry continued to talk about Harry and then, as we walked further along the street, he spoke again of the difficulties faced by many of the families who live in the neighborhood. He said that many of them were broke by the tenth of each month. "They see the American dream," he said, "And they say 'Shit! I'm going to get me some,' and they spend the money." Jerry made the connection back to his children and he talked of his inability to provide them with more opportunities. "Most important is to be friends with them," he said. "We can play, do this, do that, go to the supermarket, buy little things." As we walked back to the apartment building, he said, "If you're friends with the kids they're not afraid to come up and ask you anything." Back in the apartment Tasmika was drawing. She had made a figure and had written "Gesus" underneath it. Jerry looked at it. "She wrote a *G*," he said, then after a moment he added, "I wonder if it was spelled like that." It was another idea to explore, and we listened as Jerry talked to us about religion and Middle Eastern languages.

In the spring and early summer Jerry painted signs and tried to find work. Jemma took a job working in a factory for below minimum wage. She worked from four in the afternoon until midnight. At first Jemma seemed happy because of the extra money, but the strain of leaving for work before Tasmika came home from school was too much for her. She told us that she rarely saw Tasmika during the week and that, although Jerry and some neighbors took good care of both children, she worried about them. After a few months she stopped working. The family's financial difficulties seemed to be more difficult for them to manage. Jerry moved out. Jemma said that he had a room nearby and he saw the children every day. Jemma continued to keep the apartment clean. She spent her time with her children and often took care of neighbors' children while their parents were working. For a while she cooked extra food for a young woman who was suffering from sickle-cell anemia; on one occasion she gave a mattress to a family who had lost their home in a fire.

In the fall Jerry was back with his family. We visited early in September, just after Tasmika had returned to school. The apartment seemed to be full of people, friends who had stopped by and neighbors from upstairs. One of them opened the door for us and hesitated for a moment, but then Jemma saw us and told us to come in. Tasmika was full of the first few days of school, and she fetched her new book bag to show us. It was bigger than the one from the year before and was filled with more books. Tasmika said her dad had bought it for her. Then Jemma showed us another book bag. It was small and blue. Jemma said that Jamaine was now in nursery school in the afternoons and that Jerry had bought this book bag for him. She undid the flap and pulled out a tiny paint set. She laughed and said that whenever Jerry bought the children something there always seemed to be a paint set inside. Jemma looked inside Tasmika's bag and, sure enough, there was a paint set with her books. While we were talking Jamaine ran into the apartment with a cigarette in his hand. Jemma shouted at him and asked him where he had got it. Jamaine told her that someone had given it to him and asked him to take it in for Jemma to light. Jemma took the cigarette and told Jamaine he was not to touch them. She lit the cigarette and took it outside.

Tasmika emptied her book bag and showed us her treasures. She had an enormous pink pencil with a tiny plastic pouch attached to the blunt end. In the pouch were four little pencils. Tasmika also showed us her "new" basal. It was the same one as the year before. Jemma came back and began to cook the evening meal. We stayed for a while and then made our way to visit another family. As we were leaving we asked about Jerry. Jemma said that he was fine and that he had been mending shoes.

In October it was Jerry's birthday. We met Jemma as she was leaving to go downtown to pick up her class ring. She had had it made bigger and was giving it to Jerry. Later Jerry told us about his gift and of the party that Jemma had arranged. Jerry said they had gone to a disco and danced. He said he had felt young again, and for a moment he seemed young to us.

The next time we saw Jerry, the youthful look was gone. When we arrived he opened the door and invited us in, but he told us that he was very busy. Three of his friends were sitting in the living room. Jemma and the children were not at home. Jerry explained that they were having a meeting. He said, "Right now I'm not thinking of Jamaine or Tasmika. I have other things on my mind." Jerry went on to say that he had to make some money. Christmas was coming and he had to get ready. Then he told us that he was eligible for only one more week of unemployment money. We did not stay long. Jerry walked with us to our cars and then went back to his friends.

It was the last time that we saw him. Jerry left. Jemma said that he was looking for a place to live near his family. Jemma continued to live in the apartment. She never spoke badly of Jerry when we visited her, although there was talk in the neighborhood of his drinking and beating her. The children saw their dad occasionally, and they talked about him when we came to visit. The apartment was often filled with people, but not with Jerry's friends. Tasmika and Jamaine's godmother, who lived upstairs, was often in the apartment, and she spent much of her time with the children. Jemma's sister visited with her children, and Jemma continued to take care of neighbors' children while their mothers were at work.

In the early spring of 1985 Jerry died. Jemma told us when we visited her at that time. She said she had not known that he was ill, that nobody had told her. She said that Jerry's mother had phoned a neighbor and asked her to tell Jemma that Jerry was in the hospital on a respirator. The next day a call came to tell her that he had died. Tasmika and Jamaine were with Jemma as she told us about the death of their father. Jamaine got some paper and began to draw. A few minutes later he showed us his paper. The picture was of an angel. "This is my dad," he said.

Postscript: July 1987.   After Jerry's death Jemma managed, for a while, to maintain the apartment in which they had lived, but eventually she moved in with her mother, and the children changed schools. As of July 1987 Jemma is planning to move into an apartment in a nearby town. She says that the building is being renovated and that she hopes the renovations will be completed by September. Tasmika, who is twelve, and Jamaine, who is eight, will continue to attend the school near their grandmother's apartment. Jemma says that she does not want Tasmika to change schools again, especially as she will be graduating from the eighth grade at the end of the next school year. The children will travel the short journey to school by bus.

Jemma's family now includes a new baby—a boy, born in June 1987. Jemma is happy with her new son, and she speaks of learning again what it is like to take care of such a tiny child. Tasmika and Jamaine enjoy taking care of their new brother. Jemma says that they both help her. "Sometimes I feed him," Tasmika explains. "I wash him and I take him outside." Tasmika goes on talking. She speaks of school, of being in the "highest" reading group and continuing to study ballet. She says that Jamaine is also in the "highest" reading group, and then she adds that he also likes to wrestle and to skateboard with his friends. When Jemma talks about Jamaine she also speaks of him making good progress at school. She says that the RIF bookmobile visits their street and that Jamaine is always there taking out books and reading them.

Ieshea, Teko, Danny, Hakim, Jarasad, and Sarita

We had heard of Ieshea for months before we met her. Tanya talked about her with guarded respect. Like Tanya, Ieshea was a life-long resident of the neighborhood. The two women share in the history of the place, and their lives are intertwined through their children: Tanya's son Gary and Ieshea's young daughters, Jarasad and Sarita, have the same father. At one time Tanya and Ieshea had been in love with the same man. Perhaps it was for this reason that Tanya sometimes mentioned Ieshea and spoke of the way in which she took care of her young children.

Jemma also talked of Ieshea. We learned that they had been friends since childhood, and it was Jemma who finally introduced us to Ieshea. It was late in the afternoon on a late fall day in 1982. We had been visiting Jemma and her family. It was chilly, but the days were drawing out and there were many people on the street as we left Jemma's home. Jemma came with us as we left, and we continued talking to her as we walked to our cars. Mothers were out with their babies, and young children were riding their tricycles on the sidewalk, weaving in and out of the people who were walking along. Trucks rumbled by; the men were at their usual gathering place by the public telephone on the corner of the street. People called to Jemma; she shouted greetings to those who were across the road and spoke more softly to those who passed close by. It was in the midst of all these salutations that Jemma saw Ieshea, who was just ahead of us on the street. She was carrying Sarita in her arms, Jarasad was by her side, and her son Hakim was a few steps away. Jemma called to Ieshea and told her that she wanted her to meet her friends. She turned and greeted Jemma just as Jemma had been greeting friends who saw her as she walked along the street. Ieshea, who was then thirty-five years old, was dressed in jeans with a tweed jacket and a man's flat cap. Her slender frame gave her the appearance of being a small woman, but she was of average height and the strength of her face added to her stature. Jemma told Ieshea about the research project, and without any prompting Ieshea began to tell us about Hakim and how well he was doing in the kindergarten class. She told us that he was not in a formal reading program but that he was beginning to read. She then went on to tell us about the basal series that was used in the first-grade classroom that her son would be in the following academic year. Trucks rolled by; people continued to salute Jemma and Ieshea, and in turn the two women both acknowledged the many faces that they knew in the crowd. Ieshea balanced her greetings with our conversation about young children learning to read, and she told us of the experiences of her older sons, Danny and Teko, when they had been in first grade. Then Ieshea waved good-bye and went with the crowd down the street. Jemma talked to us for a few moments, and then we left, hoping to get another chance to talk with Ieshea and the opportunity to follow the progress of Hakim as he began his formal reading instruction in first grade.

When we next spoke with Ieshea it was early in the summer of 1983. Hakim had made the honor role in kindergarten and was beginning to read in school. We began to visit her family each week. They lived on the same street as the abandoned building that had been Tanya's home. Ieshea lived on the first floor of the house in which she had grown up. Her parents lived upstairs in the second-floor apartment. Ieshea and her five children lived in four rooms. The door in the hall led into the living room, which was furnished with a big comfortable couch and two easy chairs. A corridor led to the kitchen, in which there was a table and chairs, an old refrigerator, a stove, and a sink. Teko, Danny, and Hakim shared a bedroom at the back of the house, the entrance to which was through the kitchen. Ieshea and her two young daughters slept in the front room, which had bay windows that looked out onto the street. Their bedroom opened up into the living room; there was no partition to separate the space. Ieshea kept the apartment scrubbed clean. She often talked about how difficult it was to keep the place tidy with so many people living in such a small space. But during our early visits she talked most about her children and of their progress in school. Ieshea told us that Hakim had been in day care since he was eighteen months old and that she felt he should have skipped kindergarten because of his earlier experience. She said, "He's repeating a lot of the same things that he had in day care, so I feel personally that he would have been ready for first-grade work." Ieshea said that she was hoping to get her young daughters, Sarita and Jarasad, into day care the following September. She said, "I'm on the waiting list. I don't know if they'll get in, but I hope so." Ieshea explained that the center would take young children who were eighteen months old. Then she told us that Sarita would be eighteen months old that September and Jarasad would be three. She said that Jarasad already knew her alphabet. Then she returned to Hakim. She said he knew his alphabet "long ago" and "how to spell his first and last name." He had learned these things in day care, she said, and again spoke of the transition from day care to kindergarten. She said, "They take them up there I think at seven, but he used to go from eight-thirty and they close at five. So he's used to an all-day day care, and then when he started kindergarten it was a half-day, and by the time they file in and then they serve milk and cookies what do they have? An hour's worth of learning? Really an hour or two because he goes in at twelve and they're dismissed at two forty-five ... so there's nothing challenging for him, and he seems to have picked up everything new that they've taught him."

Ieshea talked of Hakim at home. "He draws a lot, and he'll sit down and write. He's good at penmanship, and he likes to practice things like that." She told us that she used to read to him "because he was my baby ... and I would read him a book and he would know when to turn the page, and I didn't know whether he was memorizing what I had said or if he was actually reading ... maybe it was a little bit of both, but he'd know when to turn and he knew what the words were on what page." Ieshea returned to the subject of her girls and again made comparisons between their early experiences and Hakim's. She said, "Now to Sarita and Jarasad I very seldom sit down and read to them. I may teach them Pat-a-Cake and Ring-Around-the-Roses ... [but] I very seldom sit down and read. Now Jarasad likes *Jack and the Beanstalk*, and she remembers parts of the story. She'll turn the page and she'll recite what I've been reading. She's not really reading; I know that she's memorizing it. She has a good memory." Ieshea thought again about Hakim and she continued, "I don't read to them like I should but, see, when I had Hakim, my other children one was seven and one was eleven.... They were bigger and they were going to school all day and then he was in day care and when he came home I would read to him because he loved books and liked to read.... I don't read to the girls like I should."

Speaking of her children Ieshea told us, "They all look out for each other," and then she told us of the experiences of her oldest son, Teko, who was then eighteen. She said that Teko was "really bright" but that he had dropped out of school. Ieshea explained, "When he graduated from grade school he was an A student and then he went to junior high, and I think he missed the closeness. You see, when you're in grammar school you're with that one teacher all day and you establish a certain relationship. When you go to high school it's more impersonal. The teacher may not even know your name for six months." Ieshea told us that Teko had received an academic scholarship to a private high school and that he attended the school for one and a half years before asking to return to the public high school. She said, "It was an all-boys school and he'd gotten into girls, and so I let him go to the local high. Then he didn't want to go to school, so he didn't go. I let him quit school because he was on the verge of getting put out of school, but with the stipulation that he at least got his diploma.... He got it in January, and before he would have graduated from high school in June.... He's always been very bright.... When he was in the private school his teacher didn't want him to leave, but he just didn't want to go to school and he was sixteen. I could have sent him, but I can't take him by the hand and make him stay in school, especially when he didn't want to go." Ieshea told us that Teko was talking about going into the service. She said, "If that's what he wants to do, that's what I would prefer him to do."

The conversation shifted again, this time to Danny, who was then thirteen. Ieshea told us that she was worried about Danny and that he was the only one of her children who was having difficulties. She said, "He seems to have a problem in school ... whatever test they give, every year, they said he scored on a ninth-grade reading level and on his level in math, but he doesn't have good grades in school.... They say he's reading on a fifth-grade level. His report says he's on a fifth-grade level. He's in the sixth grade, but when he tested, he tested on a ninth-grade level. He should be in the eighth grade getting ready to graduate, but he's in sixth grade." Ieshea told us that she had visited the school and had asked for the child study team to make an evaluation to "see if he has some kind of learning disability, if he has a problem, something that can be helped." Ieshea continued, "And they evaluated him, and I had to go in and talk to the psychologist, and she said that they found nothing wrong ... but he still doesn't do very well." Ieshea's voice was filled with concern. "They say he has ability, but he just doesn't do it."

That summer was good to Ieshea and her family. The family was relaxed and happy. Ieshea and Jemma visited each other nearly every day, and Hakim's father often came to spend time with his young son. Ieshea dressed Sarita and Jarasad in pretty dresses, and she watched them while they played and cleaned the apartment while they slept. Hakim and Danny spent time with their friends in the neighborhood and they came and went as they pleased, trouping in and out, smiling at us when we came to visit and sometimes sitting to listen to Ieshea as she talked to us about her children and her life. Teko was often with the young men who congregated down the street by the pay phone. At other times he brought his friends home and they listened to music in his room. Ieshea always seemed to know where her sons were, and there was rarely any discord in the house. Each of her sons talked to their little sisters as they entered or left the house, but it was Danny who picked them up or played with them if Ieshea was busy. Ieshea told us that Danny watched Sarita and Jarasad when she went to the store. He was the one who took care of them.

In September Hakim entered first grade and Danny went into the seventh grade. Teko stayed home. Ieshea enrolled Sarita and Jarasad in the local day-care center, but Sarita was so upset at being separated from her mother that

Ieshea decided to keep her at home. Jarasad, who was then three, soon settled into the routine of the day-care center and was happy. Ieshea also enrolled in school and began taking evening courses towards an associate degree. Ieshea was happy; she laughed a lot during the first few weeks of the new school year. She talked about her life and the difficulties that she had overcome, and at times she seemed invincible as she spoke with fierce determination of her hopes for her children. She told us, "If it takes all I have I'm going to help them get out of this situation."

Then one day early in October Ieshea was not at home when we came to visit, and we learned the following week that she had been attacked and beaten by the father of her two little girls. He had been released from prison and wanted to resume his relationship with Ieshea. She refused. Ieshea told us that he had grabbed her as she had returned home from school. It was dark and no one was out on the street. He dragged her onto some waste ground near her home and there he kicked and punched her until she could not see or walk. When we saw Ieshea her face was badly bruised and swollen and she was having difficulty walking. She told us that the doctor thought she might lose her hearing in her right ear because her eardrum was punctured and they were not certain of the severity of the damage. She reported the beating to the police, but there was no resolution: the man was not caught.

Ieshea did not return to school. She stayed in her apartment and rarely went outside. She took care of her children and kept her apartment clean. Very often when we visited, Ieshea would be mopping the floors or folding clean clothes. Sometimes she would be cooking, and we would talk about our favorite recipes. But whenever we visited and she stopped to talk, she would pick up Sarita and sit with the little girl on her lap. Sarita would snuggle happily against her mother and the two of them seemed to love just being together. In the late afternoon Danny would go to the day-care center to get Jarasad and bring her home. Then Ieshea and her family ate supper.

Hakim enjoyed first grade, and Ieshea talked about his progress whenever we went to see her. But it was Danny of whom she spoke the most. He was having problems in seventh grade, and she told us that he was becoming increasingly difficult at home. His father had cancer, and Danny went to visit him whenever he could. Ieshea spoke of how unhappy Danny was at school and of how difficult it was for him to cope with school while his father was dying.

Then one evening when Danny was waiting at a bus stop after visiting his father, one of his cousins drove by. He stopped the car and offered to give Danny a lift home. There was a young man sitting in the passenger seat beside his cousin, so Danny got into the back of the car and put his duffel bag at his feet on the floor. Moments later a police car drove up behind them and gave chase: the car had been stolen. The young men tried to get away. After speeding through the city streets they abandoned the vehicle and ran away on foot. Danny stayed in the back of the car. The police also gave chase on foot. A man came out of a bar and, not realizing that the car was involved in a police chase, stole it. Danny was still sitting in the back seat. Another chase ensued. The police took the man and Danny into custody. A gun was found in Danny's bag. At the police station Danny told the officer in charge that the gun was not his and that the man who had come out of the bar had put it in his bag just before the police had arrested them. Ieshea went to the police station to get Danny, who was told he would have to stand trial.

Danny continued to go to school, and he visited his father whenever he could. His father had only weeks to live. Danny was quiet and rarely spoke at home and was increasingly difficult in the classroom. Then his dad died. It was a Friday, and the funeral was the following Tuesday. Ieshea said, "I let Danny stay out of school the day after the funeral also, Wednesday. You know, I told him it would be all right if he stayed out another day. And then Thursday was his first day back at school. So, um, Thursday afternoon, the principal she called and said that, um, there had been some trouble with Danny and his teacher in the classroom and, um, I said, you know, 'Is everything all right?' Or 'What happened?' So she said, 'Well, Danny and the teacher had some kind of confrontation, and it ended up with the teacher hitting Danny.' "

Danny had been beaten by the teacher in the classroom. The school report stated that he had raised, reddened areas on the right side of his body. Ieshea took Danny to the hospital, and he was treated for contusions. (This incident is presented in detail in chapter 3.)

Danny's court case and the incident of institutional abuse collided. Ieshea tried to cope. The public defender spoke to her on the telephone and told her that if there were any witnesses to the car chase she should make sure that they appeared with Danny in court. The child study team visited her to tell her that they were considering whether Danny should be classified for special education. They showed her a report from school that stated Danny's problems as follows: "Lacks respect for authority, very disruptive, lacks interest in school (doesn't do his homework—sleeps in class), use of foul language to his peers and adults in school." Ieshea refused to agree to the placement of Danny in a special education program. At one point during the conversation the social worker who was a part of the child study team asked Ieshea, "What are Danny's strengths?" Ieshea did not hesitate. She said, "I think Danny is a leader," and she went on to say that she thought Danny could lead the class either way. After a few seconds she continued, "I think he's very good at math. I've always said it was his reading that was the problem, but I think it's his writing." Sadly, Ieshea added, "He has tended to do well in classrooms where the teacher has liked and helped him."

A few weeks later Danny went to court. Ieshea went with him, and she took Sarita with her. Sarita stayed in her mother's arms. Ieshea explained that when the children went to school she sat down and cuddled Sarita. It was the way they began each morning, quietly and together. We left the car in a parking lot and walked the two blocks to the courthouse. It was an old building with crumbling paint, which spoiled its faded splendor. Careworn faces and angry frowns met us as we jostled with the crowd towards the elevator. People were everywhere, standing, sitting, and walking about. Some were going places, while others were going nowhere, just back and forth or around and about. On the fourth floor there were benches that looked like church pews where people would sit waiting for someone to call out the hymn. They talked quietly to each other, but the noise filled the hall as it echoed up to the domed ceiling and down through the layers of the building via the massive stone staircase that connected the floors.

Most of the people in the building were black. Three white men stood talking to a court officer. One of the men looked like a lawyer. He left, and the court officer opened one of the big wooden doors to a courtroom and stepped inside and out of sight. The two white men who were left stood waiting. We watched them. Ieshea said that they looked like father and son. The "son" leaned back against one of the massive stone pillars, and the two men continued to wait. Ieshea said that we had to wait for the public defender but there were no public defenders in sight. Danny was sitting next to Ieshea. Every so often he smiled at Sarita. Sarita cuddled closer to her mother, but her eyes were shining as she watched her brother and on her mouth there was a hint of a smile.

There was nothing to do but watch the people. Mothers and sons, sisters and brothers, they looked like families, and Ieshea talked about them as we waited. A man who looked like a lawyer walked up to one of the families and talked to them. He was tall and imposing. He had silver hair that curled close to his head. He had on a dark grey pinstripe suit and was carrying a leather briefcase. The lawyer leaned forward and spoke to a mother who was sitting with a small child on her lap. We could hear him as he spoke. He told her that they had to come back the following week, they would not be called that day. The mother frowned and got up. She spoke to two young men who were standing near her. She had her back to us and she spoke quietly to the young men, who were probably still in their teens, and then she talked again to the lawyer. The lawyer listened, nodded, and then walked away. The mother walked towards the elevator, and the two young men followed her.

Ieshea commented that both the families that we observed talking to lawyers had been white. The woman whom we had just been watching was white. Just as Ieshea commented, the first lawyer returned and spoke to the father and son. Ieshea smiled and we listened as the lawyer told them to come back on the twenty-ninth of May. He said he would see them then, and they all walked away. He continued to wait, knowing that Danny would have to go before the judge without knowing who would defend him.

At last the public defender arrived and came over to where we were sitting. Danny stood expectantly. The lawyer was black. He was tall and imposing and smiled at Danny and Ieshea in a friendly but businesslike way. His immediate question was "Are there any witnesses?" Ieshea said, "No," and she looked around at the waiting people as if expecting someone to arrive. The public defender sat in the space that had been occupied by Danny and placed his briefcase on his knees. He pushed the catches to one side and opened the case, took out a folder, shuffled the papers, and found a form. He placed the form on the folder and the folder in the open briefcase. Ieshea watched him, and Danny stood quietly waiting. The lawyer took a pen from his pocket and began asking questions. He spoke to Ieshea: Name. Middle initial. Address. Phone. Danny's social security number. His date of birth. Height. Weight. Color of eyes. Race. Much of the form the lawyer filled in without asking the questions. There were other questions that he did ask Danny: School? But mostly he wrote. His head was bent forward and his hands were hidden behind the lid of the briefcase. Ieshea and Danny watched even though they could not see either the form or the writing. Sarita also watched, but her head was against her mother and her hands had gathered up the cloth of Ieshea's jacket as she held on tight. Then the lawyer's hand made a quick flourish as he signed his name. He took the form out of the briefcase, gave it to Ieshea, and asked her to sign it. Ieshea took the pen and signed her name, and then Danny was asked to sign. The lawyer did not ask them to read the document. He took it from Danny and placed it back in the folder and the folder back inside the briefcase. Then he snapped shut the lid and stood. He said he was going to see the prosecutor to try and get a better deal for Danny. Then he left.

Ieshea and Danny continued to wait. By then it was ten-thirty. Ieshea told us that the courts broke for lunch and that they closed at four. Two young men, one white, one black, were brought up the stone stairs and were taken into one of the courtrooms. They were both handcuffed, and one of the court officers held the white prisoner by the cuffs as he led both young men swiftly through the big wooden doors. Three court officers were coming in and out of the courtrooms. Ieshea said she thought that they were taking the names of those who were waiting, so Danny took the letter that they had received with the date of his court appearance and he gave it to one of the court officers. The officer shuffled through the papers he was holding and found Danny's name on the last page of the docket. He wrote a check beside his name. The young men who had arrived in handcuffs came out of the courtroom with their hands free. They walked down the stone stairs and were met by two older women, perhaps their mothers. The women turned, and the four of them walked down the stairs together.

We continued to watch. Lawyers walked up and down and between the waiting people. Ieshea commented that the lawyers never seemed to look at anybody. They walked with their gaze somewhere ahead, as if their eyes had already reached where their bodies were going. The public defender who was representing Danny had come out of one of the courtrooms and he was standing talking to the prosecutor. They stood deep in conversation, and then the public defender came over and talked with Danny and Ieshea. He told them that he had been trying to establish that there were two phases to the case and that Danny was only involved in the first. He told Ieshea that it was important that she got her witnesses to court because the witnesses for the state were there. He told us that the witnesses for the state were the young woman who owned the stolen vehicle and her father. The public defender talked with Danny. He wanted to know about the other young men who were in the car and how Danny was involved. Danny was quiet. He looked at the lawyer and said, "My cousin made me feel it was all right." Danny told him that the man who jumped in the car after the first chase had put the gun in his bag. He told him that he had told the police that it was not his gun. The lawyer listened as Danny talked. Then, after a moment, he said to Ieshea that it was really important that she got Danny's cousin to come forward, and that if not his cousin then his aunt. Ieshea nodded in agreement, and the lawyer told her that it would be best if she could get both of them to come to the court. The lawyer then said that he was going to wait in the hope that he could talk again with the prosecutor, and with that he started to walk back towards the courtroom. As he walked, he turned and looked at Danny. He told him he was due to appear in court directly after lunch.

Ieshea gave Danny some change, and he went to the pay phone on the other side of the hall to telephone his aunt. Ieshea sat with Sarita and watched the people as she waited. Then Danny returned. He looked at his mother with a worried frown and told her that his aunt had said that she was going out but that she would be back in time for them to come to court. Ieshea smiled at him and suggested that he try to find out if we could get a drink and something to eat. She gave Danny some more money and we added to it. Again we waited. Danny returned with coffee, sodas, and cake. Sarita sat up, and her mother gave her a small piece of cake, which Sarita held in her hand for a few moments before eating. The coffee was hot, and drinking it broke the monotony of the hours we had spent waiting. Just for one moment Ieshea talked of other times, of happier moments in her life, and then Danny began to laugh. He pointed at our laps, which were filled with crumbs, and then at the floor, where crumbs had landed at our feet.

The public defender came back. He asked about the witnesses. Had they arrived? Ieshea stopped smiling and her look was strained. She said that Danny had phoned his aunt and that she had said she would come. He nodded but did not look hopeful. Then he told Ieshea and Danny that it was still unclear whether there would be a trial. Again he left, telling them that he was going to continue to work to get the case dismissed.

Again Ieshea and Danny sat and waited. Earlier we had watched as another man had been led handcuffed into one of the courtrooms. Now he came out through the big oak doors, and an old man and woman who had been sitting close together and apart from the rest of the waiting people rose expectantly. Their faces looked strained as they moved towards the uncuffed man. "He's going to be released," the court officer told them, "but he'll get released from jail." The old man asked about the location of the jail, and the court officer gave them directions. Ieshea talked about the couple and she smiled as she said that there had been a change in the look on their faces. "They're no longer waiting," she said. "They know what's happening."

Ieshea was watching the people and Danny playing with Sarita. He was tickling her. His hands were in front of her and he was wiggling his fingers. Sarita was smiling at him. Danny said, "My sister. I'll tickle you." Sarita laughed, and he tickled her around the middle. Then he started again. Hands out, fingers moving, "I'll tickle you." Sarita was laughing. Danny was laughing. He stopped wiggling his fingers and held out his arms. Sarita held out her arms in return, and he picked her up off Ieshea's lap and together they walked around the circle of waiting people. He pointed up at the dome of the ceiling and then he let her look over the stone balustrade. Ieshea told him to be careful, and Danny drew back away from the edge and put Sarita down. He held her hand as they walked around together.

A court officer came out of one of the courtrooms and shouted that the judge had adjourned for lunch. There were groans from those who were waiting. One woman said, "It's not fair." Ieshea commented that many of the people who were waiting had not even spoken to a lawyer. Slowly people got up and began to leave. A few waited for the elevator, but there were so many people that most of them walked down the stone stairs. It was twelve-ten, and we continued to wait. Ieshea said that she didn't want to leave in case the public defender returned. She said, "We still don't know if there will be a trial." The building seemed empty and sounds echoed up and down the central staircase and between the floors. A few people continued to wait but most of them had gone. At twelve-thirty the public defender came to talk with Ieshea and Danny again. He held up his thumb and forefinger so they were close together but not quite touching. "We're within this much of dismissing the case," he said. Again he told us that he has been working to establish with the prosecutor that there were two phases to the case. He told Ieshea and Danny that he had talked to the young woman who owned the car and explained to her that it was not Danny who had stolen the car. The lawyer said that he had also told the young woman that although Danny had been in the car he did not run when the police gave chase. The public defender was looking at Danny as he said that he had also told the prosecutor that Danny's family had tried to help the police by providing them with information about the cousin who was driving the car. Danny looked down and Ieshea seemed troubled. The public defender left and returned to his negotiations. Ieshea and Danny continued to wait. Ieshea said it was unlikely that Danny's aunt would come. She explained that if the cousin came forward he would be arrested.

The waiting continued. Ieshea joked and said that if she had come in old jeans they would have been seen right away. But because she had curled her hair and made herself look pretty they would have to wait all day. By that time a few people had returned, but most were still out. A public defender, one that we hadn't seen before, appeared and stood near where we were sitting. He had a big stack of files and began to call out the names that appeared on the outside of them. Few of those who were called came forward. No one had told them to stay. The public defender called, looked around, and then tried another name. Eventually a few people went over to speak with him. He asked them about their cases and spoke to them as if for the first time. Ieshea said that many of these people must go into court having only spoken for a few minutes with a lawyer before their appearance before a judge. The public defender looked tired, but he listened as he wrote and he asked a quick succession of questions to each of the people that he was representing. Ieshea said that Danny was lucky to be represented by the lawyer with whom they had been working.

Danny's lawyer came back. He was smiling. The case against Danny was going to be dismissed. He explained to Danny that the prosecutor wanted to speak with him. Another lawyer walked towards us and introduced himself. Danny stood up in front of him. Danny was quiet but looked at him as he spoke. The prosecutor said that he was aware that Danny had not run away from the police and that he had not been driving the car. He said that he knew that this was the first occasion on which Danny has been in trouble. He told him that the charges had been dropped, but that he didn't want him to treat the situation lightly. Next time he wouldn't be so lucky. He told Danny to keep out of trouble and to work hard. He said he didn't want to see him in court again. Danny thanked the prosecutor, and the prosecutor said he should be thanking the young woman who was dropping the charges against him. The prosecutor left, and the public defender sat down. Ieshea thanked him and he smiled. He said that Danny seemed to be a good kid and he was pleased that everything had been worked out. He told us that Danny was lucky. He explained that he was a pool lawyer brought in because the courts were so overloaded. He said that the public defenders had so many cases to represent they could not spend the time that he had spent on just this one case. Then he looked at Danny and told him that he did not expect to see him back in court. He said that Danny had made one mistake and he could not afford to make another.

We continued to visit Ieshea. She showed us the work that Hakim brought home from school, and she gave us pictures that had been drawn by Jarasad and Sarita, but mostly we talked about Danny. Ieshea said that since he had been beaten by his teacher "things had changed for Danny." She said, "Last week he asked if he could go to the bathroom. The teacher asked him why he didn't go when they changed lessons. Danny explained that he didn't need to go then. The teacher wouldn't let him go, so Danny got up and went to the bathroom. When he went back to the room the teacher sent him to the office. They sent him home." Ieshea said she was still hoping that something would be done about the teacher but added that she had not heard anything about any disciplinary proceedings.

Several weeks passed before we saw Ieshea again. We talked with her on the telephone, and when the child study team arrived to persuade her to sign the papers so that Danny could be placed in a special education class, she telephoned us and said that she wanted us to hear what they were saying. Our conversations were about Danny. Ieshea did not talk about herself, nor did we think to ask her how she was feeling. Ieshea was a strong woman, and we thought she would come through this situation as she had come through other difficult times. But we were wrong. When we next saw Ieshea she had not eaten for two weeks. She was sitting at the kitchen table and she smiled when we arrived. Her hair was not combed and her skin was ashen, but we did not realize that it was through lack of food. We sat and talked to her for a while about the child study team. The learning consultant on the team had said that Danny was "hostile and suffering from an oppositional disorder." She had also said that he was "hateful." Hateful? Did she really say that? Ieshea said that was the word she had used. Ieshea's eyes filled with tears, but she did not cry. She sat at the table smoking a cigarette and drinking black coffee. Her hands were shaking and her mouth trembled as she tried to smile. She had not signed the papers. She told us that if she signed, Danny would be able to attend a trade school. If she did not sign, he would not be able to go. She explained that she could not have him classified as emotionally disturbed. She didn't want him labeled. On the telephone, one member of the team had told us that Danny had difficulty with visual–motor integration and that he had broad cognitive deficiences. We were also told that "because of his attitude on the days that we worked with him, he might not have been putting forth his best effort." Ieshea told us that they had said the same to her, and she also told us that she thought it would have been hard for Danny to do his best because he was evaluated in the classroom in which he had been beaten.

We told Ieshea that we had talked to a psychologist who was willing to do an independent evaluation of Danny. We explained that the psychologist had asked if Ieshea would try to get Medicaid to pay for the evaluation through the Division of Youth and Family Service. Ieshea got up from the table and went over to the phone. It was then that we realized how much weight she had lost. She made her telephone call leaning back against the wall and then she put her hand out and held onto the table as she slowly sat down. She said her caseworker was not in the office so she would phone again later. We asked her why she had lost so much weight. What had she been doing? Ieshea said it had been two weeks since she had eaten. She said that what food she had was given to the children. She explained that it was always difficult in the spring because her heating bills were so high during the winter. Ieshea smiled and said, "They won't cut you off in winter, they wait until spring." This year she had not managed to pay the bill. There had been a large telephone bill because Teko's friends often phoned and reversed the charges, and sometimes her friends did the same. She had paid the telephone bill because she didn't want to be without a phone. She said she needed the phone. Just after she had paid the phone bill, the electric company sent her a notice to say that they were going to cut off her electricity if the winter bill was not paid. Ieshea sent Danny with what money she had to pay the bill. Otherwise, she would have had to pay the bill and also a fee for turning the electricity back on. The bills had been paid, but that meant there had been no money for food.

Ieshea explained that she had been living on liquid protein that she got from one of her cousins who had had a throat injury and could not eat. By doing this she had managed to keep enough food in the apartment for her children. But two weeks ago she had finished her supply of liquid protein, and since then she had been sipping black coffee in the hopes of getting through to the end of the month. She still had three days to survive. Ieshea smiled and said they'd make it, but there was nothing in the refrigerator for the children to eat and it looked as if they too would have to go without food. We asked Ieshea to come with us to the fast-food restaurant that was just around the corner but she wouldn't. She said that she could no longer eat and that even the thought of food made her feel sick. We tried to give her some money and at first she would not take it. Finally we agreed that the money should come out of the small research fund from which each of the families participating in the study received a stipend. Ieshea promised to eat. She said she would cook a meal and eat with the children. The next morning we telephoned to make sure she had eaten. Ieshea said that had eaten with her children. She told us that she had cooked hamburgers and mashed potatoes. Then Ieshea chuckled as she added that she had also baked a cake.

In the weeks that followed Ieshea gained weight and focused her energies on her young children. Hakim made the honor roll in first grade, and she showed us the certificate that he had been given in school. Jarasad continued to attend the day-care center; Ieshea took her in the morning and brought her home in the late afternoon. Ieshea's days belonged to Sarita. It seemed that they never tired of each other's company. Sarita helped her mother clean the apartment and cook the dinner. Sometimes she played while her mother talked with friends, but mostly they talked to each other. Danny was out most of the time. Ieshea said that she was frightened for him. She told us that she was losing him. Her voice was quiet as she spoke of Danny, and she no longer dwelled on the difficulties he was facing. Then one night Danny did not come home. Ieshea told us that she had friends looking for him but that no one had seen him. She said that he had been home in the late afternoon and that he had left with some friends early in the evening. She had been expecting him to return home before dark. Ieshea asked friends to look for him, but it wasn't until the following day that she heard that he had been seen selling cartons of cigarettes at two o'clock in the morning in the parking lot of an all-night diner. Danny returned home the following evening.

Ieshea was angry and frightened. She had talked many times of "losing

Danny to his environment," and it was as if it had finally happened. Ieshea spoke of her belief in his abilities and of his attempts to survive. She was torn. She wanted to fight for him, but he was no longer listening to her. Ieshea could not control him, and she mourned him as if he were lost to her. She talked about the school and the situation with Danny's teacher. She said she did not want to go to court to try to establish the beating that Danny had received as a case of "institutional abuse." She said, "No one was on my side. I felt that they weren't going to do anything to him [the teacher] except an official reprimand." Then, speaking of Danny, she said, "He used to be my best child. He was the one I sent to the store. But now he's uncontrollable. I personally don't believe he's a bad kid, but he's developed some bad habits. I'm so disappointed in him, because he can be more than he is. He sells himself short."

In the following September Danny entered eighth grade. Ieshea still refused to sign the papers to have him classified as emotionally disturbed. Hakim entered second grade. Jarasad began her second year at the day-care center, and Sarita joined her. Each day Sarita would go to the day-care center with her mother, and for two months she cried about it. But then she began to enjoy the program, and within a short time was happily participating with the other children in the activities of the center. Teko stayed home. Ieshea again began to pursue her own career. She submitted her papers to the local community college and waited for them to be processed. She was accepted in the program to which she had applied. However, by then the process had taken so much time that she was told it was too late to apply for financial aid. Ieshea could not afford to pay for the books that she would need, so she decided to try and get a job as a secretary. It was at this time that Ieshea spoke of her relationship with her parents, which had become so strained she decided to move out of the apartment in their house and began to look for another place to live.

Eventually, Ieshea found an apartment in an old Victorian house. We visited her there. The street on which the house was located was about a mile away from her old neighborhood. It was in an old part of the city on a well-cared-for street of similar Victorian houses. None of the houses was boarded-up or pulled down. The house, in which Ieshea had taken a third-floor apartment, was surrounded by a fence, and there was a gate that opened onto the cement path that led up to the front door. Inside the fence the grass was cut and the bushes tended. Ieshea's apartment had four rooms. They were bright with sunshine, and the breeze kept them cool. The place was comfortable, clean and pretty, and fresh with flowers. On that day we spent several hours talking with Ieshea and playing with Jarasad and Sarita. Hakim was there, and he drew pictures of his family and gave them to us when we left. One of Ieshea's friends was visiting and had brought her two-year-old daughter to play with Jarasad and Sarita. While we talked, the children played. Jarasad emptied Cathé's pocketbook and played with her makeup. Then she reorganized the contents of her bag, talking as she worked. "We'll take this out of here and we'll put it in here. That's a good idea." Sarita watched and then joined in when Jarasad began to write. Ieshea told us, "Jarasad writes from the time she gets up until the time she goes to bed." She wrote her name with her left hand, and she drew letters on the paper.

Ieshea told us that when they moved, Danny had changed schools and that he had attended a nearby middle school. But then he had been involved in the theft of a car and was sent to a residential home. He had recently returned home and was living with his mother and his brothers and sisters. Ieshea said that he was happy at home and that he still helped her to take care of Jarasad and Sarita. She said, "He just doesn't want to go to school." She told us that Teko had managed to get Danny a job shining shoes and that he was pleased to be earning money. Ieshea looked troubled as she spoke of Danny being fifteen years old and not completing eighth grade. Again she told us how unhappy he was when he went to school. She added that she couldn't make him go.

We talked about the neighborhood in which Ieshea and her children were now living. Ieshea said that she didn't know any of the people who lived on the street, and she explained that when she took Jarasad and Sarita to the day-care center she went back to her old neighborhood and visited Jemma. Ieshea explained that she returned to the apartment only in the late afternoon when the children were out of school. She talked about Hakim, who had grown very chubby since they had moved. Ieshea said that in the old neighborhood he was never at home, but that now he was never out. She told us that Hakim didn't have any friends to play with in this new place. Hakim listened to his mother as she talked, and he smiled at her when she told us how well he was doing in school. He seemed quite content to be at home and spent the rest of our visit drawing a picture for us of the members of his family. Our visit came to an end with Ieshea telling us that she would be moving again soon and that we could always get in touch with her through Jemma. She told us that the apartment was too expensive for her to maintain. She said that it was $375 per month, almost all she had to live on.

Postscript: July 1987.   In July 1987, Ieshea was planning to move to a city in the South. She wanted to leave the place in which she has lived all her life so that her young children would have a better chance than Danny or Teko. In July 1987 Danny was seventeen. He had been in a juvenile detention center for eighteen months, but he was then living with his mother and was back at school. He had just finished eleventh grade and he would be in twelfth grade the next year. Teko had just been sentenced to twenty years' imprisonment for armed robbery. Hakim continued to do well at school, and Ieshea has been told that he is eligible for the gifted and talented program the next year, when he would be in fifth grade. Jarasad was also doing well. Ieshea says that she was reading before she entered first grade. Sarita had just graduated from preschool. Ieshea was working as a secretary at the community college that she worked at before Sarita and Jarasad were born. Sarita attended preschool at the college. Ieshea said that she liked the local day-care center better. She talked about the availability of facilities at the college day-care facility and of the overcrowding at the day-care center in her neighborhood. But she said that there is an impersonal atmosphere at the college that does not compare with the warm and caring atmosphere at the crowded local center. She said, "All the teachers at the college are accredited, but Sarita is learning nothing." As Ieshea talked about her children she shared her concern for their future. "Teko was just as bright or brighter than Hakim," she said. She spoke of being frightened for her sons and for her young daughters. She explained that it is for this reason that she was trying to leave the city. Ieshea said that Teko told her to go, to get away, to start over. "There's nothing I can do for Teko," she continued. "I told him to try to go to school while he's inside. Maybe he can work with the social services when he comes out. I told him, 'All you need is a piece of paper behind you.'" June 29 was Ieshea's birthday, and Teko had sent her a card. Ieshea said it had made her cry. Teko wrote that she was his older sister and his younger sister, his mother and his father. He finished by writing that he was glad that she was by his side.

In late August, Ieshea bought a car for $400 and paid a man $100 to drive the family south. But as she packed the car, Danny began to cry. Ieshea says it was only the second time that she had seen him cry since he was a little boy. She could not leave him, and he refused to go with her. The family stayed.

As of September 1987, Ieshea is trying to reestablish her life in the inner-city neighborhood. The money she had saved for the move is gone, and her landlord is talking of eviction.

Commentary

When we imagine our readers we wonder about the questions they must be asking about the lives of the families we have written about. We imagine such questions as, "What have we learned from the Shay Avenue families?" In chapter 5, we address this question. We argue that their lives do not fit any of the preconceived notions of black families or families who are poor and living on welfare. The experience and reason of the families themselves create more fragile and sensitive images. We have also asked ourselves how the families have helped us understand the social, political, and economic forces that shape their lives. However, to address these questions we need to be able to reflect upon the literate lives of the families. Ours is a literate society, and by studying the complex and involved societal contexts in which print gets written and read by ordinary people in both ordinary and critical situations, it is possible to gain a view of the workings of a social system. The Shay Avenue families can teach us in this endeavor.

Two
Literacy and the Children at Home

Children in a literate society grow up with literacy as an integral part of their personal, familial, and social histories. Interacting with their literate environment, children invent their own literacies, and their inventions often parallel the inventions of literacy by society as a whole.

Yetta Goodman

Many naturalistic studies use structured tasks that are specifically designed to enable researchers to gain insights into children's literacy (Goodman and Altwerger 1981; Harste, Woodward and Burke 1984; Sulzby 1986; for a review of this research see Teale 1986). Although no such procedures were used in this study, the work of these researchers has informed our observations. For us, it was merely a matter of observing, spending time, and hoping that we would see reflections of the literate lives of the children as we visited them in their homes. We watched for the children to write or read, and we collected examples of their work whenever an opportunity arose. Occasionally, a serendipitous moment would arise when it seemed appropriate in the context of the situation to ask a question or (at the end of the second year of the study) to provide markers and papers, but for the most part we watched and waited as we visited the families. We did not have to bide our time for long, for literacy is indeed an integral part of the children's everyday lives. What we attempted to do was to engage the "landscape" with the child (Hart 1979). Thus, this chapter is an attempt to enter a world that we have lost and to try, as adults, to recognize in the observations that we have made and the pieces of print that we have collected the authenticity of literate experiences that are a part of a child's world (see Coe 1984; and Taylor 1987). It is important to emphasize that during the first three years of the study we did not ask the children to draw or write anything for us. We collected whatever papers were given to us, and we rarely asked questions about a particular picture that was drawn or message that was written.

Houses

We will begin by considering the significance of one particular drawing that was produced and reproduced by many of the children participating in the study. The drawing is of a house or apartment building. Next to the house there is sometimes a tree, occasionally a swing set, and once in a while some flowers. One of the earliest pictures that we have was drawn by Tasmika (September 1982, age 7) in iridescent crayons, which were a gift from her father. In the picture (Figure 2–1) there is a tall house or apartment building; two flowers, and a swing set.

When Jemma gave us Tasmika's picture she also gave us another house that had been drawn on the same occasion. Jamaine, who was three years old, had been watching his sister, and he wanted to make a similar picture. Jemma explained that Tasmika had held his hand and guided his movements in the making of a house that resembled the one that Tasmika had drawn for herself. (See Figure 2–2.) We did not realize the importance of these pictures until much later, when a corpus of comparable pictures had been collected.

A few weeks later Tasmika played school with Selina, one of her friends, and they both drew houses (Figures 2–3 and 2–4).

Other houses followed, some in crayon and some using the paint boxes that Tasmika and Jamaine were given by their father. The painted pictures

Figure 2–1 • Tasmika's House in Iridescent Crayon

Figure 2–2 • Jamaine's House, Drawn with Help from Tasmika

Figure 2–3 • Tasmika's House, Drawn While Playing School

Figure 2–4 • Selina's House, Drawn While Playing School

Figure 2–5 • Sherran's First House

are blurred and the colors have run, but the shapes are of houses with sometimes a tree and maybe a sun.

More houses were given to us. In the spring of 1983 Trisha, Pauline's sister, gave us a package of her son Sherran's drawings and writing. The importance attached to the drawing of houses can be seen in these early pictures. The first (Figure 2–5) seems quite a simple drawing. But the second (Figure 2–6) is simply extraordinary. The house that fills the center of the

Figure 2–6 • Sherran's Second House

page had a door and many windows plus the beginnings of Sherran's name etched into the lower right-hand corner and into the roof up above. On one side of the house is an upside-down tree laden with apples and surrounded by clouds, and on the other side Pac-Man is gobbling up ghosts.

A year later the houses that Sherran (age five) drew were large and bold. One still makes us smile, for there at an upstairs window is Sherran smiling out of the house that he had made (Figure 2–7).

There are other houses, including one by Hakim (age seven) drawn in school, in which the tree is enormous and the house is small. (See Figure 2–8.) Under the big yellow sun people look as if they are sunbathing. One small person has climbed a ladder into the tree. On the back of this picture is another house that almost fills the paper. (See Figure 2–9.) It is drawn with perspective in pencil. Above the house is a sun and below it, a person.

The last set of houses that we want to share was drawn by Shauna, Pauline's daughter. The first group of houses (Figure 2–10, A through G) was drawn in October 1983, when Shauna was seven. Shauna drew them on lined paper taken from a college file belonging to her mother, and Pauline, who was watching Shauna as she drew, took a piece of the paper and drew one of the houses in the series. There are seven pictures altogether, and they are presented in the same order as Shauna showed them to us.

Shauna's line drawings seem to be reflections of the same place, with the selection, color, and configuration of the elements within her pictures being used as an expression of different views of that particular locale. In the first picture (Figure 2–10, A) the house is lightly colored in purple and edged more

Figure 2–7 • Sherran Smiling Out of an Upstairs Window

Figure 2–8 • Hakim's House with a Big Tree

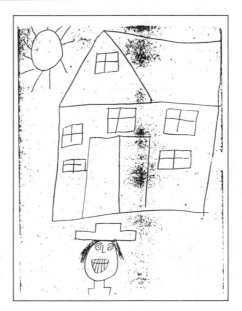

Figure 2–9 • Hakim's Big House

deeply in the same shade. A ball is also colored in the deeper shade. In one cloud Shauna has written her first name, and in the other she has written "summer." The second picture (Figure 2–10, B) is essentially the same as the first, except that there is one less flower and the house and ball are not colored. In the third picture (Figure 2–10, C) which Shauna said her mother had drawn, it is no longer summer. Pauline's picture is like Shauna's except that it is winter. There are no leaves on the trees. A snowman with a black hat stands next to the house, which is on the left side of the paper. There are two figures in the foreground of the picture. When Shauna showed us the picture she told us that the person in the orange snowsuit (the figure at the right) was her mom and that the other figure was herself. She said they were playing outside in the snow. In the fourth picture (Figure 2–10, D), a pencil drawing, the building on the left looks more like an apartment building than a house, the swing set is back, and there are apples on the tree. Two little people are standing in the foreground, and there is a ball beside them. Shauna has written her name, first and last, in the two clouds up above. In the fifth picture (Figure 2–10, E) the house is blue, with a red roof and door. Shauna has placed the house back on the right side of the paper. The ball is there but no children or flowers. Both are back in the sixth picture (Figure 2–10, F). This time there are four children, two and two, each pair holding hands. The two pairs are separated by two flowers. There are apples on the tree, and the sun and clouds are in the sky. The building is on the left beneath the sun, and it contains many more windows than in Shauna's previous buildings. In the final drawing (Figure 2–10, G) the number of windows has doubled and the children have gone, but there are still apples growing on the tree.

At about the same time as the series of pictures in Figure 2–10, Shauna drew a picture of a house while we were visiting her home. By late in the second year of the study we had begun to carry markers and paper in our bag with the tape recorder and cameras, and sometimes the children would take them out and use them. Shauna took them and drew a large house and edged it in red to match the bright red roof, chimney, and door. (See Figure 2–11.) The rest of the house she colored blue and at the top, just under the roof, she made three windows. One was brown and one was blue; both of these she edged in red. The third was just red, and she pressed harder to make the lines for the windowpanes. The tree was green, and its brown trunk was edged in green. A multicolored ball lay next to the tree, and a swing set was next to it. Two flowers, two clouds, two birds, and a bright yellow sun add to the picture, and Shauna has written in eager, cursive writing "It's a summer" next to the sun and into a cloud. We left the markers and paper for the children to use, and Shauna drew still more houses in the fall of 1983. (See Figure 2–12.)

The houses that the children drew raised many questions in our minds, which sent us delving into the literature on children's art. Kellogg (1970) in her book *Analyzing Children's Art* states, "The Building or 'houses' which

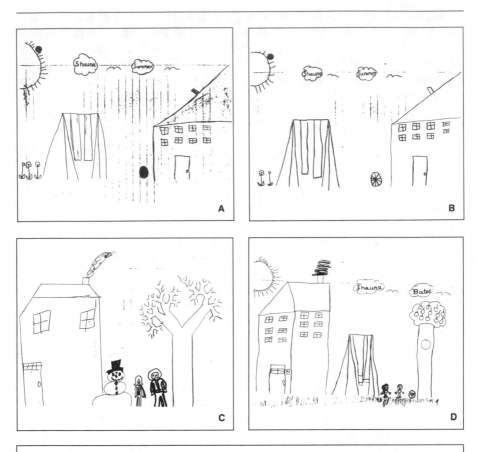

Figure 2–10 • Shauna's Houses, October 1983.   **A**: House with Purple Ball. **B**: House with Uncolored Ball.   **C**: Pauline's House.   **D**: Pencil Drawing.   **E**: A Blue House. **F**: House with Four Children.   **G**: House with Many Windows.

children make are drawn alike all over the world" (p. 123). Kellogg also points out, "The customary Vegetation items drawn by young children are Trees and Flowers" (p. 128). Kellogg uses uppercase letters for "Trees" and "Flowers" to remind us that these labels are often based on adult interpretations of children's art, and she expresses legitimate concern about the tendency of adults to project their own emotions and ideas onto the work of young children. We agree with Kellogg and find ourselves viewing with extreme caution the large body of psychological research that seeks to interpret children's drawings within the framework of some medical model.

Figure 2–10 continued

With this strong cautionary note, what can be said about the houses? First of all, some straightforward adult observations. Let's consider where the pictures were made. Some were drawn at school, but most were drawn at home. Some were drawn when the children were playing with siblings or friends, but most were drawn by children working on their own. The houses were made on whatever materials were available at home or sometimes at school: lined paper, drawing paper, or oak tag; and they were drawn with pencils, pens, crayons, and markers, or with paints and paintbrushes. The houses sometimes look like single-family dwellings, while at other times they

Figure 2–11 ● Shauna's House—"It's a Summer"

Figure 2–12 ● Two More of Shauna's Houses, Fall 1983

look like apartment buildings. The sun, swing sets, trees, flowers, and people are often featured in the pictures. It should be noted here that there are no swing sets and very few trees in the neighborhood in which the children actually live. The houses in their neighborhood are close together, and many are boarded up or knocked down. It does not seem that these pictures depict where the children live. And yet, if we consider the children's interpretations of their own drawings, we find, for example, that Sherran drew himself looking out of an upstairs window and Shauna drew herself playing outside in the street. Could it be that the houses are the children's *interpretations* of the homes in which they live? Do the pictures represent a socially constructed metaphor of place? Is this the landscape that we must engage in with the child?

We cannot answer these questions, but we can influence your thinking by sharing with you just one last picture, which was drawn by a friend of Tasmika when we were visiting her family in the spring of 1985. Three years after the study began, an occasion arose for us to ask Tasmika to draw a map of her neighborhood. We had been talking to the families about the location of essential services, and we wondered what would happen if we asked the children to draw a map of their neighborhood. Tasmika had already walked with us and talked about the places that were important to her (school, friend's house, store). Now we were asking her to draw them on a map. Tasmika's friend came into the room and asked her what she was doing. Tasmika said she was drawing her neighborhood. The friend took some paper and a couple of markers and went over to the table and began to draw. We were not watching her, as our attention was fixed on Tasmika. Just before we left, Tasmika's friend asked us how to spell *neighborhood*, and a few minutes later she showed us the picture in Figure 2–13.

Figure 2–13 • "Our Neighborhood"

Our own interpretation of these drawings centers upon what Hart and Chawla (1980) have referred to as "a special sensuous, uncritical perception of the environment" that young children enjoy. It appears to us to be an early symbolic representation of their world. As such, it is an apt place for us to begin to think about literacy and children at home.

Family and Friends

Homes are important, and so are family and friends. In *Artful Scribbles*, Howard Gardner (1980) shares with us his analysis of the child's "emerging capacity to produce configurations that function (and begin to look) like things." Gardner writes of the complexity of the transition that takes place as the child moves from simple graphic shapes to the depiction of objects. He states, "Despite all these obstacles en route to the first human representation, the magic moment eventually comes. Sometime in the first four years of life the child produces the first figure that merits the label 'man,' 'person,' 'mommy,' 'me....' " We have collected these early human representations, which Kellogg refers to as "the favored subject matter of child art," from the very young children participating in the study. They were drawn in notebooks and on

Figure 2–14 • Jamaine's Drawing, December 1982

Figure 2–15 • Jarasad's Face Drawn at the Day-Care Center, February 1984

the back of flyers, on whatever paper was available. The first face (Figure 2–14) was found in a pile of newspapers. It was drawn by Jamaine in December 1982 on the back of a notice that Tasmika had brought home from school.

Jarasad drew the faces shown in Figures 2–15 and 2–16. The large, smiling face (Figure 2–15) was drawn with crayons at the day-care center in February 1984. The four smaller faces (Figure 2–16) were drawn on notepaper with a ballpoint pen during one of our visits to her home, in April 1984.

Perhaps because of our interest in the children and their families (rather than art or even literacy per se), what interested us most about the children's drawings was their graphic depiction of themselves and members of their families. The faces that Jamaine and Jarasad drew they did not identify as depictions of particular people, but the faces that were drawn by older children were said to be representations of their families.

Figure 2–17 was given to us by Ieshea. It is a self-portrait that Hakim drew sometime during his kindergarten year. (We have replaced Hakim's real name with the pseudonym used in this book.) Figure 2–18, another self-portrait of Hakim, was drawn just after he had entered first grade. Figure 2–19 is a drawing of Hakim's father. It was drawn at about the same time that Hakim drew the second portrait of himself. (We have removed the first and last names that Hakim wrote above the portrait of his dad and have replaced

Figure 2–16 ● Jarasad's Four Faces, April 1984

Figure 2–17 ● Hakim's Self-Portrait, Kindergarten

Figure 2–18 • Hakim's Self-Portrait, First   **Figure 2–19** • Hakim's Portrait of His Father
Grade

it with the words "FATHER'S Name" to indicate the location and the upper-
and lowercase letters Hakim used.)

Many of the pictures came with "I love you" messages, and it is here that
we can begin to appreciate what Gardner (1980) has referred to as the "interesting mixes of graphic and linguistic resources, in the service of complex
conceptualization." Hakim's self-portrait in Figure 2–20 can be interpreted as
both an expression of self and the sharing of feelings.

The portraits that the children drew and the accompanying "I love you"
messages that they wrote intrigued us. Again we were trying to engage the
landscape with the children. We wanted to see the families with their eyes
and understand the ways in which literacy is used in the complex constructions of familial communication. Thus, after the end of our regular visits to
their homes, we found an occasion to ask the children to draw pictures of
their families. We believed that watching them as they drew would make us
a little more sensitive to their expressions of family, and we thought that
perhaps we would observe the writing of the "I love you" messages that we
had collected during our many prior visits to their homes. We had not realized
that the children would take the task to heart or consider it so seriously.

When we visited Shauna in April 1985, she asked us if we had any books
for her to read. We had to apologize and say that we hadn't brought any. By
way of consolation we told her that we had some markers and paper, and we
asked her if she would like to use them to draw a picture of her family. Shauna
smiled and took the markers and some paper. Joe-Joe, who was at home that

Figure 2–20 • Hakim's Self-Portrait with Message

day, also took some paper, and he sat with Shauna. Shauna's enthusiasm was quickly tempered by her first attempts at the picture. "I can't draw," she said. She watched Joe-Joe and drew her first figure much as he had done. We told her that we liked her drawing, and she seemed to relax. The portraits that Shauna and Joe-Joe drew took much longer than we had anticipated; it was several hours before they were finished. They drew one family member after another, slowly and with great care. The two children talked quietly about their families and who they were going to include. There was no discussion of those that they left out. In looking at the pictures (Shauna's in Figure 2–21; Joe-Joe's in Figure 2–22), you will find that their interpretations are not quite the same. Shauna did not include her grandmother, Cora, although she is close to her (Pauline has spoken of Shauna's writing many "I love you" notes to Cora). Joe-Joe's family portrait did not include Gina or Megan, two of his sisters. Neither of the children included their fathers. Shauna began with a picture of herself and then to the right she drew Gina and her mother, Pauline. To the left of herself she drew Sherran and then Joe-Joe. Then she returned to the right side of the paper and she drew Megan, Trevor, and Trisha. Shauna's figures show the height of each family member: Sherran is the smallest; next comes Joe-Joe and then Shauna herself. Megan follows, with Trevor and Gina. Then come Pauline and Trisha, who are about the same height. Pauline occasionally watched Shauna as she worked, and although the figures were not named she seemed to know who they were. Pauline recognized Trevor by the color of his clothes. His yellow shirt and yellow pants had family significance, and Shauna chuckled as her mother commented on her choice of color for his clothes. Shauna finished her family portrait by placing each person in a blue frame, and then in a box that she drew above each member of her family, she wrote their names. (We have included each person's initial only.) Joe-Joe was thirteen when he drew his family portrait. He drew himself, boom box in hand, and wrote "Home boy" with an arrow pointing to himself.

In June 1985 Hakim drew his family. (See Figure 2–23.) Again we were struck by the fond way in which he attended to his drawing and by the amount of time he took making each person. Once the figures were completed he wrote the name of each member of his family in the carefully formed script of his new cursive writing. (We have drawn rules in the location of the actual family names that Hakim wrote.)

Figure 2–21 • Shauna's Family Portrait

Figure 2–22 • Joe-Joe's Family Portrait

Tasmika also drew a picture of her family. At the time she drew it, Jemma's apartment was full of people. Her sister was visiting with her two children, and Tasmika's godmother, who lived upstairs, was also there. Adults and children came and went. Tasmika talked to us about school and told us that she had received an academic achievement award. During this conversation we asked her if she would like to draw a picture of her family. Tasmika took the paper and markers; found a space on the floor; and, kneeling forward, began to draw. Her cousin and a friend asked her what she was doing, and Tasmika told them what she was drawing. Requests for paper quickly followed and soon the floor was littered with children quietly drawing their families. It was on this occasion that Jemma told us of Jerry's death. The circumstances were such that we did not watch the children except to glance at them from time to time. Jamaine was close to Jemma as she talked, and it was then that he drew the picture of his father before his death and becoming an angel when he died. When Jamaine showed us his picture (Figure 2–24), he pointed

Figure 2–23 ● Hakim's Family Portrait

Figure 2–24 ● Jamaine's Portrait of His Father

to the figure he had drawn at the bottom of the piece of paper and he told us it was a picture of his dad. Then he traced his finger along the line (arrow?) that he had drawn up to the figure at the top of his paper and told us it was his dad and that his dad was an angel.

The older children drew intently for some time and then brought their pictures to show us. The first (Figure 2–25) was drawn by Tasmika's nine-year-old cousin A.J. Tasmika's picture (Figure 2–26) was of her mother, brother, and herself. At the top she wrote "My Family" and a message to her mother:

Figure 2–25 • A.J.'s Family Portrait

"Your tarrifick Mommy"; and she drew a heart with an arrow through it. Beneath her family portrait she carried on a conversation that was perhaps with her mother, although she wrote it by herself. "Arm't they Cute" she wrote in pale blue. Then, in dark blue, as if colors signified speakers, she wrote "yes." Then, again in pale blue, she responded, "thank You."

Cards

The linking of messages—of drawings with words—had begun. Without being asked, the children were drawing their families and writing "I love you" messages. Pictures became letters and cards with writing and decoration. Tasmika made a card for her mother. On the front she wrote, "To Jemma. My My Mom is My heart." Inside she wrote, "To My Mommy" and the poem "Roses Are Red." (See Figure 2–27.)

A.J.'s card was written with a question. His mother answered by circling "yes" with a blue marker. (See Figure 2–28.)

Figure 2–26 ● Tasmika's Family Portrait

Figure 2–27 ● Tasmika's Card for Her Mother

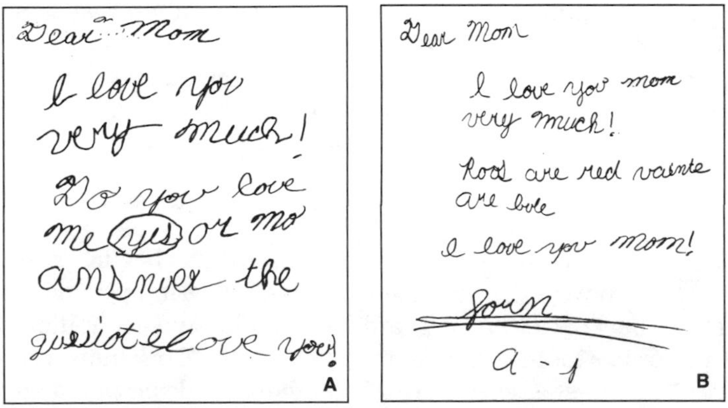

Figure 2–28 ● A.J.'s Card.   **A:** Outside.   **B:** Inside.

I love you mommey
you love me.
you is sweet
I'm is sweet
Daddy swett
sister is sweet
to. I love you !

Figure 2–29 • Tasmika's Younger Cousin's Card

Tasmika's younger cousin also made a card and drew herself and her mother. (See Figure 2–29.)

The cards the other children made were like the ones we have just shown. Sometimes the picture was the "main event"; sometimes the message that was written carried the message, and the drawing, perhaps of a heart, seemed to be there merely as decoration. The "I love you" cards and letters shown in Figures 2–30 through 2–33 are representative of the many that we collected.

Building Contextual Worlds

In focusing upon the children's interpretations of the places in which they live and upon the ways in which they communicate on multiple levels with those whom they love, we have attempted to show how the children are active participants in building and maintaining their contextual worlds. In *The Human Cycle,* Colin Turnbull (1983) writes, "In all cultures, at all times known to us, the children are a source of wonderment for they are the supreme example of the human potential for creation" (p. 25). In a place called home and with people to love, the children we observed displayed their gifts for creation. However grim the realities of life may have appeared, the children were growing up with literacy as an integral part of their personal, familial, and social histories.

Figure 2–30 • Three of Tasmika's "Big Max" Cards

Our observations of the very young children demonstrated that pens, paper, and books are first handled and held; they are physical objects to be manipulated and eventually controlled. Pens have caps to be taken off and put on. In the accompanying photographs (Figure 2–34, A through D) Sarita (aged two years and one month) is playing with some markers. She was intrigued by their small caps; in the first picture (Figure 2–34, A) she is holding a lilac marker and is slowly replacing the cap. In the second photo (Figure 2–34, B), Sarita has removed the cap and is writing. Notice that there is another marker in her hand and that she holds the one while she writes with the other. Her left hand is on the paper, and she holds the paper still as she works. After a while she stops and picks up all the pens (Figure 2–34, C). She rolls them in her hands and looks at them. The lilac pen is back in the pack

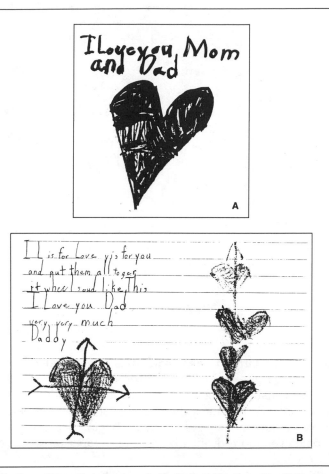

Figure 2–31 • Two of Tasmika's Cards.   **A**: To Both of Her Parents.   **B**: To Her Father.

now, and she selects another marker to take its place. Still holding the pens in her left hand, she continues to work, watching intently as she makes black marks in the corner of her picture (Figure 2–34, D). In viewing the photographs one can almost see the motor and visual (and perhaps aesthetic) pleasure of scribbling experienced by this young child (see Kellogg 1970). (Sarita's finished work is shown in Figure 2–35.)

Sarita worked beside Jarasad (aged three years and three months), whom you can see in the photographs in Figure 2–36. Notice that Jarasad is holding the pen in her right hand. Look at her face as she focuses upon her paper and the way she uses her left hand. She is holding the paper while moving her fingers as if they are a part of the production.

Figure 2–32 ● A Card of Hakim's to His
Mother

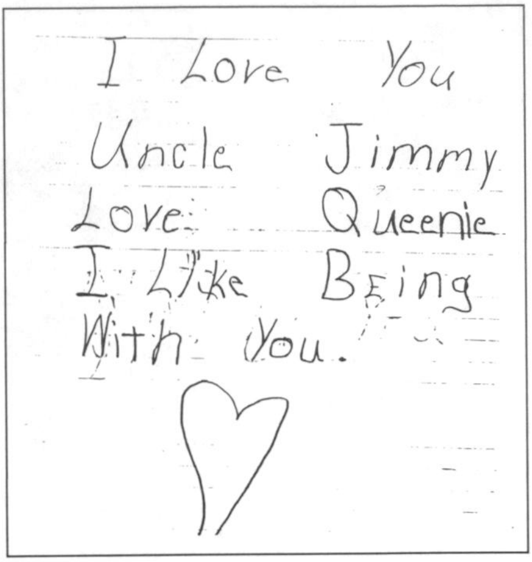

Figure 2–33 ● Queenie's Card for Her Uncle

The picture that Jarasad was making might be considered to be nothing but scribbles. (See Figure 2–37, A.) However, there is a face on the page and, with a little imagination (though this is, admittedly, adult perception of a child's work), one can find the *J* that begins her name. The letter *J* is more clearly visible on the other side of her paper (Figure 2–37, B), and her movements become even more defined on the third paper on which she worked (Figure 2–37, C).

It would be easy for us at this point to study the writing of the other young children who participated in the study, but this would give the impression that we were observing children for whom writing and reading emerged as separate processes independent of one another. Our findings are to the contrary. Drawing, writing, and reading appear closely connected. For example, on the occasion when Sarita played with the pens and drew on paper, she also stacked books and listened to a story. In the first three pictures of Figure 2–38, you can see Sarita (aged two years and one month) as she sorts and stacks the books that belong to her brother Danny. In the fourth picture, she has chosen a book that belongs to her and to her sister, Jarasad. She has opened the book and has been looking at what's on the page.

Moments later Sarita took the book to Louise Taylor, who visited the families on several occasions, and was quickly joined by Jarasad. (See Figure 2–39, A.) Louise read and listened to Jarasad, who talked about the story. Sarita left and Jarasad continued "reading" the story to Louise. (See Figure 2–39, B.)

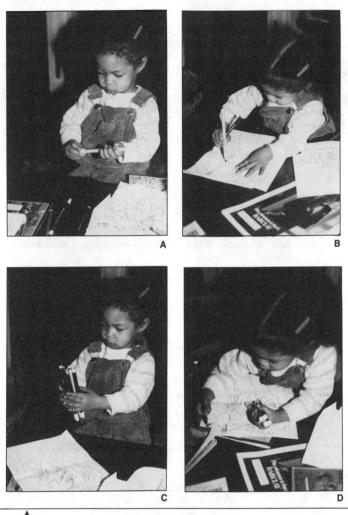

Figure 2–34 ● Sarita Playing with Markers   **Figure 2–35** ● Sarita's Finished Work
▼

A   B

C   D

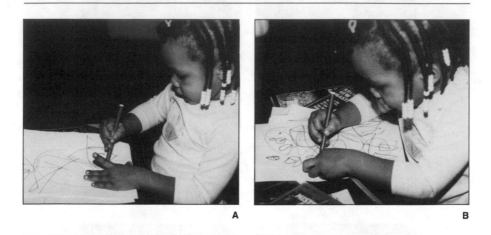

Figure 2–36 • Jarasad at Work

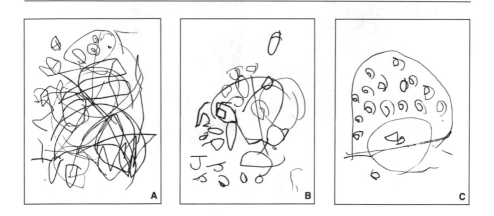

Figure 2–37 • Jarasad's Work. **A:** Her First Drawing. **B:** Her Second Drawing.
C: Her Third Drawing.

Then Jarasad found another book. She turned the pages of *Aldo Apple-sauce* with Louise looking over her shoulder and she continued to look at the book as Louise examined the elaborate braids of her hair. *Time* magazine was next on her agenda. (See Figure 2–40, A, B, and C.)

Our observations of Sarita and Jarasad illustrate the complexity of the contexts in which writing and reading are recognizable as interrelated processes in the literate activities of the children. If we tease these processes apart, we can state that all of the very young children were comfortable both

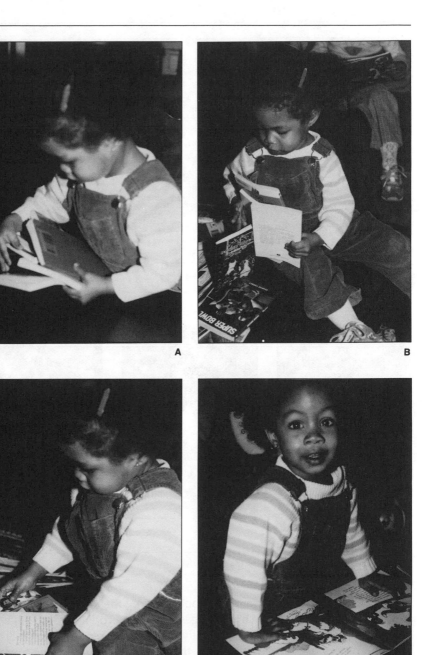

Figure 2–38 • Sarita with Books

Figure 2–39 • Sarita and Jarasad with Louise

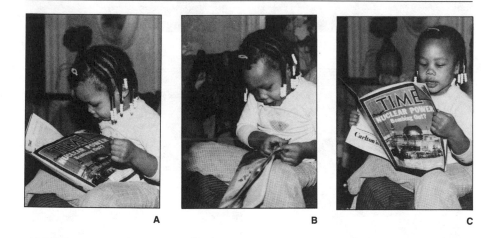

Figure 2–40 • Jarasad with *Time* Magazine

using pens and paper and handling books. During the course of the study we collected many examples of the youngest children producing letterlike forms among their scribbles. Writing gradually became differentiated from drawing. The differences are clearly visible in the card that Jamaine made when he was just four. Jamaine folded a piece of oak tag and "wrote" on the outside (Figure 2–41, A). On the inside he drew two large faces (Figure 2–41, B). On another occasion he wrote on a scrap of oak tag and gave it to us. (See Figure 2–42.) "This says 'Denny,'" he said.

Figure 2–41 • Jamaine's Card.   **A**: Outside.   **B**: Inside.

Figure 2–42 ● Jamaine's Writing: "This Says 'Denny' "

At about the same time we heard Jamaine read. Two days after his fourth birthday he showed us four books that he had received as presents. Jamaine sat beside us, turning the pages of one book after another, reading the pictures and talking the story.

In each of the families we observed the young children reading. Sherran, age three, once read in a halting voice as he looked at the pages in one of his books, "Yellow—is—the—color—of—the—sun,—I—guess." Tanya's small son Gary, age four, also read during one of our visits. Queenie was dancing to some disco music, and Gary sat on the bed with a prayer book. The music and talk drowned out most of the words, but the sound was of reading. Later Gary showed us the book. He opened it and turned over bunches of pages and then he stopped when he reached a page with a picture. Gary pointed at it and sounded out "Je-sus." Still later, as we were leaving, we observed Gary writing in the front of the prayer book. He drew a series of short lines in the right-hand corner. There was a telephone number just above and to the left of Gary's writing and he drew an O next to the last digit, which was a zero. We asked him what it was and he said, "a circle." He then drew several more circles further down the page.

In this chapter we have tried to resist the temptation to separate literacy from the contexts in which it was observed. Clearly there is much more to be said of the ways in which the parents and children communicated through print. However, our purpose has been to emphasize (1) the ways in which the children use both graphic and linguistic resources in the service of complex communications that reflect their experience of place and their conceptualizations of family; and (2) the ways in which the younger children learned through their own explorations of drawing, writing, and reading as interconnected processes that were meaningful in their everyday lives. The degree to which both parents and children were involved with print will be explored in greater depth in chapter 4, "Literacy in a Comparative Frame." In the remaining pages of the present chapter our attention is given to another kind of literacy: school literacy that comes home.

School Literacy at Home

Writing and reading at school came home and added a further dimension to the literate lives of the children. We will begin our discussion with some observations of the early literacy experiences of the preschool children. Faces were drawn, both at home and at the day-care center that many of the children attended. Many of the children's drawings in both environments included the printing of letters and the writing of names. A year after the photographs were taken of Jarasad writing (Figure 2–36), Ieshea talked about Jarasad writing her name. We met Ieshea in Jemma's apartment and she said, "If you come to my house you might not want to take the papers but you might want to take a wall." Ieshea smiled and added, "Jarasad writes all over the walls— her first name and her last." The children's intense interest in the writing of their names seems to be in accord with the attention that was given to name writing in their preschool programs. The biggest difference seems to be in the way in which their names came to be put on paper. At home, the children wrote for themselves, and most of their productions were their own. At school, names were incorporated into drawings by the children, but name writing was also specifically taught. Teachers wrote and children copied.

The children's interest in the writing of names continued as they entered kindergarten and then first and second grades. We collected examples of names written over and over again that made patterns down and across pieces of notebook paper. When Shauna was eight, she added to her own name the names of her mother, her aunts and uncles, and her cousin Sherran. On another occasion she wrote her own name—first, middle, and last—and did the same for her mother, Pauline, and for Trisha and her son Sherran. Underneath the four names she wrote her own name again, this time in red; and she wrote her mother's in blue. She drew a blue box around their names, as if linking them together in a family arrangement. Next she wrote Sherran's name in bright pink and Trisha's in purple and placed a purple box around them. Again it seemed that she was acknowledging the special relationship of mother and son that existed between Trisha and Sherran. This, together with some hearts, made up her page. In contrast, at school the children simply wrote their names at the top of each piece of paper that they received. Names were drawn carefully during "penmanship," but were written primarily to identify their work. We did not collect any examples from the children's schoolwork of the children's visual explorations of kinship or self through the writing of names. This small and seemingly insignificant difference between home and school is nevertheless illustrative of the fundamental disparities that exist between the interpretations of literacy at home and at school.

And yet the children's work in school became an important part of family life. School literacy entered the home through the work that the teachers sent home for the parents to see and through the homework that the children were given to do every night. When Tasmika was in first grade Jemma talked with us about the homework that her young daughter received. She said, "She comes home, she changes her clothes, she does her homework, and after she get finished with her homework I make her explain to me everything that she did, and then she goes out to play. But at school I haven't had much problem with her. She gets good grades. Tasmika reads good. If she see a word that she don't know, she'll sit down and try and figure it out. She'll break it down and try to figure it out. She won't just say, 'I'll skip it,' and go to the next one. She'll just try to figure it out, and if it takes her too long and you see her sittin' there and she's just thinkin'. And she asks you if she know that she can't get it. Then she'll ask you what the word is. Otherwise she rather do her homework on her own. Like, I'll sit down with her and I'll ask her, you know, 'Do you want me to help you?' And she'll say, 'No, I'll do it. I'll do it and then you can see it.' And [she] don't want me to sit down and help her. She'll do it on her own. I mean, after she get finished, then I ask her to show me what she did and how she do it. And she's pretty good. Tasmika's good."

Jemma's description of Tasmika doing her homework reflects our observations of homework in the families that we visited. We were often at their homes when the children arrived from school. After greetings and some talk, clothes were changed and homework done. On one occasion Queenie sat on one of the beds with her homework paper supported by a book that was resting on her lap. We could see her working, but we did not intrude. Eventually Queenie got up and brought the paper, a ditto, to Tanya, who was sitting with us, talking in the kitchen. Queenie gave her mother the paper and stood leaning against her as they looked together at the work that she had brought home. Tanya checked her answers. Queenie's task had been to shade in a circle next to the sentence (one of three) that described the accompanying picture. (See Figure 2–43. Note: In reproducing this ditto, we have removed Queenie's name.) Queenie read all of the sentences to Tanya. There were several words that Queenie could not read, and Tanya told her what they were. Later Queenie read her basal reader with Tanya, and again Tanya supplied the words that Queenie could not read.

Our observations of Pauline and Shauna were similar to those of Tanya and Queenie. Typical was the occasion when Shauna arrived home with a math review sheet. After changing her clothes, Shauna sat down next to her mother on the couch. She put the paper on a book, which she placed on her lap. Shauna did her work resting against her mom, and Pauline watched her daughter work. When Shauna made a mistake, Pauline pointed to the sum with her finger. Then Pauline would wait while Shauna erased, recalculated, and then wrote her revised answer. When she had completed this process Pauline removed her finger and Shauna continued working on the ditto. There was a time when we observed Shauna working beside her mother on a par-

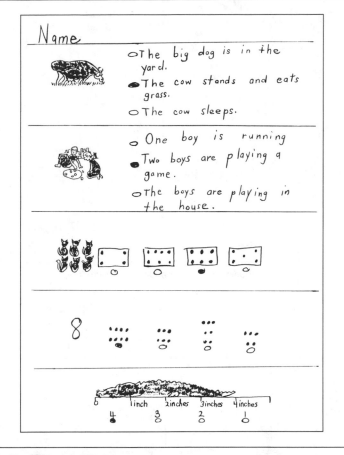

Figure 2–43 • Queenie's Ditto

ticularly difficult ditto, and Shauna resisted revising one of her answers. Pauline giggled with her. They joked, and Shauna wrote. The moment of tension quickly passed, and Shauna finished her homework with a smile for her mom. At the time that these observations took place, Pauline was attending college, and she told us that she often did her homework while Shauna did hers. Pauline also said that if Shauna finished before her, then Pauline would write some math problems for Shauna to do.

During the course of the study we collected many examples of the schoolwork that the children brought home from school. The exercises presented here are typical of the work that the parents received and then gave to us.

Figures 2–44 and 2–45 are two exercises that Queenie and Tasmika brought home during their first-grade year. The children were in different classrooms. We will resist discussing the exercises; rather, we present them to you as

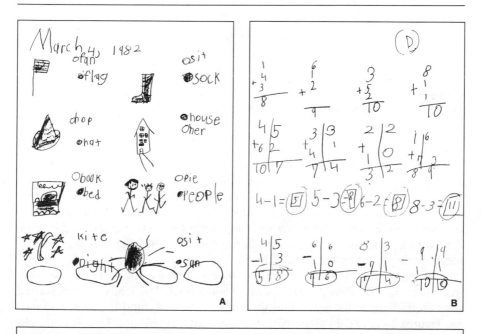

Figure 2–44 ● Queenie's Schoolwork.　A: Side One.　B: Side Two.

Figure 2–45 ● Tasmika's Schoolwork.　A: Side One.　B: Side Two.

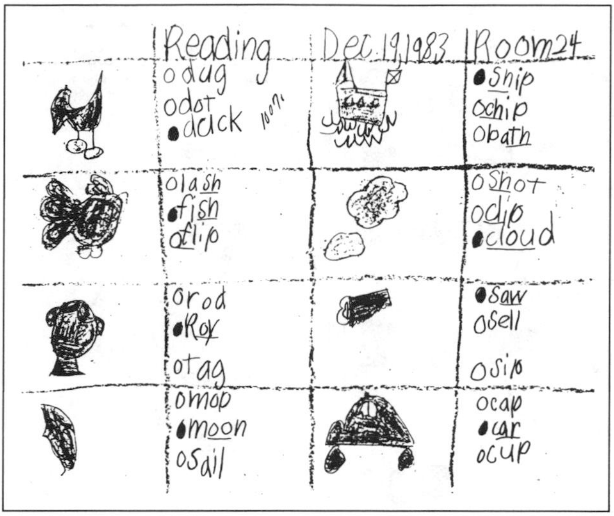

Figure 2–46 • Hakim's Schoolwork

they were presented to the parents—without any explanation about the work that the children had done. (Throughout these examples, though, we have deleted the children's names.)

Similar work was also completed by Hakim when he was in first grade the following year. (See Figure 2–46.)

Workbook pages were also sent home. Figure 2–47 presents several typical workbook exercises that Hakim brought home (from Series R, Macmillan Reading Program, 1980 edition).

Writing (penmanship) papers came home along with the workbook pages and other exercises. We collected many of these from Jemma, who saved Tasmika's work for us. Tasmika completed the papers shown in Figure 2–48 when she was in the second semester of first grade.

Most of the work that the children brought home from school was successfully completed, and their scores on standardized tests suggest that they were prepared by their teachers for the system of assessment employed by the administration. It seems that in these early years the school was taking the necessary steps to enable the children to succeed at the tasks that were set for them. The children learned their lessons well, and we have at least some indication that school literacy was meaningful. When Tasmika played school she did not write "I love you" messages. Instead she made lists of words and wrote the alphabet. Figure 2–49 is typical of this kind of writing. The "messages" carried by these activities had little to do with the meanings of the words.

A. Write the letters.
Circle the picture with the same vowel sound.

home

1.
2.

money — funny

B. Write the letters.
Circle the picture with the same **middle** sound.

1. many
2. funny
3. funny

"Izzy," Part One, pages 66-72 (Softcover: pages 66-72)

Objectives: Recognize the phoneme-grapheme correspondences for long vowels /ow/-o-e, and for medial consonants nn, nn (Decoding Skills)

Directions: Identify the key picture and read the key word with the children. Read the first set of directions and identify each picture. Have the children complete this part of the page. Follow the same procedure for the second part.

39

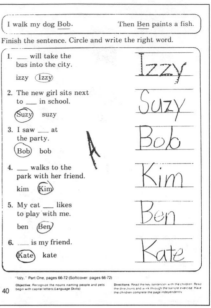

I walk my dog Bob.   Then Ben paints a fish.

Finish the sentence. Circle and write the right word.

1. ___ will take the bus into the city.
   izzy   (Izzy)

2. The new girl sits next to ___ in school.
   (Suzy)   suzy

3. I saw ___ at the party.
   (Bob)   bob

4. ___ walks to the park with her friend.
   kim   (Kim)

5. My cat ___ likes to play with me.
   ben   (Ben)

6. ___ is my friend.
   (Kate)   kate

Izzy
Suzy
Bob
Kim
Ben
Kate

"Izzy," Part One, pages 66-72 (Softcover: pages 66-72)

40

Objective: Recognize the nouns naming people and pets begin with capital letters (Language Skills)

Directions: Read the key sentences with the children. Read the directions and work through the sample exercise. Have the children complete the page independently.

Read the words. Underline the word your teacher says.

1.	2.	3.	4.	5.
again	girls	may	not	slowly
gave	fish	many	know	sees
fame	first	man	Kim	surprise
6.	**7.**	**8.**	**9.**	**10.**
help	thing	party	soon	three
her	time	play	wood	her
hill	live	pony	sees	their
11.	**12.**	**13.**	**14.**	**15.**
of	part	his	going	for
for	play	is	green	father
or	place	hers	doing	mother
16.	**17.**	**18.**	**19.**	**20.**
word	saw	may	this	thing
were	see	say	his	turtle
there	was	many	then	little
21.	**22.**	**23.**	**24.**	**25.**
bus	Izzy	Help	Many	move
boy	lives	Hat	Mindy	other
box	is	Hal	Into	mother
26.	**27.**	**28.**	**29.**	**30.**
ask	read	days	why	looked
as	rock	does	went	soon
and	look	dogs	want	liked

"Izzy," Part One, pages 66-72 (Softcover: pages 66-72)

Objective: Understand and use vocabulary appropriate to grade level, cumulative. Vocabulary Review (Comprehension/Literary Skills)

Directions: Read the directions with the children. Point out number 1 and have the children find it. Say the underlined word. Have the children complete this example. Then follow the same procedure for all the other examples.

41

"My dog is gone! Have you seen my dog?" Mindy said. She ran to find her dog.

Mindy ran fast. She looked here and there. She looked for her dog as she ran.

Finish the sentence. Underline the right word.

1. The pony runs ___ .
   fast   gone   seen

2. The dog is ___ .
   here   seen   gone

3. The boy ___ .
   sang   as   ran

4. She sang ___ she ran.
   as   fast   seen

5. A turtle can't go ___ .
   first   fish   fast

6. He looks ___ he rides.
   at   or   as

"Izzy," Part Two, pages 73-76 (Softcover: pages 73-76)

Objective: Understand and use vocabulary appropriate to grade level (Comprehension/Literary Skills)

Directions: Read the story with the children and review the underlined words with them. Read the directions and work through the sample exercise. Have the children complete the page independently.

42

Figure 2–47 • Hakim's Workbook Exercises

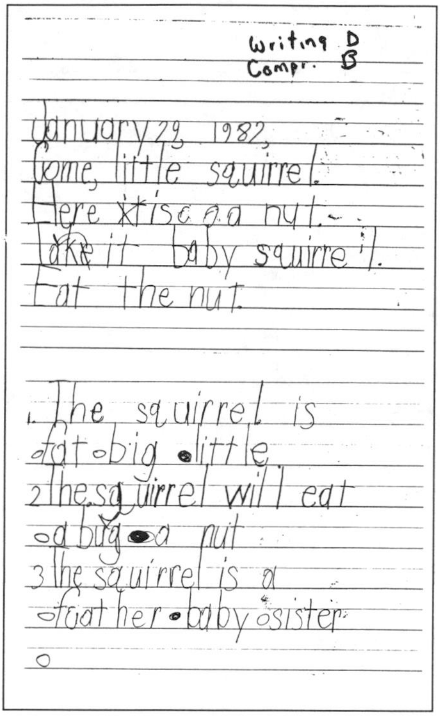

Writing D
Compr. B

January 29, 1982.
Come, little squirrel.
Here xt is a a nut.
Take it baby squirre'l.
Eat the nut.

1. The squirrel is
fat big little
2 The squirrel will eat
a big a nut
3 The squirrel is a
father baby sister

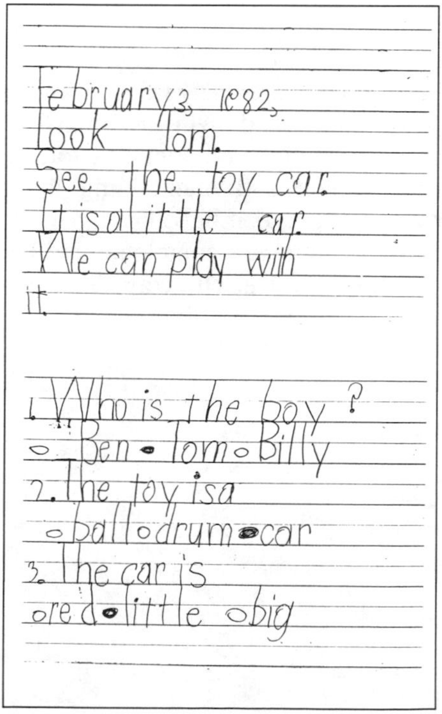

February 3, 1982.
Look Tom.
See the toy car.
It is a little car.
We can play with
it.

1. Who is the boy ?
Ben Tom Billy
2. The toy is a
ball drum car
3. The car is
red little big

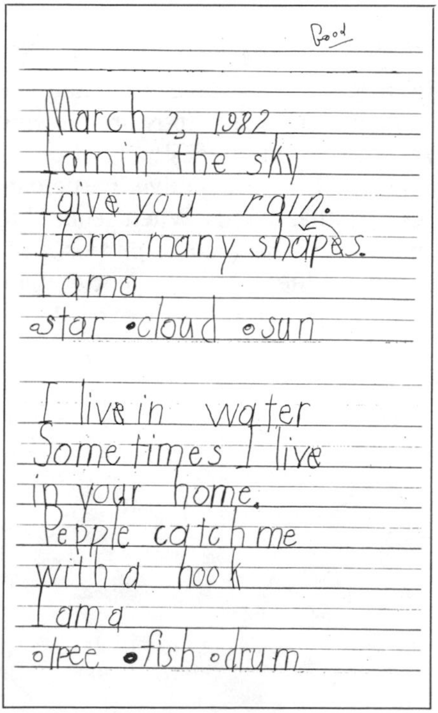

Good

March 2, 1982
I am in the sky
I give you rain.
I form many shapes.
I am a
star cloud sun

I live in water
Sometimes I live
in your home.
Pepple catch me
with a hook
I am a
tree fish drum

Figure 2–48 • Tasmika's Penmanship Papers

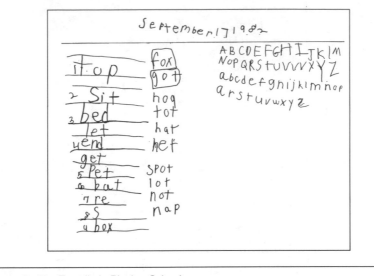

Figure 2–49 • Tasmika's Playing School

Commentary

In this section we have attempted to explore some of the many ways in which the children in our study are growing up with literacy (drawing, writing, and reading) as an integral part of their personal, familial, and social histories. The children are active participants in building and maintaining their (con)textual worlds. When school literacy comes home, it becomes a part of that world. The genuine purposes of literacy at home are complemented by a form of literacy that is not designed for practical use. The consequences of this situation will be explored in chapter 5.

Three
Literacy and the Children at School

A child moves out through concentric worlds even with her first steps, but whether these worlds are encountered as wholes or as fragments and whether they provide an entry into other spheres of imagination and experience depend on how they are presented, how attention is gradually shaped and the cosmos gradually unfolded.

Mary Catherine Bateson

In a book that focuses so specifically upon learning in families, you may be wondering, "Why a chapter on children at school?" The answer is clear: To understand the ways in which children learn at home, it is essential that we know something of the ways in which they are taught at school. What we present in this chapter are small pieces of data that we have collected: a description of four-year-old Jarasad's graduation from the day-care center that she attended; a day of observations of Shauna in her second-grade classroom; and an account of an incident in school that occurred when Danny was in seventh grade. Each piece was chosen for the insights that can be gained from them into the lives of the children we have been visiting as they move out through the concentric worlds of their own imagination and experience. It is important for us to emphasize that this tentative arrangement of data is presented to raise questions. It is not a classroom ethnography or sociolinguistic analysis. For such research we turn to the work of Bloome (1983), Florio and Shultz (1979), Gilmore and Glatthorn (1982), Green (1983), Heap (1986), and McDermott (1976a and b), whose research has helped us appreciate the extraordinary complexity of the ways in which classroom contexts are embedded in and constrained by the everyday world (social, cultural, and political) in which we live.

In the families we visited, the parents often talked of their children's early childhood experiences in pre-elementary school programs and their subsequent school achievement. When Ieshea spoke of Hakim, who was in day care from the ages of eighteen months to five years, she said, "I feel personally that he would have been ready for first-grade work, but they wouldn't take him. . . . I really believe that's why he's on the honor roll because he's repeating a lot of things that he's had already. . . ." The parents supported their children through their early years of day care, and they participated in the activities that were arranged for parents to share. The importance of this time in the lives of these young children is emphasized by the elaborate graduation ceremony that marks the end of their pre-elementary years. The following description is of the graduation of Jarasad, a proud moment in a young life that we want you to share.

Jarasad's Graduation

When Jarasad graduated from the day-care center she wore a white dress and white gloves, and Ieshea brushed her hair into pretty curls. Sarita also wore a new dress. She went with her mother to celebrate the occasion, which was held at the local Elks' Club. Ieshea wore a beige suit with a long jacket and sat near the front of the auditorium so that she could see Jarasad and the children as they marched to the music, made speeches, and sang songs. The auditorium was filled with the families of the children. There were mothers and fathers, aunts and uncles, grandparents and children; they were all dressed for the occasion in their best clothes. The hall was packed to capacity, and there was much laughter in the crowd. Some of the parents were standing in the spaces left for the children who were soon to march into the hall. A teacher spoke to them and to a photographer who was assembling his equipment, telling them that they must move so that the children could enter as they had practiced at their rehearsals. Then, just before the children entered, the audience was told not to distract them as they participated in the ceremony. The audience was hushed, and the families turned to watch as they all waited for a glimpse of their own particular child.

Marching to the rhythm of rock music and carrying flags, the children entered the hall and the ceremony began. Wearing caps and gowns and in step with one another, they made their way down the aisle to the front of the hall. Their teachers marched with them, encouraging them and guiding them as they moved forward towards their seats. Then the children stood for the opening song, the welcoming address, the valediction, and another song. The children stood tall and smiled at their families, who watched with pride. More songs were sung: "Gifted and Black," "The Greatest Love," and "You, You, You." Two-year-olds gathered on stage and sang their songs. Then the three-year-olds used lammi sticks, keeping time to the rhythm of the music to which they sang. The graduating class participated in the ceremony individually as well as together. Each child said, "Hello," in a different language, and then they sang songs, made speeches, and danced. Two guest speakers spoke of the courage of black women who raised their children with love and concern for their well-being. One of the speakers emphasized to the parents that they must support their children throughout their school careers. "Don't stop now!" was the message that the parents heard.

After the ceremony, photographs were taken and lunch served. In the basement the tables were set with food, which the families had prepared. The children were served first. They were given plates by their teachers, who helped them chose what they wanted to eat. Then the families, talking and laughing, and some latecomers, who had been taking just one more photograph, filled their plates and sat together to enjoy the ceremonial meal.

Shauna's Day at School

In our visits to the elementary school that most of the children attended, it is the rows of orderly desks, the board work, and the lines for the bathroom that stick in our memory. The children sat quietly in their seats, and there was little movement in their classrooms. The school doors were locked when the children went inside. During the course of the study we followed Queenie, Shauna, and Tasmika through six school days (Queenie for one day, Shauna for three days, and Tasmika for two days). We used Barker and Wright's *One Boy's Day* (1951) as a model for these observations. Although our efforts fall far short of their exemplary study, we do believe that the record that we have created adds a further dimension to our understanding of the lives of the children with whom we worked. Barker and Wright used eight observers throughout the day; each observable period was approximately thirty minutes in duration. For us it was a matter of recording for an entire day. We each recorded several full days of observations and several half days. When a full day of observations was made by one of us, the other observed the same child for half of that day. Thus, notes could be compared and questions raised. The use of eight observers ensures against what Barker and Wright refer to as "unconscious biases and perceptual bents." We had no such insurance. But two observers are better than one, and we have both contributed to the account that is presented in this section. It is hoped that, within the scope of the entire text, some of our own idiosyncracies will be made clear. One final comment: We have presented the entire record for the particular day of observations. There is a certain monotony in the notes; this reflects the tedium of the day. Some readers may find themselves skipping through the pages of ethnographic notes to gain a general impression of Shauna's day at school, while others may read the section in detail. But however the text gets read, it is important to remember that the notes reflect an actual day at school.

7:15 A.M. Traffic is at a standstill. It's cold and icy, but there is no fresh snow. Trucks edge forward, breathing out fumes, and commuters are trying to keep warm in their cars, holding Styrofoam cups of coffee and smoking as they move slowly forward towards the light, where the traffic will break and move off in different directions. A young girl in a yellow ski jacket and sneakers is selling roses. She holds them out to the drivers of the slowly moving cars, but nobody buys.

7:50 A.M.   Philadelphia Avenue, near Shay Avenue, is quiet. A few people are walking along the street, hats down, collars up. The door to Shauna's house is not locked. We go inside and climb the stairs. When we reach the second floor we knock and wait. The house is quiet—sleepy. Megan opens the door. Pauline is sitting by the window, and Shauna is standing in front of her. Pauline is arranging Shauna's coat. She tells Shauna to go and wash a dirty mark off her face.

7:55 A.M.   Pauline looks at Shauna's face and makes sure it is clean. Shauna turns and leaves. Gina and Megan follow her down the stairs. The three girls walk to school. Shauna walks in front with Gina. Megan waits for us to catch up. She says that Gina and Shauna walk together every morning.

8:00 A.M.   When we reach the playground Shauna goes in. There is a guard on duty, so we go around to the front office. Inside the door, another guard sits behind a table. Arrangements have been made, so brief explanations are quickly given and we are allowed to sign the visitors' book and enter the school.

8:05 A.M.   We look for Shauna in the cafeteria, where children are eating breakfast, but she isn't there. Megan comes in and tells us that Shauna is in the playground.

8:10 A.M.   Outside, Shauna is standing at the top of some concrete steps by the door that she will go through when the bell rings.

8:15 A.M.   Shauna is still standing quietly, but then she drops her bag by the door and goes into the playground to speak to some friends.

8:16 A.M.   Shauna returns and resumes her position by her bag at the door.

8:20 A.M.   A woman asks us to return to the office. Inside, we talk to the principal, who is sitting at a typewriter, straightening some paper, ready to type. She smiles and asks us which classroom we will be visiting.

8:28 A.M.   Back outside, the playground is full of children. None of them seems to be bothered by the cold. Most of them are playing, running, jumping, and clapping hands. Some are lining up, while others are on top of a pile of snow that has been cleared from the path and steps that lead to the door through which they will go when the bell rings for classes to begin.

8:30 A.M.   Shauna is standing in front of the door.

8:33 A.M.   Shauna continues to wait. She moves into the doorway and watches the children who go in and out as they move between the cafeteria and the playground.

8:35 A.M.   The bell rings. Shauna goes in and is out of sight. We follow, but we are on the third floor before we see her again. Shauna is standing by the door to her classroom. She is first in a long line of children from her class who are all waiting for their teacher to arrive.

8:40 A.M.   Shauna's teacher arrives. She tells the children to go into the classroom; then she questions us with a quick smile. We introduce ourselves and quickly realize that she has not been told about our visit. After a brief explanation, Shauna's teacher says that it is O.K. for us to visit.

8:45 A.M.   The children are taking off their coats and jostling for space to hang them up in a closet at the side of the room. Shauna is in the middle of a group of children who are taking off their coats. She hangs hers up and goes to her place and sits down. Her teacher is writing on the chalkboard.

8:48 A.M.   Shauna sits in her chair and looks at the board. Then she gets out her reading book and opens it.

8:50 A.M.   Two girls arrive. Shauna's teacher asks them why they are late. One of them explains that she had to go to her baby-sitter's house. She says that her friend had gone with her. The teacher tells the other girl that she should not have gone and tells them that there is no need for them both to be late.

8:52 A.M.   Shauna puts her reading book away. She has not spoken since she came into the classroom.

8:53 A.M.   Shauna gets her book out again and turns the pages, slowly gazing down at the book. She looks up at the chalkboard and then at a friend, but continues to turn the pages of her book.

8:55 A.M.   The teacher finishes writing on the board, sits down, and calls for the first row to show her their work. Shauna goes and stands in line. She is next to last. The teacher praises a boy for good work and asks him if he took his time. The next boy hands her a crumpled sheet, and she asks him if she gave it to him like that. He says no. She tells him not to bring his work back in that condition. The teacher takes the pencil that the boy hands to her. She sharpens it and gives it back to him. The boy goes back to his place and sits down.

8:58 A.M.   Shauna shows her work. The teacher speaks quietly to her, and Shauna answers in a quiet voice that we cannot hear. The teacher looks at each of the homework sheets that Shauna has given to her and then sharpens Shauna's pencil. Shauna takes the pencil when it is offered and sits down. She opens her book and looks down as she slowly turns the pages.

9:02 A.M.   Holding the book to her chest, Shauna looks around. Then, standing the book on her desk, she continues to turn the pages. She leans her face on her left hand and continues moving the pages. Her next-door neighbor, one of the girls who came late from the baby-sitter, puts her arm around her. No words are spoken.

9:06 A.M. Shauna puts her book face down on the desk and draws on a piece of paper.

9:07 A.M. The children are told to get out their spelling books. They get their books and leaf through the pages. The teacher tells them to point to the words that they are studying. Shauna points and with the class she says, "Book." The children then spell the word—"B–o–o–k"—and finish off by saying the word "Book" one more time. Say; spell; say. Shauna chants each word with the class. Then she closes her book and puts it in her desk.

9:10 A.M. Shauna's teacher gives each child a piece of paper, and Shauna writes her name on it. She is sitting up straight but looking down at her paper as she writes. She finishes her name and looks up. Shauna raises her hand and her teacher asks her what she wants. Shauna says that the person who changes the date on the calendar is absent. Her teacher thanks her, walks over to the calendar, and turns over the number 18.

9:15 A.M. Shauna is sitting. Her teacher is organizing her desk. She tells the children that she will say the words from their spelling list and then say each word in a sentence. As the words are read out, Shauna writes them down. "*Book*. She is reading an interesting *book*."

9:18 A.M. Shauna erases and writes. Her teacher finishes the list and tells the children to put their papers face down and put their pencils down. Shauna obeys and sits, looking forward, as the papers are collected.

9:20 A.M. The teacher has been writing on the board. She shows the children and tells them to do numbers 1 through 6 on the front of the paper that is being given out and then do numbers 7 through 10 on the back.

**Board Exercise ●
Homonyms**

1. no	ate	7. blue	new
2. sea	right	8. here	sun
3. two	know	9. son	hear
4. eight	flower	10. knew	blew
5. flour	see		
6. write	to		

9:26 A.M. Shauna is working on the board exercise.

9:29 A.M. Shauna continues to look at the board and then down at her paper.

9:30 A.M. Children are getting up and going to the teacher's desk. Shauna doesn't look at them. She continues writing. Then she abruptly gets up, puts her pencil on her desk, and goes over to her teacher, leaving her paper. Then she returns to her desk.

9:32 A.M.   Shauna gets another sheet of paper. She folds it and looks at the next exercise, which her teacher wrote on the board at the beginning of the morning.

Second Board Exercise

1. Find the words that have the same ending sound as *sink*.
   bank   rug   think   thing   tank   rink

2. Find the words that have the same ending sound as *plant*.
   play   elephant   sent   present   want

3. Find the words that have the same beginning as *squirt*.
   squirrel   quiet   squaw   seat   squat

9:37 A.M.   Shauna continues to write. She writes each sentence and the words that go with them. She yawns and puts her hand over her mouth; then she continues.

9:40 A.M.   Shauna is working on the third question. Children are quietly looking from the board to their papers. There is very little talk.

9:44 A.M.   Shauna finishes the third problem. She gets up and takes it to her teacher's desk. She picks up a ditto on George Washington and returns to her seat.

9:45 A.M.   Shauna peels the paper off a white crayon and shows it to her neighbor. Then she colors George Washington's face. Shauna puts the white crayon down and picks up a red one. She continues to color George Washington's face. Still coloring, she hitches in her chair with her feet, which are curled around the chair legs.

9:48 A.M.   Shauna goes on coloring. The girl sitting next to Shauna brings Shauna her picture and asks about the colors she has used to shade George Washington's face. Another child brings a picture. Shauna looks up and then continues to color. The children sit down. Shauna looks around at the other George Washingtons on the desks beside and behind her.

9:52 A.M.   Shauna continues to color.

9:54 A.M.   A mother enters the classroom and asks the teacher if she may speak to her daughter. She has lost a gold chain and asks her daughter if she has it. The mother goes through her daughter's coat pockets. The teacher offers to help. Shauna looks up at them and then at us. She holds up her picture of George Washington for us to see.

9:56 A.M.   Shauna's teacher is working with a reading group. Shauna continues to color. She stops and looks again at the George Washingtons around her. She turns around and looks at a girl who is walking towards the back of the room. Shauna shifts her gaze to the desks behind her. She picks up a box of crayons from one of the other desks and sits, going through the crayons. She selects a peach-colored crayon and uses it to add another layer of color to George Washington's face.

10:03 A.M.   Children are moving. They are getting other things to do. Shauna goes on coloring. Then she puts down her crayon and gets up. Shauna comes over and looks at our notes. We ask her if she is working hard. She says, "Not too hard." She goes to the back of the room, returns to her desk, and then goes back again. She returns to her desk with an old cigar box. She puts it on her desk and sits down.

10:06 A.M.   Shauna fixes the box by pressing the tape that has come loose. She opens the box and takes out one card at a time. The first card says APE. After looking at three of the cards, she puts them into the box, gets up, and returns the box to the back of the room. She takes another box and goes back to her seat. This time she has a box of dominoes. She puts the box in her desk and takes the dominoes out one at a time.

10:09 A.M.   Shauna lines up the dominoes. Almost at once they fall, one after another, until they are flat on Shauna's desk. Shauna tries to stand them up all at once, but when it doesn't work she sets them upright one at a time.

10:12 A.M.   Shauna takes the box out of her desk and removes the rest of the dominoes. The line of dominoes falls down. Shauna puts them all in the box and takes them to the back of the room. There is a seat at the back where some children are sitting with books. Shauna sits down. She picks up a book, turns the pages as she looks at the two girls who are sitting beside her, and then pretends to read, mouthing the words as one of the girls reads a page. She looks up and smiles at the two girls. They each have a book; one reads a page and then the other reads a page. Shauna has found the same page, and she waits as the two girls argue about whose turn it is to read. The argument goes on until the two girls get different books and read on their own.

10:18 A.M.   Shauna selects another book from the table and turns the pages. She stops turning and looks at one page. Then she closes the book and puts it back on the table with the other books.

10:20 A.M.   Shauna comes over to where one of us is sitting and takes the notebook. She turns the pages and stops at a diagram of her classroom. "What's that?" She asks.

"Your classroom."

Shauna looks at the location of the desks, the chalkboard, and the other objects in the room and then gives back the notebook.

10:23 A.M.   Shauna gets a box with pictures that have cut-out parts. One is of a tiger. She looks through the box of cards and then puts them back. She picks up another box and returns with it to her desk.

10:26 A.M. Shauna puts some of the cards on the desk, and then she turns towards the back of the room and starts a game with the girl who sits behind her. The girl shows Shauna the word without the initial letters and she has to guess the word. The girl holds up the cards and Shauna reads.

sm ell   p en   p ot

10:30 A.M. Shauna continues to guess. Smiling, she picks up the cards that she has guessed and counts them. She puts them in a neat pile in front of her on her friend's desk.

10:32 A.M. The children are told to put away their activities and get ready for library. Shauna turns around, gets her book out, and sits up straight. Her teacher comments on how nicely she is sitting.

10:34 A.M. The children are told to line up, boys in one line and girls in a line perpendicular to the boys':

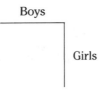

Shauna is second in line.

The children leave the room in their lines. They are told to go as far as the alarm box.

10:38 A.M. We arrive at our destination: the library. The teacher tells the librarian that we are following Shauna through a school day. He smiles and greets us.

Shauna asks where we are going to sit. We ask her if it would be O.K. to sit near the chalkboard, away from the area where the children are finding seats at tables. Shauna sits down.

10:41 A.M. The librarian reads out the cards from the books that the children have taken out. Each of the children raises their hands as his or her title is called.

10:43 A.M. The librarian calls "*Summer Story*." Shauna raises her hand. She takes the class card out of her book and hands it to the librarian. He in turn gives her the call card that belongs in the book, and she puts it in the book.

10:45 A.M. Shauna raises her hand. The librarian says, "I don't want to hear about it, honey." Shauna frowns and turns around.

10:47 A.M.   The librarian talks about the cards.

10:48 A.M.   The librarian shows the children an enlarged version of a card, which he has drawn on the board. Shauna sits and watches. The thumb on her right hand is in her mouth and her elbow is on the table.

10:51 A.M.   The librarian asks a boy to fill in the card—name and room number. The boy comes up and fills it in. The librarian asks what he could have done better. Shauna raises her hand and shakes it back and forth. The librarian calls on her. She says that the boy missed a line. The librarian says, "Right." He then asks for more volunteers. Shauna does not raise her hand. She sits watching. Her elbows are on the table and her head is in her hands.

10:55 A.M.   The librarian says that the clock on the wall tells him it's time to move on. Shauna raises her hand and, when acknowledged, asks if she can turn out the lights. The librarian says that someone has already asked him to do the lights.

10:56 A.M.   The lights are out. The librarian switches on the projector for the children to see a film on going to the library. Shauna faces the screen and sits watching.

11:02 A.M.   Shauna hasn't moved.

11:09 A.M.   The lights go on. The film has ended. Shauna hasn't moved.

11:10 A.M.   The librarian and the children are talking about the film. Shauna sits, listening. Shauna's table is told to select books. Shauna and the other children get up quickly and move to the shelves.

11:12 A.M.   Shauna picks up a large yellow book, looks through the pages, and then goes to the front desk. She takes out the card, takes a pencil from the container, and writes her name on the card. She is the first child to get a book.

11:13 A.M.   Shauna shows us the book. It is *A Silly Book of Animals*. We ask her how she chose it and she replies, "I know how to read it."

11:16 A.M.   Shauna is kneeling on her seat, reading. She picks the book up from the table and shows a page to the girl sitting opposite. Another girl tries to look at the book. Shauna frowns and positions the book so the girl can't see. Then she puts the book back on the table and continues to read. She is saying the words quietly to herself.

11:19 A.M.   Shauna continues to read, standing the book on the table. She stands up and shows a picture to a friend. Then she sits down and continues to read. The girl sitting next to her listens for a few moments, then returns to her own book. Shauna continues to read. Some children are still choosing books.

11:21 A.M.   Shauna's table is told to line up. Shauna is up and in the girls' line. She is the second girl in the line.

11:23 A.M.   In the corridor, Shauna stands watching as a group of eighth graders line up and move out of their classroom. A man (a teacher?) stops to ask them about their books. The girls' line breaks as they show their books, but it is quickly re-formed after the books are shown.

11:26 A.M.   Shauna leaves the line and asks to see our notes. She looks at them and returns to her place in the girls' line.

11:27 A.M.   Shauna's teacher arrives and tells the children to line up in front of her. She tells them to hold their books under their arms.

11:28 A.M.   The children line up outside the bathroom. The doors are held open and a child outside the girls' bathroom takes the girls' books as they go in. The girl gives the books back as they come out. The children (boys and girls) go into the bathrooms in threes. They are told not to talk.

11:30 A.M.   Shauna is in and out and goes to the back of the line without her book. She is called back.

11:34 A.M.   The teacher locks the boys' bathroom and stands by the girls' bathroom, waiting. Shauna speaks briefly to the girl standing next to her. The girls' bathroom is locked.

11:36 A.M.   The children are told to "face the room." They go back to their classroom. Girls in; boys in.

11:37 A.M.   The children are sitting in their places. They are told that they can read their library books.

11:38 A.M.   Shauna opens her book and shows a picture to the girl sitting next to her. Her teacher tells the class that she doesn't want to keep anyone else in (that she doesn't want to have to make anyone else stay after school for misbehaving). Shauna reads.

11:40 A.M.   The girl sitting in the seat next but one to Shauna asks her to write a cursive *o*. Shauna carefully writes one and then goes back to her book. On one page of her book, the writing is on many lines. Shauna follows the lines with her fingers and reads the text out loud. Then she closes the book and looks around.

11:42 A.M.   Shauna's teacher tells the children to put their books away. They are told to get out their George Washington pictures and to read the story at the bottom of the page. The children read in unison.

11:46 A.M.   The teacher reads from a book on George Washington. Shauna sits up with her arms on the desk.

11:51 A.M. The story continues. The teacher says, "George Washington was a born leader," and two little girls clap their hands together.

11:53 A.M. Shauna looks up at the clock and then turns around, resting her chin in her hands.

The children sit. There is very little movement.

Shauna's teacher says the Americans didn't want to obey the English laws. She looks at Denny (who is English), grins, and says, "No offense."

Denny laughs and says, "That's fine."

The children are told to line up and get washed for lunch.

12:00 NOON. Shauna's teacher leaves to wash up. We are invited to accompany her.

12:03 P.M. The children are waiting in two lines. Shauna is first in the girls' line. They leave the classroom and walk to the stairway. The children take the stairs from the third floor to the basement. At the bottom of each flight of stairs, the two lines stop; wait; then continue.

12:09 P.M. In the cafeteria we are invited to sit with the teachers. We can see Shauna. She lines up for her lunch and laughs with her friends. She sits and eats quickly.

The children leave the cafeteria and go outside for a short time.

Tasmika introduces us to her teacher, and we talk of following Shauna through a school day.

12:31 P.M. The children are returning to their classrooms. They go in lines with their teachers. Shauna's class goes up the stairs.

12:43 P.M. Several of the children look at the research notes that are being made. Shauna picks up the picture that she started drawing first thing in the morning.

12:45 P.M. Some children are reading, some are drawing, and others are writing. Shauna is writing. She looks around and then goes back to the task that she has set for herself. She taps the person sitting next to her and says something. Then she goes back to her drawing.

12:49 P.M. Children are talking. There is a lot of movement.

12:50 P.M. Shauna's teacher calls for the children's attention. She gives out scrap paper and test booklets. The children are told to leave them where they are put on their desks.

12:53 P.M. A boy sitting near one of us says that his uncle has a book about Martin Luther King. He says that he (the boy) has also written a story about him.

12:55 P.M. All the test booklets are given out. Shauna is sitting. The children are told to use the markers they were given to make sure that they line up their answers.

12:59 P.M.   The teacher reads the directions.

1:00 P.M.   The teacher asks, "What is the first picture?" in the booklet. Shauna raises her hand. Another child is called on and answers.

1:02 P.M.   "What else do we have?" asks the teacher. Shauna raises her hand. She is called on and answers correctly.

1:03 P.M.   Shauna raises her hand in response to each question that her teacher asks. Her teacher writes a money sum on the board. Shauna is called on to add up the cents, and she does so correctly.

1:04 P.M.   The children are given further instructions:
"Use the scrap paper. When you've finished, put the guide over the answers and sit up."
"Close your mouth."
"Get to work, J——."
"I don't want a sound."
"I don't want to hear that."
"Excuse me. Don't you make a sound."

1:08 P.M.   Shauna has done the two examples. Her pencil is by her book.

1:09 P.M.   The girl sitting next to Shauna gets out a reading book. The teacher tells her not to and says to sit up straight.
"I don't want anything else out. Put the booklet on the desk and leave it there.... Put the guide down and leave it there."

1:11 P.M.   "T——, do not talk." Shauna is sitting, looking in front of her as if at the wall below the chalkboard.

1:15 P.M.   "Everybody, pencils down, eyes here, sit up in the seats.... Put your finger under the sentence which tells you what to do. Read it."

1:19 P.M.   The children start to read. Shauna's teacher stops them. "I want everyone's finger under the sentence. We are reading the first sentence."
The children read:

"He had 8 🌰.
"He lost 2 🌰.
"How many 🌰 are left?"

1:22 P.M.   Shauna is sitting quietly. Her teacher writes some children's initials on the board. These are the children who are going to be kept after school:

FK
DP

DR

AR

1:24 P.M.   The teacher continues with the test instructions. Shauna continues to sit.

1:25 P.M.   The children follow the teacher's instructions by turning to page 10 and looking at it. They are told that they will do this page when they have done page 9. They are told to move to page 9 and to use the scrap paper.

1:26 P.M.   Shauna is working. The teacher smiles at one of us and rolls her eyes.

1:28 P.M.   Shauna is working. Her teacher continues to talk to the children. "I don't want to see anybody with a blank scrap paper." Shauna is using her fingers to count. Her teacher says, "Don't let me see anybody rushing through this."

1:30 P.M.   "I don't like what I see over here. Get busy, young lady—now."

1:31 P.M.   Shauna is following the steps. She is writing the sums on the scrap paper, looking in the book, then at the answer sheet.

1:32 P.M.   Shauna continues to work. Shauna's teacher tells the children to put their papers together and put their heads down when they have finished. Shauna and a boy in the row behind her are the only ones who put their heads down.

1:35 P.M.   The teacher repeats, "Put your head down if you have finished and checked it over." More heads go down. Shauna's teacher says that she is going to try something else that might make it a little easier. She waits, glancing several times at the clock.

1:38 P.M.   Shauna's head is still down.

1:39 P.M.   The teacher tells the children again to put their heads down when they finish.

1:45 P.M.   The booklets are being collected. Shauna is now sitting, with her arms on her desk.

1:46 P.M.   Shauna looks around. Some boys are talking to her. Shauna yawns and continues to sit.

1:48 P.M.   Her teacher asks the children if they want to play a game. The children say, "Yes," and some of them clap.

1:50 P.M.   The children are told to get into their lines. Shauna is third in the girls' line. They leave the class and head for the bathroom.

1:52 P.M.   The children wait at the top of the stairs.

1:53 P.M. The children are standing and waiting. Another class is using the bathroom. Shauna's class waits for them to leave.

1:54 P.M. The line is moving. Groups of four are going into the bathroom. Shauna is in the first group.

1:56 P.M. A girl comes out of the bathroom and tells the teacher that Shauna pushed her. She says again, "She pushed me." Shauna smiles and there is a sparkle in her eyes.

1:58 P.M. Another class arrives, lines up, and goes into the library, which is nearby. Still another class lines up for the bathroom.

1:59 P.M. Shauna is with two girls at the front of the line.

2:01 P.M. We wait for one little girl. The children turn to go back to their classroom. Shauna turns. She is now third from the back of the line.

2:04 P.M. Back in the classroom, Shauna's teacher tells the children that they are going to play Seven-Up. She picks one boy. The boy picks three children, all big boys, and then one girl. The girl won't go to the front of the class, so he picks a second girl. The rest of the children sit with their heads down and their hands on their desks with their thumbs up. The five children at the front of the class go around the room, and each one touches a seated child on the thumb. The five children then return to the front of the room. The five children who were touched on the thumb stand up in their places. They are each given a chance to say who touched them. At this point there is some confusion over whose thumbs were touched.

2:10 P.M. The children have changed places, and the game begins again. Heads down, thumbs up. One of the girls who is "up front" touches the thumb of a child who has already had a turn. She then touches another thumb.

2:11 P.M. The teacher tells the children, "Heads up, stand up." Shauna was touched. She stands and guesses correctly that it was one of the boys.

2:12 P.M. Shauna walks around the room and touches someone. A boy is called to say who touched him. He says Shauna. He is incorrect. Shauna smiles and says, "No."

2:14 P.M. The guessing is finished, and another round begins. Shauna quickly says, "Heads down, thumbs up." The children up front walk around the room and then back to the front, and they ask the class to guess who has touched their thumbs.

2:17 P.M. A child says that she thinks Shauna touched her thumb. Shauna says, "No." Then another child guesses Shauna. Shauna smiles and sits down.

2:19 P.M. The game goes on. Shauna sits with her elbows on her desk. Shauna is touched again.

2:20 P.M.   Shauna's teacher stops the game in the middle of a round.

2:22 P.M.   The classroom aide comes in, and the children are told to sit and listen to her. Shauna's teacher calls Shauna over to her desk so that she can help Shauna with some sections of a math test that she missed.

2:23 P.M.   Shauna sits by her teacher, who helps her with the directions to the test.

2:24 P.M.   The aide has been reading the last part of the story about George Washington. She finishes and the children clap. Then she asks them some questions.

2:27 P.M.   Shauna's teacher tells the children to read until two-thirty.

One of the boys cleans the board. The teacher tells us that this boy is nine years old and that he will be going up into his right grade soon.

2:30 P.M.   The children read and talk. One of the boys jumps out of his seat, pretends to punch one of the boys, says "I got him," looks at the teacher, sits down quickly, and begins to leaf through the pages of his book.

2:34 P.M.   The children are told to sit up and get ready to get their coats.

2:36 P.M.   Shauna leaves the test and gets her coat and hat with the other children. She puts her papers into her book bag.

2:40 P.M.   Shauna sits while the children pick up the things that they have given to their teacher to look after. The children also collect a few things that have been taken away during the day, such as a bottle of perfume that one girl had brought to school.

2:41 P.M.   Shauna's teacher tells the children that they can take home their report cards but that they must bring them back to school on the following Tuesday.

Chairs are placed on desks, and the girls line up. Shauna is second in line.

The children move out of the classroom. They go as far as the fire alarm.

In the corridor Shauna meets Megan and asks her if she has her report card. The two girls leave the school and walk home together.

They reach their house and go upstairs. Shauna has her report card out. She shows it to her grandmother. No one else is home. Shauna has her Metropolitan Achievement Test (MAT) scores: Reading, 3.7; Math, 2.1. Megan's mother (Shauna's grandmother) is cross with Megan. She failed science, social studies, and math. She is in fifth grade and has the following scores on the M.A.T: Reading, 3.1; Math, 4.7.

3:10 P.M.   Shauna is sitting next to her grandmother. She has a record sleeve on her lap and is practicing her letters in cursive writing on a piece of paper.

3:24 P.M. Pauline arrives home, and Shauna shows her mother her report card. Then Gina follows; she, too, is given the card to read.

Danny at School

For the families with whom we worked, the parents' provision of a literate environment and support of their children's education are somehow balanced (albeit precariously) with the strong need for the children to become independent survivors in a sometimes hostile world. On many occasions during the period that we worked with the families, we were asked what happens to children for whom this sensitive balance is not possible. What happens to the children whose families are surviving under such stress that they cannot support the education of their children? What happens to the children who have learned to survive, who are productive members of a social world, but who cannot translate their productivity into the ways in which the schools are expecting them to learn? The account that follows is presented as a response to these questions.

In February 1984, we asked Danny, then age fourteen, about school. He told us about his classroom and about himself and the teacher. Danny said, "It's just regular, with a teacher's desk. That's it. Ordinary. Nothing else. Just a plain ol' square." Danny went on to tell us that he didn't work. He said he played. Smiling, he explained to us, "I don't know. I just like to play a lot in class. It's a lot of kids and they talking a lot. I just get in a lot of conversation." Danny spoke of not liking the girls in the class. He explained that they were too wild and that they never did any work. "At least I do my work sometimes," he said. We asked him if he had a special friend. He told us about him. "He likes to play a lot, just like me," Danny said, and then he added, "That's why I like him. He don't work too much either. He likes comic books." Speaking of his teacher, he explained, "He play with us. He be cracking jokes with us and everything." Danny spoke of the testing that was taking place in his classroom and of the teacher working "with papers at his desk." Danny explained, "He doesn't really work with us. He give us work and don't tell us what to do. He just tell us the page." Then later he said, "He just lets us sit there and play. He don't tell them to stop or nothing. He just lets them keep on going. All he do is write their names down. I don't know what for, because he don't give them no assignments no more—like, to write a hundred times or something like that."

Danny told us that math was his favorite subject in school. He said that the class was working on problem solving. He talked about spelling. He said, "I can't spell." Danny paused. "I can spell, you know, when I really want to, but I don't ever study." We asked him why he didn't study and Danny said,

"I play too much." Danny spoke in a similar way when he talked about his reading and writing assignments. "You see," he said, "I know them all. It's just that I don't do it. But I can do it all. Every time I do it, I get an A or B. I don't get anything lower than a B. I can do it easy. It's just that I don't do it. I play too much with the class. I just keep talking a lot." We asked Danny about science. He said, "We don't really have too much science ... we just read, then we have written assignments." Danny told us that that they "had to draw a couple of times," and he explained that they had drawn diagrams of the eye and the inner ear. The question had arisen on several occasions as to whether Danny would be able to go on to the eighth grade. We asked him if he thought he would make it. Danny said that he wanted to graduate out of seventh. "I know I ain't, though," he said. "I might." He paused and then added, "It's too late now."

In the following month, March, Ieshea told us that Danny had been beaten by his teacher in the classroom. His father had died on a Friday, Ieshea said, and the funeral was on the following Tuesday. Ieshea explained, "I let Danny stay out of school the day after the funeral also, Wednesday. You know, I told him it would be all right if he stayed out another day. And then Thursday was his first day back at school. So, um, Thursday afternoon, the principal she called and she said that, um, there had been some trouble with Danny and his teacher in the classroom and, um, I said, you know, 'Is everything all right?' Or 'What happened?' So she said, 'Well, Danny and the teacher had some kind of confrontation, and it ended up with the teacher hitting Danny.' And I asked her, 'The teacher hit him?' So she said, 'Yes.' So I said, like, 'What happened?' So she asked me if I was coming in because I was already sched-uled to go in for a parent-teacher conference later that afternoon. And she said that, um, she told me that, um, Danny's teacher had hit him and she said that she explained to the teacher that, um, not to hit any of the children, that if something was wrong then he should send them down to the office, you know, not to hit them. So I told her all right, that I would be here, you know, because she said that she wanted me to talk to the teacher himself to find out exactly what had happened, you know.

"So wait. Danny came home from school, I didn't even question him about it because I was waiting for him to tell me about it because Danny has got into trouble before in school, you know, and I didn't know whether it was something that he had provoked, and plus I knew it was his first day back since his father died. I didn't know whether someone had made a comment that he didn't like or, you know, what frame of mind he might've been in, and I didn't know whether he had, um, provoked the incident. I didn't know what had happened. So after Danny didn't volunteer any information like what had happened, when it was time to go to the conferences—because the confer-ences were scheduled from three to five—so when it was time to go, I told Danny, I said, 'You come go with me down to the conference so that you can be there when the teacher tells me what happened.' You know. 'So that if the teacher says something that you don't feel is correct you can tell what your side of the story is.' You know. So we went and, um, the conferences were held in the classroom, and, um, we went up to the class and we were the first one in there. There were other teachers with Danny's teacher, but then they left and then it was just Danny and I and his teacher. So the teacher started telling me about, you know, Danny's grades and the tests and various things. He didn't speak about the incident at all, you know. So I let him talk about, you know, the tests and the scores and this and that, you know, and then I —I asked him, 'Mr. ———, can I ask you what happened in here today?' So he said, 'Yes. We were doing a writing assignment—starting a writing assignment,' and he said, 'Danny wrote "Seventh Grade" on the paper, on the heading of his paper, and I told Danny to put "Grade Seven." ' And he said, 'Danny wanted to know what was the difference, that technically they meant the same thing, so if he had wrote "Seventh Grade" why did he have to change it? Why did he have to put "Grade Seven?" ' And that's when he went into the explanation about if he gave Danny a parable, like if someone has five pennies and they're at a parking meter and have to put in a nickle, they can't use the five pennies; then he wanted it to say 'Grade Seven' and not 'Seventh Grade.' So I guess at that point he said that Danny became aggravated or angry or exasperated or whatever and he flung the sheet of paper, and the teacher said the sheet of paper hit him and he said that's when he hit Danny.

"But still I'm under the assumption that he just, er, snatched him or, you know, I thought it was one lick, you know. So I told the teacher, 'I would rather that you not put your hands on Danny. If something goes wrong in here,' I said, 'you send Danny to the office, and I'll take care of him if he does something wrong.' And I told the teacher, I said, 'Don't put your hands on my child.' I said, 'He has just gone through a very bad experience. His father has just died, and he doesn't need this,' you know, and I said, 'If someone hits my children I'm going to hit them, and if I can't hit them I'll get someone who can, or if I can't do that I'll go to the police.' And I said, 'So I don't ever want that to happen again in the class.' So the teacher said, 'O.K.' You know, he wouldn't let it happen again. So then Danny and I left, right? Then his class is on the third floor. So we left, and after we got all the way down to the first floor, and, er, Danny says, 'Momma, he didn't just hit me, he beat me with the stick.' So I looked at Danny. I said, 'He did what?' He said, 'He beat me with—' I said, 'What kind of stick?' So he said, you know, the pointer that you go to the chalkboard with. He said, 'He beat me with the stick, that— you know—the pointer.' And he said, um, 'I have whips all over my body.' He said, 'Because when he was beating me, after the stick broke I walked out of the class and I went down to the office, and the principal took me to the nurse's office.' And then Danny gave me, um, um, a sheet of paper from the nurse and it, um, said 'Reddened marks on his shoulder, his upper arm, his thigh, and his legs,' you know. So we were all on the first floor then, and so we were right outside the office, so I told Danny, I said, 'Come on. Let's go in here to the principal because the principal and the teacher both told me that he just hit you. I thought it was just one lick or something.' So I went in to the principal and I said, 'Mrs. ———, you gave me the impression that he just hit Danny.' And I said, 'He beat Danny with the stick,' you know, and I said, 'He beat him viciously for him to have left so many welts and bruises all over his body.' You know. And I told the principal, 'I talked to the teacher, but when I spoke with him I was under the assumption that it was one lick.' I said, 'But now I can't let it go just like that.' You know, I told her, at that time I told her, I said, 'I'm going to have to sleep on this and decide what I'm going to do about it,' I said, 'because something has to be done.' I said, 'The teacher needs some help. If he beat Danny so badly,' I said, 'he needs some help, and he shouldn't be in that classroom beatin' on those kids like that.' And all she did was nod her head in agreement. She just said, 'I understand.' And she just shook her head in total agreement, which led me to believe that she knew what the teacher did was, like, totally, you know, outrageous and that it had no business happening like that and that Danny was, you know, completely innocent. It was nothing that Danny did that could possibly have motivated this teacher to do that to him. Because had the teacher told me that Danny, um, came at him in a threatening manner, or he had something in his hand getting ready to hit him, or if the teacher had told me that he was trying to defend himself when he hit Danny, or that Danny was fighting with someone else and he was trying to break them up, or, I mean, anything like that, maybe I could have accep—underst—no, I couldn't have accepted him hitting him, but I could better understand it, you know. But I told the teacher, I said, 'You overreacted.' I said, 'If all Danny did was fling a sheet of paper, and the sheet of paper hit you, and you picked up a stick and started beatin', you overreacted.' "*

Ieshea showed us the paper that she had from the school. It was a standard form that said that Danny needed to be seen by the "appropriate professional practitioner." The printed section of the form stated, "As a result of an examination by the physician/dentist/<u>nurse</u>, your <u>son</u>/daughter seems to show the following condition which needs attention." Then, written by hand, "Raised redden [sic] area on right shoulder, right upper arm, right thigh and right leg." On the other side of the form, written in script, was the statement that Danny was referred to a hospital for "x rays etc." Later that afternoon Ieshea took Danny to a physician, but when he was told of the incident in school the physician refused to treat Danny. Ieshea told us that he had told her that he did not want to be involved in a possible court case. Danny was subsequently examined in the emergency room of a hospital. The faint carbon copy of the hospital form states that he had contusions of the arm and right leg. The box is checked beside "SPRAIN AND FRACTURE, SEVERE BRUISES." In the section

---

*In July 1987, Ieshea commented, in response to this statement in the manuscript, "If I had done that to my child, they would have taken my child away from me."

"OTHER INSTRUCTIONS," someone (doctor or nurse) had written, "Rest, ice pack for 24–48 hours. Remove ice bandage when sleeping." Then, slightly to the side, as if an afterthought, was written, "No gym."

Ieshea told us that she had spoken to the police and to a caseworker at the Division of Youth and Family Service, but the teacher continued to teach, and Danny returned to school. A few weeks later a social worker visited Ieshea. We arrived during that meeting. Ieshea told us that the child study team was considering whether Danny should be classified for special education. On the table was the report from the school. Ieshea gave it to us to read. The form carried the heading "School Referral to the Child Study Team." It was written by Danny's seventh-grade teacher. The problem was stated as follows: "Lacks respect for authority, very disruptive, lacks interest in school (doesn't do his homework—sleeps in class), use of foul language to his peers and adults in school." Under "Steps Taken" was written, "Conferences with child, his previous teacher, the principal and his mother." Under "Weak Areas" was written, "Math seems to be one of his weaker areas but he does so little (if anything) it is difficult to determine." The report stated that his peer relationships were "good"; adult relationships, "Fair to poor"; school relationships, "Fair to poor." The results of the tests (the California Test of Basic Skills, or CTBS) that Danny took in May 1983 were given as follows: 5.3 in reading; 8.0 in math; and 7.9 in language arts. Beneath these scores was written, "There are times when his behavior warrants his removal from among the rest of the class (placed in the back or suspension)."

Danny remained in school. The child study team evaluated him and reached their conclusions. They visited Ieshea and asked her to sign the forms so that Danny could be classified as emotionally disturbed.* Ieshea told us that she had been told that if Danny was so classified, he would be able to attend a trade school in a special education class the following semester. Ieshea telephoned us and said that they had told her that she must make the decision quickly, since it was already June and the arrangements had to be made. While the team was at her home, Ieshea asked them to talk with us. In the telephone conversation that followed, a person who identified herself as a learning consultant said that Danny was "hostile and suffering from an oppositional disorder." She also said he was "hateful." The woman continued by saying that the evaluation showed that Danny had an inability to relate to his peers and to adults and that he constantly seemed to defeat himself. She said that the team wanted to classify him as "emotionally disturbed." A psychologist also participated in the conversation, and the telephone went back and forth between the two of them as they stated that academically there was a three-year lag in Danny's development and that he had difficulty with

---

*In response to this statement in the manuscript Ieshea said, "They wanted to punish him. He exhibited self-restraint. My son showed an immeasurable amount of strength to walk away. He showed strength that even I don't know that I have."

vision–motor integration and broad cognitive deficiencies. However, one of them qualified this "diagnosis" by adding that "because of his attitude on the days that we worked with him, he might not have been putting forth his best effort." Again it is important to emphasize that the evaluation had taken place in Danny's classroom where Ieshea had talked of him being beaten by his teacher.*

During this time we tried to help Ieshea and Danny. We arranged for Danny to see a private psychologist for an independent evaluation, and we arranged for him to attend a celebration of the telecommunications program for high school students that was being given by the Institute of Urban and Minority Education at Teachers College, Columbia University. It was our hope that Danny would be able to participate in the program during its next session. On the day that he was to attend, we telephoned Ieshea to say that we would be arriving to take Danny into New York. Ieshea told us not to come. Danny had not been home since the previous day. She said that he had been seen selling cartons of cigarettes outside an all-night diner. Ieshea was angry and hurt. The difficulties that she faced with Danny had coincided with her lack of money to buy food, and for a moment it seemed that she had no personal reserves on which to draw. We telephoned the Division of Youth and Family Service in the hope that Ieshea's caseworker would be able to help her. It was then that we were told that Ieshea had dropped the complaint against Danny's teacher. Later Ieshea said, "I had no one on my side to go with me. I felt that they weren't going to do anything to him except an official reprimand. He used to be my best child. He was the one I sent to the store. But now he's uncontrollable. I personally don't believe he's a bad kid, but he's developed some bad habits. I'm so disappointed in him, because he can be more than he is. He sells himself short."

Ieshea did not sign the papers for Danny to be classified as emotionally disturbed, and in the following September Danny returned to his school to repeat the seventh grade. He was fourteen years old. Just after school began we saw him on the steps outside his mother's home. He was laughing and talking to his younger brother Hakim. We asked him how he was doing. He smiled and said that he was O.K. In the summer of 1985 we talked with Ieshea about her year. She had moved twice during the year and was once again looking for a place to live. Danny had left his old school when they moved and had been going to a junior high school. Ieshea told us that Danny was not happy and had stopped attending school. Ieshea said that he had been involved in the theft of an automobile and had been placed in a residential home. Then he had returned home. At fifteen, Danny had not finished eighth grade and was working shining shoes at the airport. Ieshea told us that Danny

---

*In July 1987, Ieshea talked about how she imagined Danny must have felt during the evaluation. She said, as if talking to the child study team or the teacher, "You don't like me. You've hit me. I wouldn't do shit for you."

was still very good to Jarasad and Sarita and that he was very happy working. She said that he just didn't like going to school.

Commentary

We began this chapter with a quotation from Mary Catherine Bateson in which she speaks of the importance of the "concentric worlds" of childhood. She states, "but whether these worlds are encountered as wholes or as fragments and whether they provide an entry into other spheres of imagination and experience depend on how they are presented, how attention is gradually shaped and the cosmos gradually unfolded." If we think about the concentric worlds of the children in the Shay Avenue families, we are overwhelmed by the fragmentation that takes place as they move from the hopes of their families and the promise of their early years through an educational system that gradually disconnects their lives. In the final question that we ask in chapter 5, we try to address this issue and place it within the broader framework established in the next chapter, "Literacy in a Comparative Frame."

Four
Literacy in a Comparative Frame

Viewed as a social process, reading is used to demonstrate group membership, acquire status or position, control others, control oneself, gain access to social rewards and privileges, to socialize and transmit cultural knowledge, and to engage in a broad spectrum of social interactions.

David Bloome

In focusing upon the types and uses of literacy that are evident within the homes of the families we visited in the Shay Avenue neighborhood, we have been able to build a comparative, theoretical frame that we believe provides further opportunities for researchers and educators to consider the meanings that we give to literacy, as well as the myths and stereotypes that pervade the literature on Black families and on families who are poor. In building a comparative frame, we have used the data presented by Heath (1983) in *Ways with Words* and Taylor (1983) in *Family Literacy*. In *Ways with Words*, Heath presents an ethnographic description and an analysis and explanation of literacy and associated values in a "mainstream" community of Black and White families and of two non-mainstream communities, Roadville and Trackton, White and Black working-class communities respectively. In *Family Literacy*, Taylor presents an ethnographic description and an analysis and explanation of literacy and associated values in the White middle-class homes of children who were successfully learning to read and write. We have used the primary categories that Heath defined in her study to establish tables of the types and uses of reading and writing that have been found in the three studies (Heath 1983; Taylor 1983; Taylor and Dorsey-Gaines, present study). We would note that where Heath used mixed categories ("Recreational/Educational") we have placed the uses and examples under both primary categories ("Recreational" and "Critical/Educational") so that comparisons can be made between the three studies. Additional primary categories have also emerged from the Shay Avenue study; these categories are presented following the comparison of data from the three studies.

It is important to emphasize that the categories Heath established and that we have used and elaborated upon are useful for the purposes of coherence in theoretical description. They do not necessarily reflect the real world, nor do they reflect the (con)textual tying together that takes place in everyday life. We may say that reading cases in criminal law is "confirmational" because one is reading to check or confirm facts about the law in archival material, while at the same time it may be "social-interactional" as one reads to help a fellow prisoner with a particular case. It is undoubtedly "critical/educational," as one's understanding and ability to discuss the cases one is studying are enhanced by reading, and in another sense it is "instrumental" in that it is reading to gain information for meeting the practical needs of everyday life. Eventually, the books one has read and the notes one has taken become "autobiographical"—memories of another time and another place. Thus, in focusing upon the categories, an openness of meaning is essential, for at any one time multiple interpretations are possible for any specific activity, and the possibilities for different interpretations are created over time.

One final word of explanation. In our discussion of the categories, we have focused upon the types and uses of reading and writing in the Shay Avenue neighborhood study. The tables are presented so that comparisons can be made. In presenting the types and uses of reading and writing in the Shay Avenue study, we have tried to give as detailed an account as we can. Thus, the types and uses are "broken down" (that is, examples of documents are given) to a greater extent than was done in the two other studies. We would urge the reader to examine the tables, but also to read Heath's *Ways With Words* and Taylor's *Family Literacy* to establish a more in-depth comparative framework for the data collected in the Shay Avenue study.

Types and Uses of Reading

Instrumental reading (Table 4–1). For the families in the Shay Avenue neighborhood, dealing with public agencies was a way of life. Contrary to popular belief, assistance was not always readily available, and access could sometimes only be gained through continual negotiations via the established channels—reading and filling in forms. Personal presentation of difficulties often required the reading of documents and the provision of specific information *prior* to an interview. For example, before Tanya spoke to Ms. Deignan of the Urban League, she was given a statement to read and sign and a form to read and then fill out. The "Application for Counseling" form given to Tanya

Table 4–1 ● Instrumental Types and Uses of Reading

Group Studied	Types and Uses of Reading	Examples
Townspeople (*Ways With Words*, S. B. Heath)	Reading to gain information for meeting practical needs and scheduling daily life.	Labels; telephone dials; clocks; wattage figures on light bulbs; bills and checks; school, church, and voluntary association notices; directions for repairing or assembling household items or toys.
Roadville (*Ways With Words*, S. B. Heath)—combined category recreational/educational	Reading to gain information for practical needs of daily life.	Telephone dials; bills and checks; labels on products; notes; school messages; patterns for dressmaking.
Trackton (*Ways With Words*, S. B. Heath)	Reading to accomplish practical goals of daily life.	Price tags; checks; bills; telephone dials; clocks; street signs; house numbers.
Suburban families (*Family Literacy*, D. Taylor)	Reading to gain information for meeting practical needs of scheduling daily life.	Notes to oneself and others; lists; notices; monthly numbers (near phone and address books); address books; bills and checks; recipes; knitting and dressmaking patterns and directions; price tags and care instructions; food coupons in papers and magazines.
Shay Avenue neighborhood (*Growing Up Literate*, D. Taylor and C. Dorsey-Gaines)	Reading to gain information for meeting practical needs, dealing with public agencies, and scheduling daily life.	Directions on toys, watches, and radios sold in the street or bought in stores; labels, telephone dials, clocks; addresses in address books; telephone numbers in address books and written on old envelopes or scraps of paper (sometimes placed inside address books); *T.V. Guide*; recipes; notes left on refrigerator of items to buy at the store, to be read and acted upon by another family member; applications for food stamps, AFDC, WICS; reminders of obligations to report changes of circumstances to welfare board; notice on assignment of support rights; applications for Housing Assistance Payments Program; application for Counseling Policy of Urban League; "What to bring with you when you apply for Home Energy Assistance"; letter of default for nonpayment of rent; hospital bracelet worn to show need of assistance; job applications; notices of graduations; food coupons.

included a "Counseling Agreement," which she was expected to read and sign. The statement read:

I agree to participate in counseling for a period of not less that one (1) session or more than (3) three years, from the date of this agreement. I further agree to provide to the counseling agency whatever financial records and family information the agency needs to provide the counseling which they deem necessary.

The form (shown later in this chapter, as Figure 4–11) asked for information regarding Tanya's marital status, family composition, employment, other income, public assistance, and bank accounts. Another form that Tanya was given during her visit to the Urban League was issued by the Department of Community Affairs Division of Housing Bureau of Rental Assistance. Again there was a statement for Tanya to read and sign. This one began with a description of the agency and focused upon the purpose of the rent subsidy program, eligibility for the program, and a description of the progam. Following these statements there were instructions on what to do with the form once it was completed. Tanya took this particular form home with her, and she was told to send it in to the appropriate agency.

During that first winter when we visited Tanya in the abandoned building that was her home, she made many attempts to improve her living situation. In addition to visiting the Urban League and reading the advertisements in the local newspapers for apartments to rent, Tanya tried to improve the conditions in the apartment in which she was living. She explored the possibility of receiving home energy assistance so that the family could fix the furnace and heat their apartment instead of relying on the heat from the stove and the small electric heater that they used when it was very cold. Tanya managed to obtain the forms (Figure 4–1); but, although she could fill them in, she quickly realized that she was ineligible. Tanya had fallen through the net. The Urban League could not help her find a place to live, and the apartment in which she was living would remain without heat. However carefully she read the forms and affidavits, it would not change her situation. In desperation, she continued to wear the hospital bracelet from the time when she was hospitalized before Christmas. Her name was on the bracelet, but as the weeks passed, the writing became smudged and faded. It remained on her arm until the writing was gone. When we visited, we looked to see if she was still wearing it but it was many weeks before we asked her why she had not taken it off. Tanya's eyes filled with tears as she explained that she thought if she wore it when she went looking for somewhere to live, people would know that she had just got out of the hospital and that she needed help to find somewhere to live.

Sometimes the affidavits that had to be read and signed did indeed result in the agency's providing assistance. In February 1977 Ieshea applied for Aid to Families with Dependent Children. On the back of the preliminary form that Ieshea was given was a statement that began, "Please read carefully before signing." It stated:

By signing this document, I agree that the statements made in connection with my application for public assistance are true to the best of my knowledge. I know that it is against the law for me to obtain assistance by lying about my circumstances, or by purposely withholding information, or by persuading others to do these things for me.

I understand that any information which the county welfare board or the Division of Public Welfare obtains about my circumstances will be used only for the purpose of finding out if I am eligible for public assistance.

I am aware that the county welfare board and/or the Division of Public Welfare will investigate my statements, and may seek further information in regard to my public assistance claim. I will give complete and accurate information and will get, or help to get, new documents or information when requested by the county welfare board. If I am unable to do so, I hereby authorize the county welfare board to contact, for the sole purpose of verifying the statements I have made, any individual or other source who may have knowledge about my circumstances.

I have been informed that it is my duty to tell the county welfare board, at once, of any change in my income, assets, living arrangements, and/or place of residence. I understand that a home visit may be required in determining my eligibility.

I am aware that, if I am not satisfied with the action taken by the county welfare board, I have the right to request a fair hearing. I am also aware that, in accordance with the Civil Rights Act of 1964, no person seeking or receiving public assistance shall be subject to discrimination because of race, color, creed, sex or national origin.

Ieshea signed this statement and then added her name to another:

I, Ieshea, being sworn according to law, attest that I have read and agree to the above statement and fully realize that the county welfare board relies upon the truth and accuracy of my statements recorded elsewhere in the case records.

On the same day Ieshea was given several other statements to read and to sign. One was entitled "ASSIGNMENT OF SUPPORT RIGHTS." It stated:

I, Ieshea, of Shay Avenue, in consideration of receiving assistance for myself and/or other members of my family, do hereby assign to the County Welfare Board any right to support from any other person for myself or any other family member for whom I am applying for or receiving aid. I further agree that support rights which have accrued as of the time of this assignment may be used to reimburse the State for the amount of assistance received and to be received. The amount collected as child support shall be distributed in accord with Section 457 of Title IV of the Social Security Act.

I have been informed by a representative of the County Welfare Board that, by making this assignment of support rights, I will receive on a regular basis the full amount of public assistance to which I may be entitled for myself and members of my family. I have made this assignment relying on such information.

The statement was signed and witnessed, as was the next statement that Ieshea was given to read and expected to sign. This time the document was a testimony entitled "IMPORTANT REMINDER OF YOUR OBLIGATION TO REPORT CHANGES."

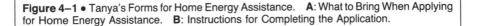

WHAT TO BRING WITH YOU WHEN YOU APPLY FOR HOME ENERGY ASSISTANCE...

In order for the State to process your application for Home Energy Assistance, your cooperation in providing verification of certain eligibility requirements is needed. All information regarding your application is confidential and will be used or disclosed only for purposes directly connected with the administration of Home Energy Assistance.

The following items of verification will be required in processing your application. If you do not have such items and are unable to obtain them, your County Welfare Agency will try to assist you in obtaining them.

1. Personal Identification – Driver license, credit card, or other types of personal identification cards, birth certificate, etc.

2. Social Security Number – your Social Security card and those of other adult household members, if available.

3. Proof of Residence – current utility bill or telephone bill in your name; rent receipt showing name, address and telephone number of landlord; mortgage contract and proof of payment, etc.

4. Proof of U.I.B., Social Security Benefits, Veteran's Benefits, Worker's Compensation, etc. – letter of entitlement for benefits, uncashed check or photostatic copy, etc.

5. Proof of Earnings – check stub for most recent week's earnings.

6. Living Arrangement – fuel bill or contract from supplier in your name (utility bill if gas or electric heat); lease, if heat/utilities are included in the rent; affidavit from landlord if you are responsible for heating costs but the bill is not in your name.

The information listed above is the minimum amount of information needed to process an application, therefore, you may be required to produce additional verification.

If you have any questions, or need assistance in obtaining verification, ask your worker.

A

Figure 4–1 • Tanya's Forms for Home Energy Assistance.   **A**: What to Bring When Applying for Home Energy Assistance.   **B**: Instructions for Completing the Application.

(Figure 4–2 presents the central section of that document.) Ieshea signed her name underneath this statement, above the place where it said, "I have read the 'Important Reminder of Your Obligation to Report Changes'. I understand my obligations as stated in this notice." It was then countersigned by a County Welfare Board representative.

In focusing upon the instrumental uses of literacy to deal with public agencies, we have deliberately skewed the data to share with you a type of reading that is seldom explored or acknowledged when researchers examine the everyday uses of literacy. We believe it is a fair assumption on our part

INSTRUCTIONS FOR COMPLETION OF HOME ENERGY ASSISTANCE APPLICATION

Do not write in the area marked OFFICE USE ONLY. This section will be completed by the HEA worker.

1. Print your full name.

2. Enter the actual address at which your household resides, including apartment number, if applicable.

3. Enter your telephone number, one number in each block.

4. Enter your Social Security number.

5. If your household's mailing address is different from the actual address of your residence, enter the mailing address here. (Example: P.O. Box #, R.D. #, etc.)

6. An authorized representative is an individual whom an applicant designates orally or in writing to act on his/her behalf; or in cases of incompetency, the person designated to act for the applicant. If your affairs are handled by an authorized representative, print his/her name here.

7. Check 'yes' or 'no'.

8. Enter the total number of persons in your household.

9. Place a check mark in the block in front of the phrase that best describes how your primary heating costs are paid. Do not designate the type of fuel used unless you pay your fuel vendor directly for your primary source of heat.

10. Check 'yes' or 'no'.

11. Weatherization includes installing storm windows, caulking, weatherstripping and other improvements to reduce heat loss and conserve energy. If you are interested in these services, check 'yes' and your name will be given to the local weatherization agency in your area.

12. Enter the name and Social Security number of all other members of your household who are age 18 or older.

13. Enter the main language spoken in your home.

14. If you or any member of your household are employed, enter the name of the person employed, the name of their employer, and their monthly earnings in the space provided.

   If you or any member of your household have income from a source other than employment, list the name of the person receiving income, claim or case number and amount received monthly next to the type of income received.

Read the affidavit carefully.   Sign and date the application.   B

Figure 4–1 continued

---

that many of those who read this book have never had to (and probably never will have to) read or sign their names to documents such as the ones we have presented. For this reason it is important that these documents are included here and highlighted. However, it is also important to remember that dealing with public agencies was just one of the instrumental uses of literacy that we found in our study of the Shay Avenue families. There were many other ways in which the families read to gain information for meeting practical needs and scheduling everyday life. As we have been sharing the documents that Ieshea had to read to gain support from public agencies, let's

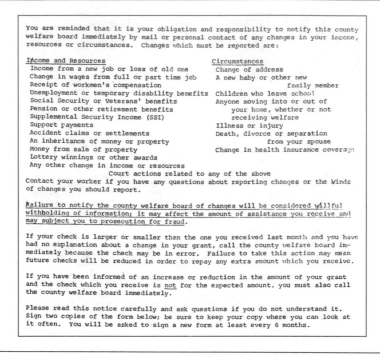

You are reminded that it is your obligation and responsibility to notify this county
welfare board immediately by mail or personal contact of any changes in your income,
resources or circumstances. Changes which must be reported are:

Income and Resources   Circumstances
 Income from a new job or loss of old one   Change of address
 Change in wages from full or part time job   A new baby or other new
 Receipt of workmen's compensation   family member
 Unemployment or temporary disability benefits Children who leave school
 Social Security or Veterans' benefits   Anyone moving into or out of
 Pension or other retirement benefits   your home, whether or not
 Supplemental Security Income (SSI)   receiving welfare
 Support payments   Illness or injury
 Accident claims or settlements   Death, divorce or separation
 An inheritance of money or property   from your spouse
 Money from sale of property   Change in health insurance coverage
 Lottery winnings or other awards
 Any other change in income or resources
                Court actions related to any of the above
Contact your worker if you have any questions about reporting changes or the kinds
of changes you should report.

Failure to notify the county welfare board of changes will be considered willful
withholding of information; it may affect the amount of assistance you receive and
may subject you to prosecution for fraud.

If your check is larger or smaller than the one you received last month and you have
had no explanation about a change in your grant, call the county welfare board immediately because the check may be in error. Failure to take this action may mean
future checks will be reduced in order to repay any extra amount which you receive.

If you have been informed of an increase or reduction in the amount of your grant
and the check which you receive is not for the expected amount, you must also call
the county welfare board immediately.

Please read this notice carefully and ask questions if you do not understand it.
Sign two copies of the form below; be sure to keep your copy where you can look at
it often. You will be asked to sign a new form at least every 6 months.

Figure 4–2 • Ieshea's Reminder of Obligation to Report Changes (Excerpt)

stay with her and examine some of the other instrumental uses of reading
that were a part of her everyday life. The comments that follow were made
by Ieshea as we made a literacy search of her home.

Discussing the use of the calendar that was in her kitchen, Ieshea explained that she wrote "important things" on the calendar. She said, "I'll read
so many things like, Hakim, they're going to take his school photos on the
third. Like, they send the notices home from school, but all these papers
accumulate and I'll forget, you know."

Going through a pile of papers on a cupboard in the kitchen, Ieshea said,
"That's the parents' board meeting at the day-care center. And they're having
a turkey raffle, too, for the school.... Mostly that's most what all this is, just
notices from their school. And coupons from the store."

Speaking of coupons, Ieshea continued, "I save money with the coupons.
We've even got coupons for Roy Rogers. Buy one hamburger, get one free.
And these are coupons for the supermarket—weekly specials. Then I cut out
manufacturers' coupons. I save everything.... Now these are, like, coupons
that come through the mail—you know, manufacturers' coupons."

Thumbing through her address book, Ieshea told us, "This is my telephone and address book, and I put, like, um, bills that have to be paid. You can look. . . . I don't care! I have so much junk that you'll think [*laughing*] you'll think I'm so junky! . . .

"Yeah, and then I put, um, things to remind myself of things I have to do. O.K., hon, mostly addresses, and this was a message I was supposed to deliver. . . . Then I put my current month's bills inside my telephone book; that way I don't lose them."

Ieshea opened a box and told us about collecting recipes and cooking: "This is my junk [*laughing*] recipe box. Don't laugh at it because it's the pits. . . . Some I took off boxes—because this is a good lasagna recipe. It's on the box of Muller's . . . that's my favorite lasagna recipe."

Ieshea talked about the recipes on boxes. "They say that they're tested in their kitchens, you know, and they're supposed to be good. Now, this is a good Maxwell House coffee—you had to send away for this one and order it. Um, it's got a coupon in it too, but this coconut pineapple cake I made [*reading*] this is the one I made with the, err [*reading*], yeah, because it's got rum in it. Oh, this is delicious."

Ieshea then showed us recipes that she had written down and saved. "These are my recipes," she said. "Those are bean pies and, let me see, my girlfriend, two different people gave me the recipes, right? And they're two different [*reading*], um, they vary a little. Sometimes when I make it, you know, like, I'll just take both recipes out and I'll, you know, combine each one. . . . I'm telling you, bean pie is very hard. I've made it like three times, and one time they were perfect, two times they came out different. . . . Yeah, bean pie is hard to make, you know, and it takes so much ingredients that when you fail it's the pits, you know. . . . [*reading*] There's one in here for two sticks of butter, four eggs, a whole can of Pet milk, and you take lots of sugar."

Social-interactional reading (Table 4–2).   Reading was one of the ways in which individual family members built and maintained relationships with other members of their families and with friends.

"Dear Sunshine," the letter began. It was lying on the floor in the bedroom. It must have fallen as the children played, since there were pens and paper scattered on one of the beds. Tanya had written the letter, either to her brother, who was then in jail, or to her friend, with whom she had once lived. Without easy access to a telephone and with no money to call, Tanya wrote letters to both of them. She also wrote to some of the men she had met when visiting her brother. "No one writes to them," she said. For Tanya, letters written meant letters to read. Her brother wrote to her, and so did her friend. She also received many letters from the men serving time. Ieshea also received letters from the prisoners that she met when she took Danny to the "lifers" program at the state prison. The envelopes were fat, filled with paper and messages for her to read. Ieshea also received letters from a man in prison with whom she had been friends since she was thirteen. Speaking of her

Table 4–2 ● Social-Interactional Types and Uses of Reading

Group Studied	Types and Uses of Reading	Examples
Townspeople (*Ways With Words*, S. B. Heath)	Reading to gain information pertinent to social relationships.	Greeting cards; letters from family and friends; newspaper features; college alumni magazine.
Roadville (*Ways With Words*, S. B. Heath)—primarily used by women and children	Reading to gain information pertinent to social linkages and forthcoming activities.	Church newsletters; greeting cards; letters; newspaper features—especially on sports page.
Suburban families (*Family Literacy*, D. Taylor)	Reading to gain information pertinent to building and maintaining social relationships.	Letters from family and friends; greeting cards; telephone messages; storybooks shared with young children; newspaper features; notices of school and church social events.
Shay Avenue neighborhood (*Growing Up Literate*, D. Taylor and C. Dorsey-Gaines)	Reading to gain information pertinent to building and maintaining social relationships.	Letters from friends; letters from children away for the summer; letters received from prisoners (some of whom one has never met, others one has visited, many of whom are serving life sentences); greeting cards; flyers; newspaper features; notices of local events, births, and deaths; storybooks shared with young children.
Trackton (*Ways With Words*, S. B. Heath)—combined category social-interactional/ recreational	Reading to maintain social relationships, make plans, and introduce topics for discussion and storytelling.	Greeting cards; cartoons; letters; newspaper features; political flyers; announcements of community meetings.

friend, Ieshea said, "I get two letters a day, and in fact I got three in today's mail." She told us that he wrote about "what's happening to him in there, different things he's feeling, things he's going through." Ieshea said she wrote back to her friend and smiled as she added, "Not as often as I should, but I do write to him." Other letters that she received came from friends, and occasionally a letter would be written by one of her children who was away for the summer and anxious to get home. Teko wrote Ieshea such a letter in the summer of 1976, and Ieshea had kept it in her box to read and reread.

"Dear Mom," the letter began:

I haven't had too much fun on this trip. First of all a boy named John Davidson he is one of the stupidest kids here he thinks he can beat everybody. Second of all the lady who takes care of me is nice but she doesn't let us have too much fun. Third of all I have lost a dollar. I hope you are having as much luck as me. I have a surprise for you momma and Danny. I will be back soon.

Sincerely yours,

Teko

Greeting cards were sent to family and friends, and children made greeting cards and gave them to their parents.

In addition, many flyers were collected during the time that the study took place. Most were from the elementary school and the day-care center, often announcing fund-raising events. Each year graduation notices were sent home, and each year the celebrations brought the families together with other families in the community. Flyers were also collected from the Civic Association. One announced "A Youth Soda Sip and Dance Contest" with a price set at "Adults $2.00" and "LITTLE PEOPLE $1.00." Occasionally, flyers were sent home from a church or temple. One such flyer announced a picnic and "Celebration Activities" and stated that there would be "Food, Films, Guest Speakers, Sports, Games and Prizes for Children" and a "Martial Arts Demonstration."

Newspaper reading was also of importance in the building and maintaining of social relationships. There were always many local and national papers in Pauline's apartment. Cora told us that on Sundays there were often five copies of the same paper as everyone went out and bought their own. Reading together and sharing opinions and views on topics read was a frequent pastime for Pauline, Trisha, and their friends. Sometimes it was magazine articles that they discussed, but often it was a particular newspaper article. Someone would read an article, comment to whoever might be listening, and listen to the response that usually followed. On one occasion Pauline, Trisha, and Trisha's boyfriend Jack were in one of the bedrooms trying to keep cool from the shallow breeze that traveled the narrow passageway between the house in which they lived and the one next door. The three young people were sitting and lying across the bed, taking full advantage of the cool air that came in through the window. There was a newspaper on the bed, and from time to time each of them picked it up and read. Talking and reading, they enjoyed a respite from the heat. It was the day that Alexander Haig resigned as Secretary of State. Pauline said she wondered who would be the next Secretary of State and commented on statements she had read about the political situation. Cora came into the bedroom as this conversation took place, and she commented that Reagan wasn't interested in the poor. She said that it was bad that Reagan had cut so many of the subsidies that go into services for children, and the conversation reached a local level as the family talked about the recent cutting of the playground program that had existed for several years previously. By then, Jack was reading again. The talk about the political and local situation ended as Cora told Jack, who was wearing shorts, that he had better not go into the diner where she worked, as the waitresses would be caressing his legs. Jack laughed and went on reading. It was on this occasion that we asked Pauline how often she read the newspaper. "Every day," she said, and then she added, "I have to." We asked her why she had to read the paper. Pauline smiled. "I don't know. I just have to," she said. But then, more seriously, she told us that she had "always" read the newspaper every day.

Storybook reading also belongs in the social-interactional category of the types and uses of reading that we observed or found evidence of in the Shay Avenue study. In Pauline's family Shauna sometimes read stories aloud to her mother, and Trisha told us that she often read to Sherran. On one occasion we observed Shauna, sitting next to Pauline, reading her school basal and then reading one of the books that Trisha had just bought for Sherran. We both noticed the monotone that Shauna used for the controlled text of her reader, compared to the lilt of her voice as she read the new storybook that belonged to Sherran. Trisha told us that she had just bought some new books at a discount store and some at a hospital when she had been visiting a friend. We asked her if we could see them. She went into her bedroom and came back with a plastic bag filled with books. The books from the discount store were published by Merrigold Press:

1. *A Brown Puppy and A Falling Star*, by Elizabeth Ross.
2. *The Gingerbread Man*, by Patricia Martin Zens.
3. *The Three Bears* (no name for the retelling).
4. *The Little Red Bicycle*, by Dorothy Urfer King.
5. *The Three Little Pigs*, with pictures by Louise W. Myers (no name for the retelling).
6. *Johnny Appleseed*, as retold by Solveig Paulson Russell.
7. *Lazy Fox and Red Hen*, with pictures by Suzanne.
8. *Whoa Joey*, by Daphne Hogstornn.
9. *ABC: A Tale of a Sale*, by Joyce Hovelsrud.
10. *Mimi: The Merry-Go-Round Cat*, by Dorothy Haas.
11. *Train Coming!* by Betty Ren Wright.

Trisha bought the following books from Golden Press at the hospital:

1. *My Little Golden Book About God*, by Jane Werner Watson.
2. *Bible Stories from the Old Testament* (no name for the retelling).
3. *Beep Beep the Road Runner*, A Golden Shape Book (no author cited).

On the day that we noted the titles of the books that Trisha had bought, her brother Mike came to visit. He talked about his two children, a little girl the same age as Sherran and a baby girl who was about six months of age. Mike talked about reading stories to his daughters, and he confirmed what Jack had said during one of our previous visits. Jack's sister was Mike's girlfriend, and Jack had told us that his sister and Mike read to their children on a regular basis. The emphasis that Mike and his girlfriend placed on reading books to their children seemed to indicate that they spent more time with their children in this activity than Pauline and Trisha spent with Shauna and Sherran. With Pauline and Trisha, books were certainly shared, but not necessarily on a regular basis.

The variation in the time spent sharing storybooks in Pauline's extended family of mothers and fathers and their children brings us to the variation that we noted in the amount of time spent in storybook reading with siblings in the same family. Ieshea read storybooks on a regular basis to Hakim when he was a small child, but she did not read with any regularity to Jarasad and Sarita. Ieshea explained, "I used to read quite a bit to Hakim. Now to Sarita and Jarasad I very seldom sit down and read to them. Now I may teach them games like Pat-a-Cake and Ring-Around-the-Roses, and they pick up songs really easily.... Now Hakim, I used to read to him a lot because he was my baby and I didn't have those two, see. Now my hands are rather full and I would read him a book and he would know when to turn the page. I didn't know whether he was memorizing what I said or if he was actually reading, I don't know which it was. Maybe a little of both, but he knew when to turn and he knew what words were on what page.... Now with the girls I very seldom sit down and read to them. Jarasad likes to because she likes *Jack and the Beanstalk* and she remembers parts of the story. She'll turn the pages and she'll recite what I've been reading. Now she's not reading, I know she's memorizing it, but she has a very good memory.... I don't read to them like I should. But, see, when I had Hakim, my other children, one was seven and one was eleven, you know. They were bigger and they were going to school all day, and then he was in day care and then when he came home I would read to him because he loved books and liked to read."

From time to time the social situations in which parents and children shared storybooks were talked about during our visits to the families. Tanya talked of reading to Queenie and of reading the same books to Gary. Tanya said that Gary would get Queenie's books for himself. She explained, "And if there's something there that I think he should know, then I bring that into the conversation and we talk about that for a while." She talked about them coming across the word "yo-yo" and Gary not knowing what it was. Tanya said, "After I had told him what it was, he kept saying, 'Mom, are you going to buy me a yo-yo?'" Tanya then showed us a book in which there were pictures of deep-sea diving and she laughed. "With this over here," she said, pointing to one of the pictures, "he wanted me to buy him a vest and flippers to go deep-sea diving." For Tanya, reading books with her children was one of the ways in which she helped them as they learned to read and write, but she also liked to read, and it was one of the pleasures of her own life that she could share with her children.

In the same way, Jerry shared books with Tasmika and Jamaine. In our conversations with Jerry it soon became evident that literature of all kinds played an important part in his everyday life. He was a philosopher and a poet. Once, holding a notebook of poetry that he had copied while he was in prison, he said, "This stuff I love. Like this is my money." Then Jerry opened the book and read one of the poems. It was this love of literature that Jerry shared with his children. We never talked with him at length about the books that he read to them, but Tasmika often told us of the books that her dad kept on top of a cupboard in his bedroom, and of his taking them down to read to her and to her brother Jamaine. Tasmika talked of bedtime, of getting ready to go to sleep and of the bedtime story that her father read. It was a special time for her, and we think it was also a special time for Jamaine, who listened to the stories with his sister. From our observations of Jamaine as he sat with a book, turning the pages and talking the stories, we were left in no doubt that he was used to handling books and that the experience of reading was pleasurable for him.

News-related reading (Table 4–3).   Reading to gain information about local, state, and national events played an important role in the everyday lives of the families that we visited. Tanya did not have a television in her apartment, and the televisions in the homes of the other families were old and temperamental; sometimes they worked and sometimes they didn't. However, there were always newspapers, and often magazines, in the apartments when we visited. Tanya told us that she read the newspaper every day. When we asked her what sections of the paper she liked to read, she smiled and said, "Whatever interests me." Tanya explained that she looked through the paper, scanning the headlines and stopping to read when an article caught her eye. She read the front-page news in the local and national papers and always seemed to be well informed. She also read the obituaries and the pages of apartment advertisements. Tanya "followed" the apartment advertisements from week to week and often knew where particular apartments were located. Some of the apartments she went to see, but most were too expensive. Tanya used to comment on apartments that were advertised for several weeks by telling us why nobody was renting them. Some were too much money and some, she said, were in worse condition than the city-abandoned building in which she was living. Just before we began to visit Tanya, she had responded to an advertisement in the local newspaper that stated that for $60 a rental agency would provide a listing of available apartments. Tanya paid $60 and received a list. On reading the listings Tanya found that she already knew about the apartments. The list was taken straight from the local paper that she read every week and in which she had read the advertisement to which she had responded.

	Table 4–3 • News-Related Types and Uses of Reading	
Group Studied	Types and Uses of Reading	Examples
Townspeople (*Ways With Words*, S. B. Heath)	Reading to gain information about third parties or distant events.	Newspaper items; news magazines; political flyers; reports from local congressmen.
Roadville (*Ways With Words*, S. B. Heath)	Reading to gain information about third parties or distant events	Newspaper items; church denominational magazines; memos from the mill on the union, health and safety issues, etc.
Trackton (*Ways With Words*, S. B. Heath)	Reading to learn about third parties or distant events.	Local news items; circulars from the community center or school.
Suburban families (*Family Literacy*, D. Taylor)	Reading to gain information about third parties or distant events, or reading to gain information about local, state, and national events.	Newspapers; news magazines; flyers (on community, school, and local politics); news items related to work/career interests.
Shay Avenue neighborhood (*Growing Up Literate*, D. Taylor and C. Dorsey-Gaines)	Reading to gain information about third parties or distant events, or reading to gain information about local, state, and national events.	Newspaper items; news magazines (*Time* and *Newsweek*); flyers ("Community Forum & Political Education Seminar"; flyer for disco for Boys Club given by Civics Association; "Missing," a flyer with photographs and information about children missing from the area in which families live); news items about local politics; news items about present governor and the candidates in state primaries; news items about national politics.

Pauline also read the advertisements. But she said that she always read the sports page first. Pauline told us that once she had read the sports page, she looked through the rest of the paper and, like Tanya, read the headlines and then any article that caught her attention. Later we learned that there were other sections of the paper that Pauline read. During one of our visits to her home Pauline said something about the stock market. It was just one of those odd comments that are difficult to remember once they are made. But on this occasion Pauline's remark was met by a confession from both of us: neither of us knew much about stocks and shares, nor of how they were bought and sold. Pauline smiled and said that she kept in touch with the market through the stock reports in the paper. She then talked to us about the shares that she followed and spoke at some length about the rise in share prices that was taking place at that time. Pauline ended the conversation by telling us that she hoped to be able to invest in the stock market when she started working.

Other news-related material came in the form of flyers that announced meetings of political groups. One such flyer, distributed by an organization for the support of black women, announced a political education seminar. Under the place and time of the seminar was the statement "Everything you always wanted to know about politics ... but didn't know who to ask." Democrats and Republicans were announced on the billing. A mayor of a nearby town was to be the keynote speaker. The panelists included a state senator, freeholders, assemblymen and women, and directors and presidents of civic organizations. According to the flyer, the sessions would focus on:

1. Choosing a political party.
2. The power of grass-roots politics.
3. The making of a candidate, or getting a piece of the action.
4. Know your government: Are elected officials doing their jobs?
5. Coalition politics, or the power of group action.

News of missing children also reached the families through the use of flyers. Ieshea showed us a flyer that she had kept because she knew one of the boys. The photographs of five local teenagers and their descriptions were featured on the left side of the flyer. To the right was information on whom to contact if anyone had news of any of the missing teenagers. This was followed by the announcement of several rewards that were being offered by local organizations to anyone "for information leading to the finding of these children."

Recreational reading (Table 4–4).   Reading for pleasure was a prominent feature of family life in each of the homes that we visited. On one occasion Tanya told us that she liked mysteries. Smiling, she said, "But they have to be *very* mysterious." Tanya talked of reading love stories and religious books, and she read for many hours each day when she lived in Cathé's house. Pauline read newspapers and magazines. Sometimes she would buy a magazine and one of her sisters would buy another. Then they would have two magazines to read and talk about. *Ebony, Essence, Jet*, and *Black Enterprise* were among the magazines that they bought, and there were usually comic books lying around. Once, while we were visiting, Gina sat drying her hair under a plastic hood, and while she waited for her hair to dry she looked through a copy of *Ebony*. Pauline told Gina that the magazine belonged to her, and after some argument the two young women sat and read the magazine together. Then Gina studied the pictures and commented on the ones she

Table 4–4 • Recreational Types and Uses of Reading

Group Studied	Types and Uses of Reading	Examples
Townspeople (*Ways With Words*, S. B. Heath)	Reading during leisure time or in planning recreational events.	Comics; sports section of newspaper, sports magazines; novels; movie ads; invitations to parties; motel or campground directories.
Suburban families (*Family Literacy*, D. Taylor)	Reading during leisure time or in planning recreational events.	Local and national newspapers and magazines (*Newsweek, Time, Smithsonian*); magazines pertaining to specific recreational interests (sailing, motor mechanics); books—fiction and nonfiction; notices of local events.
Shay Avenue neighborhood (*Growing Up Literate*, D. Taylor and C. Dorsey-Gaines)	Reading during leisure time or in planning recreational events.	Local and national newspapers and magazines (*Time, Newsweek, Ebony, Essence, Jet, Black Enterprise*); books; poetry written by friends or cut from the newspaper; unknown child's school journal that was found in the street (kept for warmth and humor of entries); the clues to crossword puzzles and conundrums; comics and cartoons.
Roadville (*Ways with Words*, S. B. Heath)—combined category recreational/educational	Reading for temporary entertainment or planning recreational events.	"Funny papers" or comics in newspapers; brochures on campgrounds; advertisements for home shows, movies, or musical programs; ball game schedules, scores, and line-ups; bedtime stories (to preschoolers).
Trackton (*Ways with Words*, S. B. Heath)—combined category social-interactional/recreational	Reading to maintain social relationships, make plans, and introduce topics for discussion and storytelling.	Greeting cards; cartoons; letters; newspaper features; political flyers; announcements of community meetings.

would like to put on the walls of her room. Pauline gave an exasperated smile and, as if to provide a reason for her exasperation, she said, "You should see her room." Pauline laughed and said that the walls were covered with pictures from the magazines that she had bought. Good-humoredly, Gina took us through the kitchen to the room in which she slept. Tucked away at the back of the apartment, the room was empty except for a cupboard, a broken bed, and the pictures that she had used to cover the walls. Gina told us that she had cut all the pictures out of magazines and added that she was always putting up new pictures and taking old ones down.

Jemma also read magazines, especially fashion magazines, but it was Jerry who took us by surprise. On the day the conversation we related in chapter 1 took place, we noticed a small stack of used books in Jerry's apartment that we hadn't seen before. At one point during our visit, Jerry went to talk with someone who called to him from outside, and while we were waiting for him to return we began to write down the titles of the books. Jerry came back into the apartment as we were writing and he laughed. He told us that he hadn't read the books yet, that he had only just "found" them. With that, Jerry began to talk about his books. "I had all the works of J. A. Rogers, Carter G. Woodson," he said. "I used to order from Henry's Bookstore in New York, and you name it, *The Bible Unmasked* ... everything, you know." Jerry left the room; a few moments later he returned. In his hands were some sheets of paper. "O.K., you ain't got to copy," he said. "Here's a list: all the books I've owned and read, and these are the ones I've wanted to buy." Jerry's lists are shown in Figures 4–3 and 4–4.

During this visit with Jerry we talked to him about the poems that we had found written as graffiti on the walls of the school. It was then that Jerry spoke of his love of poetry. "When I get into that type of thing, you know, I really go in. Kahlil Gibran, er, Kahlil Gibran? *The Prophet? The Prophet, The Spirit Rebellious, Tears and Laughter*, stuff like that—you know what I mean. I go into the heavy poets, you know. Even Shakespeare.... Have you ever read 'If'? [Rudyard Kipling] 'Parable of the Porcupines?' 'The Lion, the Jackal, and the Wolf?' 'The Mills of the Gods?' That's really nice, you know. 'The Two Glasses? The Glass of Water and the Glass of Wine?' " Jerry talked on at length about the books he had read and the poems he had copied into notebooks while he was in prison. As he talked we quickly learned that his interest in literature was much more than a leisure-time activity. For this reason we will present more of Jerry's conversation about reading in later sections of this chapter, when we discuss confirmational and sociohistorical reading.

Ieshea also presented us with recreational reading that we had not anticipated. There were always magazines such as *Glamour* and *McCall's* in Ieshea's apartment, and she talked about the ones that she liked to read. There were also many books. Some of the books were from courses that she had taken, a few were religious texts, while others were biographical/historical books that focused on the lives of Black people in American society. Ieshea

```
                    LITERATURE READ AND OWNED

The Proud Land .........Logan  Forrester
Genghis Khan ..........Harold Lamb
The Earth Is The Lords ...Tylor Caldwell
Master Of The World .......Cartwrite O'Neal
The Crusades ......Harold Lamb
Tears and Laughter....Khalil Gibran
The Prophet........Khalil Gibran
Spirits Rebellious.....Khalil Gibran
Self-Portrait of Gibran....Khalil Gibran
Black Glory In Retrospect....
Africa's Gift To America.......J.A.Rogers
From Superman To man.......J.A.Rogers
Sex & Race......J.A. Rogers
The Carpetbaggers.....Harold Robins
The Power Of Sexual Surrender....Dr. Rosemary Robinson, Md.
The Messenger.....Charles Wright
Kama Sutra.....Vatsyayana
Hannibal.....Harold Lamb
Indian's Of The America's......National Geographical Society
Mandingo......Kyle Onstott
Drum.........Kyle Onstott
100 Years Of Lynching....
Kama Kalpa......
The Fountainhead....Ayn Rand
We The Living.......Ayn Rand
Atlas Shrugged......Ayn Rand
Sanskirt Book Of Riddles....
Rubyiat Of Omar Khayyam.....Trans. by Fritzgerald
Sex and Dreams.......Sigmund Freud
Beloved Infidel .....
Rise and Fall Of The Third Reich....William L. Shirer
Julis Ceasar....Shakesphere
Nine Hours To Rama......Stanley Wolpert
Mecca....National Geographic Society
Another Country...James Baldwin
The Fire Next Time....James Baldwin
Another Country....James Baldwin
Islam The True Religion.....
Lydia Bailey.....Kenneth Roberts
The Undiscovered Self.....C.G.Jung
Why We Can't Wait.....Martin Luther King Jr.
Public Speaking.....Dale Carnegie
The Greek Philosophers....Rex Warner
The Pelopanesian Wars.....
The Black March......Peter Newmann
The Scourage Of The Swasticka....Lord Russel Of Liverpool
The Perfumed Gardens......
The Hallowed Earth.......
Lady Chatterley's Lover.....D.H.Lawrence
None Dare Call It Treason....
Daniel and The Revelation.....Uriah Smith
The Ancient Greeks.....William Prentice
Autobiography Of a Yogi.....Parambansa Yogananda
An Atheist Manifesto....Joseph Lewis
The Bible Unmasked.......Joseph Lewis
This Is Liberia......Stanley A. Davis
Africa Land Of Contrast.....Ronald Hines
Black Mans Country.....Karl Eskelund
Plutarch's Lives......Henry Regnery Company
Applications Of Psychology.....Fred A. Moss, Md., Ph.D.
```

Figure 4–3 ● Jerry's List "Literature Read and Owned"

Continued

```
Black Liberator.........
Decisive Moments In The History Of Islam...Muhammad Abdullah Enan
The New Face Of Africa......Hughes
Negro Pictorial History....Langston Hughes
Lets Look at Advertising....Pryor
From Prison To Power......Follett
Tropical Africa......Life World Library
Marketing Research......Crisp Publication
Ben Hur......Wallace
Livingston In Africa.....Simmons
The Jews In Modern Capitalism...........Sombart
The Negro In American History....Board of Ed. Publication (for teachers)
Four False Weapons......John Dickerson Carr
Buccaneer Surgeon......Frank G. Slaughter
Muslim Prayer Book....Maulana Muhammad Ali
Holy Qur'an......Maulana Muhammad Ali
The Prince....Machiavelli
The Statecraft Of Machiavelli ....Herbert Butterfield
War In The Modern World.......Theodore Ropp
Dantes Inferno....H.W.Longfellow
Strange World.....Frank Edwards
Sexual Behavior and Personality Characteristics.....Manfred E. DeMartino
Teach Yourself Arabic....A.S.Tritton, D. Litt.
Practical Dictionary of Colloquial Arabic....Elis
Practical Grammer and Vocabulary Arabic....Elias
Man For Himself......Erich Fromm
White Mans God.....Rhonda Churchill
The Great Controversy....Ellen G. White
Notebooks Of Leonardo Da Vinci.....Edward MacCurdy
Notes Of a Native Son.......James Baldwin
Muslim Contributions to Science and Culture...Muhammad Abdur Rahman Khan
Al-Ghazzali.....Syed Nawab Ali
An Easy History Of The Prophet......Syed Muzaffar - Ud Din Nadui
First Book Of Islam.......Ashraf Publication
Second Book of Islam......  "      "
Third Book Of Islam.......  "      "
Muslim Contribution To Geography.......Nafis Ahmad
Economic Geography....Charles C. Colby
High Speed Math......Meyers
Scottsboro Boys.....Heywood Patterson and Earl Conrad
Law Verses Law Enforcement.....Alan Barth
Brothers Under The Skin.....
Autobiography Of Malcolm X......
The Care Of Devils.......Sylvia Press
Physics......Sammuel Rapport and Helen Wright
The Invisible Government....David Wise and Thomas B.Ross
The Invisible Man.......
From Plantation to Ghetto.....August Meier and Elliott M. Rudaick
On Love and Sexuality......Dr. Edrita Fried....
Physical Science........Harbeck and Johnson
For Us The Living....Mrs. Medgar Evers
Message To The Blackman.......Hon. Elijah Muhammad
Facts On Flying Saucers.....Howard V. Chambers
China......Herni Cartier - Bresson
Soloman and Sheba.......Jay Williams
The Spy Who Loved Me........Ian Fleming
Goldfinger..........Ian Fleming
Dr. No..............Ian Fleming
Casino Royale.......Ian Fleming
Diamonds Are Forever....Ian Fleming
For Your Eyes Only......Ian Fleming
From Russia With Love...Ian Fleming
Live and Let Die........Ian Fleming
Moonraker..............Ian Fleming
```

Figure 4–3 continued

```
Thunderball.....Ian Fleming
The Spy Who Loved Me......Ian Fleming
On Her Majesty's Secret Service.......Ian Fleming
Shamelady......James Mayo
Guinness Book of World Records....Norris and Ross MaWhirter
Young Tiger......Richard E. Geis
American Thought.......Morris Raphael Cohen
The Grand Portage....Walter O'Meara
How Life Began.......Irving Adler
Phot Offset Fundamentals.....John E. Cogoli
Biology For Better Living......Bayles & Burnett
Psychology, Understanding Human Behavior.....Three book College set by
        Aaron Quinn Sartain - Alvin John North - Kack Roy Strange and
        Harold Martin Chapman
Readings in Psychology.......James A. Dyal
Physical Science.....Harbeck /Johnson
Study Guide for Psychology......(college volumn)
World History The Easy Way.....Cambridge Pub.
General Science.......Lemkin (Oxford Book Co.)
Exploring The Electron........Alfred Bender
The Creative Process......Brewster Ghiselin
Spanish Dictionary.....Castillo & Bond
Oracles Of Nostradamus......Charles A. Ward
Bartlett's Familiar Quotations.....
Yes I Can ....Sammy Davis Jr.
Paul and Mary......Bruno Bettelheim
Woman Times Seven......Charles Einstein
Sinatra and His Rat Pack.....Richard Gehman
A Star Called The Sun.....George Gamow
The Young Lions......Irwin Shaw
The Sterile Cuckoo......John Nichols
Nightmare County........Frank Harvey
The Tobacco Men......Borden Deal
The Black Art......Rollo Ahmed
Democracy Today....William N.Chambers - Robert H.Salisbury
How Life Began......Irving Adler
Arabic Reader.....C. Rabin / H.M.Nahmad
Cyrano deBergerac.......Edmond Roatand
The Silken Baroness.....Philip Atlee
The Deadly Kitten.....Carter Brown
The Walsingham Woman......Jan Westcott
The Idiot......Fyodor Dostoevsky
The Dame.....Carter Brown
Judgment On Deltchev.....Eric Ambler
Giovanni's Room .......James Baldwin
Vocational Mathematics.....Herman G. Schumacher
Amateur Builder's Handbook......Hubbard Cobb
To Sir With Love......E.R.Braithwaite
Dara The Cypriot......Louis Paul
What A Way To Go........Sean O'Shea
Modern Method For Cornet or Trumpet.....Ernest S. Williams
Psychadellic Spy.......A.T.Waters
```

Figure 4–3 continued

```
                           BOOKS TO BUY

                      Henry's Book Store
     ─────────────────────────────────────────────────

Before the Mayflower...Lerone Bennett....$6.95
The Crusade Against Slavery 1830-1860...Louis Filler....5.00
Negro Education in America...Virgil Clift & Gordon Hulfish....5.95
Negroes with Guns...Robert Williams.......3.50
The Potential Negro Market.....Joseph T. Johnson....4.50
Adam Clayton Powell...Neil Hickey & Ed Edwin....6.50
The Ku Klux Klan...William Peirce Randel....5.95
Negro Freemasonry and Segregation....Cass....3.50
The Negro in The United States....E. Franklin Frazier....8.00
Negro Orators and their Orations....Carter Woodson...5.25
Negro In Our History...Carter Woodson....8.00
Negro Makers of History...Carter Woodson....4.50
Negro History Retold...Carter Woodson....5,50
Pictorical History Of The American Negro...Langston Hughes....5.95
The Negro Protest.... 2.50
The Life and Writing of Frederick Douglass Vol. I, II..Philip Foner..9.50
       "     "      "        "        "    " III, IV "      "     9.50
Almost White....Brewton Berry....$.95
The Black Muslims In America...C.Eric Lincoln....4.95
Black Nationalism...Essien Udom....6.95
Black Like Me....John Griffin...3.50
Black Man's Portion....D.H.Reader...6.40
All The Rest Have Died...Bill Gunn....3.95
The Black Anglo-Saxons...Nathan Hare...3.50
Race: A Study In Superstition....Jacques Barzun...5.00
Strength To Love...Martin Luther King Jr. ...3.50
And Then We Heard The Thunder...John Oliver Killens...5.95
Shadow and Act...Ralph Ellison...5195
Why We Can't Wait...Martin Luther King Jr....60.¢
A Different Drummer...William Kelley....60¢
Negro Slave Songs In The United States....Miles Fisher...1.95
The Premier....Earl Conrad....60¢
If He Hollers Let Him Go...Chester Himes///...60¢
Notes Of a Native Son....James Baldwin....1.45
The Fire Next Time....James Baldwin....1.65
Go Tell It On The Mountain....James Baldwin....1.45
Nobody Knows My Name....James Baldwin....50¢
Another Country....James Baldwin....75¢
White Man Listen...Richard Wright.....95¢
The World and Africa....W.E.B.DuBois....1.95
Brothers Under The Skin....Cary McWilliams....1.95
John Brown....W.E.B.DuBois......2.25
Mr. Kennedy and The Negroes....Harry Golden....60¢
From The Back Of The Bus....Dick Gregory...60¢
Black Reconstruction In America...W.E.B.DuBois....3.45
The Messenger....Charles Wright....50¢
When The Word Is Given...Louis Lomax.....60¢
The Invissible Man.....Ralph Ellison.....75¢
The Black Jacobins....C.L.R.James.....1.95
Black Bourgeoisie.....E.Franklin Frazier....95¢
The Cassius Clay Story....George Sullivan....3.95
Black Religion....Joseph Washington Jr.....5.00
Black Man in Red Russia.....Homer Smith.....4.95
Black Champion (Jack Johnson)....Finis Farr.....4.95
George Washington Carver....Rackham Holt....4.95
Mary Mcleod Bethune.......Rackham Holt......4.95
Her Names Was Sojourner Truth....Hertha Pauli....4.95
Harriet Tubman: Conductor......Ann Petry....3.50
Garvey and Garveyism.....A.Jacques Garvey.....6.50
The Autobiography of Malcolm X.....Alex Haley....7.50
Manchild In The Promised Land....Claude Brown...5.95
The Defeat of John Hawkins........Rayner Unwin...5.00
Cotton Comes To Harlem....Chester Himes.....4.50
The Bible Unmas ed......Joseph Lewis....2.50.
The Black Jews of Harlem....Howard Brotz....4.50   ...
```

Figure 4–4 • Jerry's List "Books to Buy"

said that she had read most of the books she owned but that she did not have the time to sit and read while Jarasad and Sarita were so young. For Ieshea, leisure-time reading had become a momentary experience that left her with time to reflect as she went about her daily activities. One day, when she was walking home with her children, she found some old school journals that had been dropped or discarded by children on the last day of the spring semester of a nearby private school. Ieshea picked them up and took them home. She told us that she was fascinated by one young girl's journal and that she loved to read it. She said the child wrote so much about herself and that some of the entries were funny and some were sad. The girl wrote about being fat and of having a beautiful friend. Ieshea's eye's sparkled and she smiled as she told us that the young girl had given her friend the name Beauty and that she had written about the differences between them and the things that happened in their day-to-day lives. Ieshea commented on the way the child wrote of her feelings about her life, and she told us that she thought she understood how the young girl felt, as Ieshea remembered having similar feelings when she was young.

Ieshea sometimes cut poems out of the newspaper during her leisure-time reading. Showing us an old newspaper cutting, Ieshea thought for a moment and then explained. "All right," she said. "Now this is, er—" Ieshea paused. "Oh, I pick things out of the paper that are interesting to me. Why did I pick this out? It's not the picture, I know that. Maybe this article here because I pick certain things out that interest me, you know, and sometimes I'll cut out, like, a poem that has some—'Heloise' or whatever, you know." Ieshea also kept poems that friends had given her, although these might well have been held on to as much to remember the pleasure of receiving as for the pleasure of reading. (Two of the poems that Ieshea kept are shown in Figure 4–5.)

Ieshea also kept notes she received. Ieshea explained, "I keep notes to me because people write them." One of the notes Ieshea had kept was written by Cathé on a day that we had called to see Ieshea and she wasn't at home. Ieshea said, "I thought it was so cute because Hakim told you Teko's name was Tiskie and you wrote it down in the letter and I started laughing. So I said, 'Let me keep this note because it made me laugh.' " Ieshea was laughing. "This is his nickname," she said.

Also in the category of recreational reading are crossword puzzles and conundrums. For example, the following puzzle circulated through the neighborhood during the time of our visits. We were unable to find out from where it originated, but it was worked on by all the families at one time or another during the course of our visits:

1. $36 = I$ in a Y   Inches in a yard.
2. $6 = W$ of H and E
3. $212 = D$ at W B
4. $3 = P$ for a F G in F
5. $20 = Y$ that R V W S 6. $101 = D$
6. $101 = D$

7. 60 = S in a M
8. 7 = H of R
9. 56 = S of the D of I
10. 5 = F on the H
11. 40 = T (with A B)
12. 30 = D H S A J and N
13. 1 = D at a T
14. 10 = A of the B of R
15. 435 = M of the H of R
16. 16 = 0 in a P
17. 31 = 1 C F at B R
18. 50 = C in a H D
19. 2 = T D (and a P in a P T)
20. 4 = H of the A
21. 13 = C in a S
22. 6 = P of S in the E L
23. 20,000 = L U the S
24. 9 = I in a B G

JADE WARRIOR

In the madness I search for the strength to
carry on
Thru the madness I wander a chocolate
covered candy bar - sweet madness
Your thoughts attack me as I sleep thru
the madness
I went downtown today and saw your
reflection beckoning to me from a ring in
a window documenting my madness
its spheres sparkle its feline eyes
reflect its point of death its image springs
and its jaws exhale its savage funeral
breath - could this be madness
I laugh at the moon and cry to the
sun - in the madness in the madness
in the madness Ha Ha Ha Ha Ha Ha Ha Ha
Ha Ha-aaaaaH Ha-aah
Hysteria making music in my ears
while the tears flood my lips with the
salted taste of ------------?
there must be a reason why I don't know
in the madness I reached for the fire
extinguisher but it only fanned the fire
along with the madness now they both
run rampant thru my mind
But it's all clear - you were meant
to be here - from the beginning
thru the madness the flames of love
burn content in their purpose
as I watch the ambers glow I see your
image dancing silhouetted by the fire
I feel its warmth extending itself to
my person titillating my loins its hot moistness
flowing up my thighs enveloping my whole
Killing my resistence enslaving me
reducing my soul to voluntary servitude
in the madness
The bus is coming I'd better hurry
dreaming my life away in the facet - of some
stupid ring - I saw your picture today
reflected in arain puddle and I
wept - imagine me getting dust in my
eyes on a windless day and the tears
strained my pants so I put my shades on
but it was cool - it was madness

I saw your face today your printed
features.replacing the stripes on my

Pillow case - you were laughing at me thru
strange eyes and with a tongue of fire -

I must remind myself to learn that
foreign language - was it Greek
this is madness - I heard the weather
report it was singing tears in the
midst of the storm its strange melody
harmonizing with my inner consciousness
was this madness - streams of consciousness.
merging with other tributaries of
awareness uniting with the cosmic bond and
intent of driving me insane - manifested
thus in you - madness executed with wicked
precision and tears pierced the madness.
and punctuated the silence still the weather
report sang disregarding the approaching
storm laughing at my hysterical craving for
sanity as if it was madness
even now I hear the sirenic wail of tears
beckoning me to the eye of the
hurricane knowing full well I would
be utteredly destroyed skewered long before.
I reached its tranquil midst - still I
am drawn to you like a moth to the flame
Hellbent on destruction is this not
madness - as the unknown soldier sings out
its agony - sing on weather report sing
of my date with fate for my destiny is
that of the jade warrior.

Figure 4–5 • Two of the Poems Ieshea Kept

Confirmational reading (Table 4–5). In the Shay Avenue neighborhood, we found that the families with whom we worked saved all kinds of print that became archival materials to be referred to when necessary or read on special occasions. Birth certificates and social security cards were kept; so were copies of applications for welfare. School report cards were kept and shown to us with pride, as most of the children in the families that we were visiting received good progress reports from their schools. But there were other papers that also came our way. Some of these pieces of print were given to us by leshea, who stored many papers in a box in her room under the bed. Among the papers that she had kept was her secondary school transcript and a paper she had written when she took an English course at a nearby college.

Table 4–5 • Confirmational Types and Uses of Reading		
Group Studied	Types and Uses of Reading	Examples
Townspeople (*Ways With Words*, S. B. Heath)	Reading to check or confirm facts or beliefs, often from archival materials stored and retrieved only on special occasions.	Wills; income tax forms; bills; birth certificates; passports.
Roadville (*Ways With Words*, S. B. Heath)	Reading to check, confirm, or announce facts or beliefs.	The Bible; Sunday school materials; camper or sports magazines; newspaper stories; appliance warranties and directions.
Trackton (*Ways With Words*, S. B. Heath)	Reading to gain support for attitudes or beliefs already held.	Bible; brochures on cars; loan notes; bills.
Suburban families (*Family Literacy*, D. Taylor)	Reading to check or confirm facts or beliefs, often from archival materials stored and retrieved only on special occasions.	Financial records; wills; birth certificates; Bible; novels and journal articles written by deceased family members; letters and drawings of children; appliance warranties and directions.
Shay Avenue neighborhood (*Growing Up Literate*, D. Taylor and C. Dorsey-Gaines)	Reading to check or confirm facts or beliefs, often from archival materials stored and retrieved only on special occasions.	Birth certificates; social security cards; school report cards; honor roll cards; facts about law; personal attendance records for work; letter of recommendation; children's letters, poems, and drawings; food stamp certificates (kept as a reminder of the times when people who are poor receive their change in the form of tickets rather than money); newspaper cuttings.

The professor had given her an A for the paper and had written "Nice!" Ieshea's paper focused upon the question "Does Being Old Mean Being Useless?" Under the title Ieshea had written as her thesis, "With a little motivation, the 'Golden Years' can be the best years of your life." It was this message that Ieshea carried through her paper to the final paragraph, in which she wrote:

Above all, don't abandon your life or lose [crossed out] waste it in useless folly because you've become older. The "Golden Years" should present you with a new [insert] challenge. You've persevered, you've made it! Use the wisdom and knowledge you've gained through the years to do something good for yourself, and maybe even someone else.

Also in the box was a recommendation from the community college where she worked as a secretary. The recommendation begins:

I should like to thank you and commend you for the outstanding service that you provided to me and to the entire Department. . . .
Your maturity, cooperation, thoughtfulness, and professionalism helped me immeasurably in the execution of my administrative duties and are deeply appreciated.
Thanks again for all of your help and support.

Ieshea sat reading the recommendation; when she put it back in the box, Sarita picked it up. Ieshea said, "Don't lose my paper. I need it." Then, almost to herself, she said, "Though none of this is like, um, permanent and it isn't appropriate now, but, you know, I hold on to it. I don't know what I would need this for. . . . I don't think I'll ever need any of this, but I just keep it."

Ieshea had also kept the papers from a time when she had got into debt and had to appear in court. She also had an old form from a catalogue order that she made one year at a Sears, Roebuck store. The order was for children's pajamas and toys that she had bought for her children one Christmas. For a few seconds Ieshea puzzled over the form; then she remembered. She remembered the Christmas and some of the presents she had bought that were marked on the order form as "toys" and "PJ's." Much of Ieshea's box focused upon her children, from letters they had written and pictures they had made (see the section below, on social-historical reading) to an Ann Landers column that contained a poem for parents. The headline reads, "Poem urges parents to make more time for their children," and underneath was a letter asking Ann Landers to republish the poem. "The writer said, 'How I wish I had taken more time to play with my children, to hug them and kiss them more.'" The poem followed:

To My Grown-up Son •

My hands were busy through the day
I didn't have much time to play
The little games you asked me to.
I didn't have much time for you.
I'd wash your clothes, I'd sew and cook,

> But when you'd bring your picture book
> And ask me please to share your fun,
> I'd say: "A little later, son."
> I'd tuck you in all safe at night
> And hear your prayers, turn out the light,
> Then tiptoe softly to the door . . .
> I wish I'd stayed a minute more.
> For life is short, the years rush past . . .
> A little boy grows up so fast.
> No longer is he at your side,
> His precious secrets to confide.
> The picture books are put away,
> There are no longer games to play,
> No good-night kiss, no prayers to hear . . .
> All that belongs to yesteryear.
> My hands, once busy, now are still.
> The days are long and hard to fill.
> I wish I could go back and do
> The little things you asked me to.
> —Author Unknown

Ieshea had other poems and pieces that she read when she thought of her children. One piece she showed us had been typed and copied in purple ink on a duplicating machine:

> all those years nobody loved me
> except then I screamed at them spanked them
> threw them on the bed slammed the door when
> i was angry desperate for their father's love,
> i can't undo all those times i frightened them
> they loved me, they still love me, i can't undo needing
> being tortured with loneliness until i cried out at them,
> who loved me even in my needy loneliness. how
> do mothers, unloved, love their children?
> the wonder is that we do, we
> do not leave them, we do not destroy
> we cry out in terror we love our little children
> who must have a better life. . . .

Going through her papers Ieshea spoke of the poems that she saved, "Sometimes I'll read and at that particular time I'll like the thought." She talked of the poems such as the one in the Ann Landers column and she said, "Sometimes I'll cut it [a poem] out and save it." Some of the poems that Ieshea had saved were called "Sketches by Ben Burroughs." She had torn or cut them out of the local paper. One of the sketches went as follows:

In every group of people you're always sure to find a few not to be trusted, for they act in ways unkind. I'm speaking of the people who are always quick to talk. Those who find it second nature to ridicule and squawk. You must never confide in them because surely if we do we'll find our confidence betrayed and end us in a stew. People who delight in gossip must believe their shady ways help to elevate their standing so they hand out false bouquets. But this fact is far from certain because those who tell the tales are regarded as unworthy to be placed on justice scales. So it is and always will be tattletales will come and go. Only one thing is for certain: They cause untold grief and woe.

Ieshea explained, "When I cut that out someone must have hurt my feelings or said something about me that hurt me, and when I read that, you know, I said, 'Oh, this is really what I'm feeling when I'm thinking about this person,' you know." Ieshea had another piece, called "Defining a Real Friend," and as we talked about it, she said, "I'm kind of an impulsive person and I feel I'm really emotional and sometimes I overreact to things and . . . things will happen and I'll see a story and I'll cry or I'll read something and I'll cry."

Ieshea also cut or tore out newspaper panels called "Graffiti." Often the ones she chose were confirmational of the beliefs she held; for example, two of the panels she had torn out said, "Those Who Wait Get Leftovers" and "The Cost of Failure Is Greater Than the Price of Success."

Similarly, Ieshea kept food stamp certificates. We had not seen such certificates, so Ieshea explained that for years if someone used food stamps in certain stores they would not receive money as change. Instead they would be given certificates that looked like tickets. These pieces of paper could be used to purchase food, but only at the store that had given them as change. Ieshea had kept two tickets (Figure 4–6).

Jerry kept a family Bible, and he showed it to us during one of our visits. "This goes back," he said. "This has all my family tree in it." The Bible recorded the births and deaths of Jerry's family from 1887 to the present. He talked to us about the places they had lived, the kindness of one and the gifts of another, and the tragedies of some of their lives. What we felt as Jerry talked was that much of Jerry's commitment to life and his belief in himself was held tight, because of the people he had known and the literature he had read. He held his Bible as if it comforted him. He held his notebook in a similar way. Opening the notebook, he sat looking at the typed pages that he had written. "Quotations—I love them," Jerry said. "I love quotations." He looked up and smiled. " 'Ability is of little account without opportunity.' " Jerry looked down and then back up at us. " 'Any fool can criticize, condemn, and complain,' " he said; then he added with relish, " 'And most fools do!' " Jerry marked the next quotation with merry anticipation. " 'Here lies the body of William Jay,' " he read, " 'who died maintaining his right of way.' " Jerry paused and looked at us before dropping his voice in mock solemnity, " 'Dead right as he sped along.' " Jerry was laughing and his voice bubbled up in confirmation of the ending: " 'but he's just as dead as if he was wrong!' "

Critical/educational reading (Table 4–6). Critical/educational uses of reading played a crucial role in the lives of the families that we visited in the Shay Avenue neighborhood. In each of the families, both parents and children were engaged in reading to fulfill educational requirements of school or college courses. When Tanya gave birth to Queenie she was thirteen. When she talks

Figure 4–6 • Ieshea's Food Stamp Change Certificates

of that time she speaks of doing her homework and not falling behind in school. Each day when she came home, she says, her mother was there to take care of Queenie, and Tanya kept up with her studies. Right from the start Queenie was with her mother as she worked. By the time Tanya finished high school she had two children, Queenie and Gary, to see her graduate. By then Queenie was in a day-care program; her own education was well under way. Homework was a part of the routine that joined mother and daughter together. Tanya had done her homework; now Queenie did hers. At times when Tanya was back in school they did their homework together. Tanya studied the paralegal textbooks that she brought home, and Queenie had her basal reader and dittos.

In a similar way, Shauna had been exposed to and a part of the homework routines that took place in her home. Pauline was also thirteen when she gave birth to Shauna, and her mother, Cora, helped her through her high school years. Pauline did her homework and then spent each evening taking care of her baby. Shauna was in the room with Pauline as she worked, and when she entered first grade Pauline enrolled in the local community college, so their working relationship continued. We often observed them as they sat side by side on the couch, working on the assignments that they had been given.

Table 4–6 • Critical/Educational Types and Uses of Reading

Group Studied	Types and Uses of Reading	Examples
Townspeople (*Ways With Words*, S. B. Heath)	Reading to increase one's abilities to consider and/or discuss political, social, aesthetic, or religious knowledge.	Popular novels and nonfiction books; news magazines and out-of-town newspapers; denominational newsletters and magazines; the Bible; reviews of Broadway plays and ballet or symphony performances in New York or Washington.
Suburban families (*Family Literacy*, D. Taylor)	Reading to build and maintain career; reading to fulfill educational requirements of school and college courses; reading to increase one's abilities to consider and/or discuss political, social, aesthetic, or religious knowledge.	Books; journal articles; financial papers; paperwork brought home from the office; textbooks and papers; journal articles; novels; nonfiction books; magazines; children's magazines; computer visuals and printouts; stories for young children.
Shay Avenue neighborhood (*Growing Up Literate*, D. Taylor and C. Dorsey-Gaines)	Reading to fulfill educational requirements of school and college courses; reading to increase one's abilities to consider and/or discuss political, social, aesthetic, or religious knowledge; reading to educate oneself.	Textbooks and papers, especially for computer programming courses, real estate, paralegal, insurance, and general courses in sociology and psychology; magazines; stories for young children; books on criminal law; "The Canons of Professional Ethics"; facts on individual cases; literature to help one with one's own political and social situation.
Roadville (*Ways With Words*, S. B. Heath)—combined category recreational/educational	Reading for temporary entertainment or for planning a recreational event.	Funny papers or comics in newspapers; brochures on campgrounds; advertisements for home shows, movies, or musical programs; ball game schedules, scores, and line-ups; bedtime stories for preschoolers.

Not every parent had such experiences with their children. Ieshea had worked for her high school diploma (GED) after she had finished school, and so had Jerry. Neither of them had children during their early years of schooling. Ieshea completed her GED early in 1976, when she was twenty-nine. She subsequently tried on several occasions to fulfill the course requirements for a two-year associate degree. When we looked at the books in her home she told us that many of them were course books from the late seventies, when she was attending college. During that time she had taken general sociology and psychology courses, but she had dropped out of school when she was pregnant with Hakim. New textbooks had come into the house when she returned to college in 1983; however, these had hardly been used before she dropped out of school following the beating that she had received on her way home one night from the community college.

Like Ieshea, Jerry had received his GED after he left school. He also took courses and eventually received a diploma from Chicago Technical College for his studies in commercial art. Although they had very different life histories, in Ieshea's and Jerry's homes, as well as in Tanya's and Pauline's, the children were similarly exposed to the educational readings of their parents. Going to school and doing homework were a part of day-to-day life.

However, for these families if the educational system did not work for them, they worked to educate themselves. When Tanya could not both support her family and pay for a college education, she took courses in paralegal studies with the intention of finding a job and working her way through college. When Pauline found that there were no jobs in computer programming within commuting distance of her home, she dropped out for a while, but then she managed to get a job in the office where Trisha was working, and she took real estate courses at night. Trisha did the same, only for her the courses she took in paralegal studies were just the beginning. She wanted to become a lawyer, and she often talked about her attempts to save enough money to put herself through school. On one occasion we asked Trisha about the books she was studying. She showed us some of the texts that she was using at that time:

- *Paralegal Practice and Procedure: A Practical Guide for the Legal Assistant*, by Deborah E. Labalestrier.
- *Basic Estate Planning*, by Robert J. Pinto.
- *Law Dictionary: Barron's Educational Series*, by Steven H. Gifis.
- *Contemporary Business Law: Principles and Cases*, by R. C. Hoeber, J. David Reitzel, Donal P. Lyden, Nathan J. Roberts, and Gordon B. Severance.

We could present such lists for members of each of the families that we visited. The desire to be educated in the traditional sense was displayed in the courses that family members elected to take as they attempted to educate themselves. But the love of learning appeared in other ways. Conversations about paintings and poetry, economic and political issues, and religious and philosophical matters were supported by books that had been read. Ieshea's favorite book was *The Book of Lists*, but she also read her Islamic prayer book, studying the Arabic writings and translating one particular prayer into English. When Ieshea looked through her books with us she showed us books on yoga and on raising children, and she talked as she took books out of her bookcase. "Then I have *The Great Dialogues of Plato*," she said. "Because this guy, I had gotten this book because he told me something about this book was so sexy and sensual...." Ieshea said she had read parts of it and then she talked more generally. "I may not have read the whole book, but almost every book here, there is something in it that I have read. There's very few books that I have read cover to cover, but always some section of just about every book I've been into for some reason or other." Two other books that Ieshea showed us that day were *The Mathematics of Business* and *Communicating Clearly the Effective Message. Time, Newsweek, Ebony,* and *Black Enterprise,* together with the newspapers, were also read. The educational importance of these journals can perhaps be gauged by the special issues of *Ebony* that appeared in the last thirteen years, dealing with such topics as the Black child (1974), the Black woman (1977), Black love (1981), the Black woman of the eighties (1982), and the crisis of the Black male (1983). The 1986 special issue was entitled "The Crisis of the Black Family" and included articles by Maya Angelou, Alvin F. Poussaint, and Marian Wright Edelman. We do not know if this special issue of *Ebony* has found its way into the homes of the families we visited, but we do know and can say with certainty that the families' understanding of their own personal situations was informed not only by their experiences of daily life, but also by the literature that they read. Their education of themselves was an important aspect of their everyday lives.

Understanding the dilemmas of finding somewhere to live led Tanya to read a brochure entitled "A Guide to the Rights and Responsibilities of Residential Tenants and Landlords." Wanting to know more about the law in order to counsel fellow prisoners led Jerry to study legal textbooks while he was imprisoned. "I do legal work," Jerry said. "Law work. Criminal law.... I had so many cases and everything." Jerry showed us his notebook. "All this is handwritten.... Habeas corpus, ... com novases.... I had to send to the United States Supreme Court and everything, you know." He turned through the crowded pages of his writings and continued to talk as he read: "It goes right into the *Canons of Professional Ethics,* right here, forty-seven of them." Still turning, he continued. "I went right on into everything.... You look up cases and you fight and you put different grounds together of those who won cases on this and that." Jerry talked about trying to help some of the men with whom he was incarcerated. He developed information and tried to help them understand their own particular situations, but he told us that that was all he could do. Jerry emphasized that he had never had an opportunity "to get nobody out." It was his interest and reading of cases that was important. It was in this way that Jerry educated himself, and by so doing he assisted in the education of others. It is perhaps appropriate to add a note here about a conversation that we had with Ieshea a few months after Jerry's death. We talked about him and about Jemma for a while, and Ieshea commented on how much he had loved his children. Then she spoke of his love of learning. She talked about his talents as an artist, of how he had taught himself through the correspondence courses he had taken and the books that he had read.

Examples of the types and uses of reading beyond those identified by Heath emerged from the Shay Avenue study. These are presented, with further examples of the types and uses of writing, later in this chapter. We now turn to the categories of writing that Heath defined in her study, *Ways With Words*.

Types and Uses of Writing

Reinforcement or substitute for oral message writing (Table 4–7). In the Shay Avenue neighborhood the families we visited used writing when oral communication was not possible or when a written message was needed for legal purposes. Messages were written to family members. Jemma left notes for Jerry if she had to go out before he came home. She would tell him where she was, and sometimes she would ask him to go to the store or start preparing

Table 4–7 ● Reinforcement or Substitute for Oral Message Types and Uses of Writing		
Group Studied	Types and Uses of Writing	Examples
Townspeople (*Ways With Words*, S. B. Heath)	Writing used when direct oral communication was not possible or a written message was needed for legal purposes.	Notes for tardiness to school; message left by adults for children coming home before parent arrived home (and vice versa); business letters related to consumer goods or politics.
Roadville (*Ways With Words*, S. B. Heath)—substitutes for or reaffirmation of oral messages	Writing used when direct oral communication was not possible or to follow up on oral exchanges.	Notes for tardiness and absence from school; assignments following class discussions; messages left by adults for children coming home before parent.
Trackton (*Ways With Words*, S. B. Heath)—substitutes for oral messages; primarily used by women	Writing used when direct oral communication was not possible or would prove embarrassing.	Notes for tardiness or absence from school; greeting cards; letters.
Suburban families (*Family Literacy*, D. Taylor)	Writing used when direct oral communication was not possible or a written message was needed for legal purposes.	Messages written to children (from children) and other family members; letters to teachers; letters related to consumer goods or politics.
Shay Avenue neighborhood (*Growing Up Literate*, D. Taylor and C. Dorsey-Gaines)	Writing used when direct oral communication was not possible or a written message was needed for legal purposes.	Messages written to children and other family members; letters written to teachers regarding homework, immunization, etc.; letter requesting a copy of high school record.

the evening meal. Jemma also wrote notes to Tasmika. One note was written to remind Tasmika that she had to bring her bicycle into the apartment before 6:00 P.M. Jemma also stated in the note that no one was to ride the bicycle except Tasmika and Jamaine. Ieshea sometimes left notes for her children to tell them where she was going and what time she would be home. Pauline's family also wrote notes, and occasionally they were written and passed to one another in a teasing game that they sometimes played. The note would contain a message about someone in the room; it would be passed without that person seeing the note change hands. Pauline said that the notes were always thrown away after they had been passed, so we never managed to collect any examples of this use of writing. Tanya wrote notes that Queenie took to the store. During the last few weeks that Tanya was living in the abandoned building, she left the apartment as little as possible. She stood guard over her few possessions and hesitated to leave, even to go to the local store. Queenie went for her, and Tanya sent notes to the shopkeeper about the products that Queenie had come to buy.

Other notes were written to teachers. Ieshea wrote many letters in response to the situations that arose as her children progressed through school. She kept drafts of some of these letters. When we looked through the box of papers that she had saved, she gave some to us. One draft letter was dated March 14, 1977. It was addressed to Teko's teacher:

Dear Ms. ———,
    Thank you for your note regarding Teko's failure to complete his homework assignments. Except for one occasion when he told me that he had left his book in class, I was under the impression that he was completing his homework* [see insertion below]. I do not want, nor expect, Teko to be excluded from doing any mandatory school assignments. Furthermore, I cannot conceive of him having told you that he couldn't complete his assignment because he was not home in the evening. Teko is in the house *every* evening before dark, which provides him with ample time to do his homework before his ["his" crossed out] bedtime.
    Your note seemed to have been directed towards me in the form of a reprimand for preventing my son from doing his homework. Needless to say, I resent the implication.*

When Ieshea studied the letter she told us that the last two sentences were an insert that she would have liked to put into the actual letter, but she said that she didn't think she had actually included the statement in the letter that she had sent.

Iesha gave us another draft of a letter, this one to Danny's school nurse, regarding the fact that the school's provisional entry clause made it possible to refuse admittance to children who had not had their shots:

(*And it seems to me ["to me" inserted above line] that you are being over zealous in carrying out your responsibilities as school nurse.) I have read, and understood fully, the law governing provisional admittance of a pupil.*
    My son, Danny ———, has been receiving his shots at regular intervals. Intervals determined by his physician, not by you, a school nurse. I fully realize the im-

portance of these shots not only to my child but also, to other children with whom he has daily contact. However, I strongly object the ["the" crossed out] to the manner in which you have acted relative to the inforcement of the provisional entry clause.

Ieshea said, "I was so mad at her I didn't know what to do! So I would write it and rewrite it."

Letters were also written for information that could not be obtained firsthand. Jerry wrote letters to request legal documents when he was in prison and studying law; Tanya wrote letters to the managers of particular apartment buildings asking them to put her on their waiting lists; and Ieshea wrote letters regarding the changing of her name and to obtain a copy of her high school transcript so that she could apply for a GED:

[Ieshea's address]

[High school address]

Dear Sir/Ms.

I would like to request that an unofficial transcript of my grades be sent to me. I've enclosed the $1.00 fee for such services. The following information will assist you in your search:

NAME: Ms. Ieshea ——— ———

DATE OF BIRTH: June 29, 1946

Dates Attended:
I transferred to ——— High School from ——— in September 1963. I attended ——— from 9/63 to 6/64. This was my last year of high school however, I was not awarded a certificate of graduation because I lacked some necessary credits.

My reason for requesting this transcript is so that I might review it in an effort to determine what options are available to me for obtaining my high school diploma.

Thank you.

Enclosure   Yours truly,

                                                                    Ms. Ieshea ———

Ieshea's letter had been sent back to her with a brief note scrawled on the bottom. The note said, "You can attend ——— Evening NS. in September and get their diploma Call them in August (last week)." Underneath the message was the telephone number of the school that Ieshea was to attend and the name of the person who had written the note. After the name was written "clerk."

Social-interactional writing (Table 4–8).   Just as letters were read (see "Social-Interactional Reading" above), so were they written. Without the use of a telephone, the families wrote letters to establish, build, and maintain social relationships. Tanya wrote letters to her friends and to her brother in

Table 4–8 • Social-Interactional Types and Uses of Writing		
Group Studied	Types and Uses of Writing	Examples
Townspeople (*Ways With Words*, S. B. Heath)	Writing to give information pertinent to social relationships or parental role responsibilities.	Thank-you notes; letters; "practice" writing or drawing for and with preschoolers, joint parent–child negotiation of written homework assignments.
Roadville (*Ways With Words*, S. B. Heath)	Writing to give information and extend courtesies and greetings pertinent for maintaining social linkages.	Letters; notes on commercial greeting cards; thank-you notes.
Trackton (*Ways With Words*, S. B. Heath)	—	—
Suburban families (*Family Literacy*, D. Taylor)	Writing to establish, build, and maintain social relationships; writing to negotiate family responsibilities.	Few letters to family and friends (phone calls are spoken of as replacing letter writing); letters to and from children; greeting cards; writing and drawing with young children; helping with homework assignments.
Shay Avenue neighborhood (*Growing Up Literate*, D. Taylor and C. Dorsey-Gaines)	Writing to establish, build, and maintain social relationships; writing to negotiate family responsibilities	Letters to family members and friends (many families do not have a phone); letters to prisoners; letters to children ("I love you" letters, informational letters, "clean up your room" letters); thank-you letters; cards sent at Christmas, Valentine's Day, and birthdays; writing and drawing with young children; helping with homework assignments.

order to maintain friendships and family ties. She also established new friendships through the letters that she wrote to some of the prisoners she had met when visiting her brother. Ieshea also wrote letters to prisoners, and Teko wrote letters to her. "I love you" letters from the children in the families were often written. On one occasion, Pauline told us that Shauna often wrote "I love you" notes to her grandmother. The children also made and gave cards to family members for birthdays, Christmas, Valentine's Day, Easter, and Thanksgiving. In addition, the very young children gave their drawings to their parents. As the children entered elementary school, helping with homework assignments became a social event. The children did the writing, and their work was observed and checked by their parents.

Parents also wrote to negotiate family responsibilities, although from our discussions with parents, their attempts were not always successful. Pauline once told us that they had stopped writing notes to the children, since most of the notes were about chores and the children eventually ceased reading them. On the other hand, Jemma wrote such notes to Tasmika. She said that Tasmika attended to the notes better than if she had been told to do something. Perhaps the most extraordinary example of these notes is one that Ieshea wrote to Teko and Danny when she was frustrated by their lack of help. It was printed in capital letters:

1. FED UP W/GENERAL ATTITUDE AROUND HERE BEGINNING W/TEKO
YOU THINK THAT BECAUSE YOU GO OUT TO WORK EVERY DAY—YOU SHOULDN'T BE ASKED TO DO TOO MUCH AROUND THIS HOUSE—WELL, YOU'RE WRONG. YOU GO TO WORK FOR YOURSELF—NOT FOR ME, OR THIS FAMILY IN GENERAL—FOR YOU ALONE, AND WHETHER YOU LIKE IT OR NOT—YOU'RE GOING TO CONTRIBUTE MORE TO THIS HOUSEHOLD.

AND DANNY—I REALIZE YOU DO A LOT OF RUNNING BACK AND FORTH TO THE STORE AND I'VE TRIED TO EASE UP ON THAT BY MAKING TEKO GO IN THE MORNINGS & SOMETIMES IN THE EVENING—BUT GOING TO THE STORE IS JUST ABOUT ALL YOU DO.

NOW I AM TIRED OF HOLLERING AND CURSING AND HITTING YOU AND PUNISH-ING YOU BOTH.

I AM GOING TO ESTABLISH SOME GENERAL RULES AROUND HERE AND ["here and" inserted] I WANT THEM FOLLOWED BECAUSE THIS SITUATION /////// [crossed-out word] HAS GOT TO CHANGE.

FIRST OF ALL WE'RE GOING TO GET SOME RULES SET REGARDING CHORES.

OK, AGAIN WITH YOU TEKO, RIGHT NOW YOU 1 [number circled] GO TO THE STORE IN THE MORNINGS, 2 [number circled] WASH A FEW DINNER DISHES, 3 [number circled] AND DO THE BATHROOM ON SATURDAYS. THAT'S IT—OCCA-SIONALLY YOU GO TO THE STORE AT OTHER TIMES.

NOW HERE IS HOW IT'S GOING TO BE FOR YOU BOTH—

TEKO YOU STILL GO THE STORE IN THE MORNINGS.

1) AND AT OTHER TIME BEFORE ANYONE GOES OUT OF THIS HOUSE FOR ANY DESTINATION THE QUESTION WILL BE "DO I NEED ANYTHING BEFORE YOU GO OUT." THIS GOES ESPECIALLY FOR YOU TEKO BECAUSE YOU HAVE A HABIT OF PUTTING ON YOUR COAT A JUST WALKING OUT. AS IF YOU DON'T HAVE TO RE-LATE TO ANYONE. WELL YOU DO—ME.

2) NOW ABOUT THE DISHES. BY THE TIME YOU GET TO THEM—MOST OF THEM HAVE BEEN DONE—BY ME. SO THAT'S REALY NO BIG DEAL. BUT YOU SEEM TO THINK SO. THE FEW TIMES YOU HAVE HAD ["had" inserted] TO DO THE FULL DINNER DISHES OR A FEW MORE THINGS THAN USUAL ["ly" crossed out] YOU REACT WITH AN ATTITUDE. WHAT YOU SHOULD BE FEELING IS RELIEF THAT I HAVE DONE MOST OF THEM AND YOU GENERALLY HAVE SO FEW EVERY OTHER DAY. FROM NOW ON YOU AREN'T FINISHED IN THE KITCHEN UNTIL YOU'VE CLEANED THE SINK, COUNTER AND DISH DRAIN AND CHECKED TO SEE IF THE GARBAGE NEEDS TO GO OUT //// [word crossed out]

3) DANNY, THE DISHES THAT I WASH IN THE EVENING, IF I LEAVE THEM ON THE SINK THEN YOU AUTOMATICALLY DRY THEM AND PUT THEM UP—DON'T WAIT TO BE TOLD—JUST DO IT.

AND WHEN YOU COME HOME AFTER SCHOOL—GET RIGHT TO YOUR HOME-WORK.

4) NOW THIS GOES FOR YOU BOTH.—YOUR BEDROOMS ARE THE PITS AND I'M SICK AND TIRED OF THE HALF-ASS CLEANING YOU GIVE THEM.

THIS SATURDAY YOU ARE GOING TO GIVE THOSE ROOMS A <u>THOROUGH</u> CLEAN-ING AND THERE'S GOING TO BE <u>DAILY</u> GENERAL UPKEEP SO THAT THEY DON'T GET IN THE SHAPE THEY'RE IN AGAIN

AND I MEAN I WANT FLOORS CLEANED AND MIRRORS WASHED, TABLES AND DRESSERS WASHED OFF CURTAINS FIXED—EVERYTHING!

AND I WANT THOSE NASTY SHEETS TAKEN OFF AND WASHED.

5) OK DANNY OTHER THAN THE HALF-ASS CLEANING YOU GIVE YOUR ROOM ON SATURDAY YOU REALLY HAVE NO SET CHORES.
SO HERE ARE SOME—EVERY SATURDAY YOU ARE TO WASH THE WOODWORK IN THE KITCHEN—HALLWAY AND BATHROOM DOOR ALSO THE KITCHEN APPLI-ANCES WASHING MACHINE, STOVE AND REFRIGERTOR AND YELLOW STAND

6) AND I WANT THE FRONT HALLWAY—THE LANDING ON OUR FLOOR AND THE STAIRS DOWN TO THE SECOND FLOOR SWEPT. YOU WILL ALSO MOP THE LAND-ING.

7) TEKO—YOU STILL HAVE THE BATHROOM BUT THEY ARE GOING TO BE SOME CHANGES IN THE WAY IT'S BEING DONE. YOU'VE BEEN HALF-ASS CLEANING THAT ALSO. THERE ARE SOAP AND TOOTHPASTE STAINS ALL OVER THE WALLPAPER AND WOOD—DUST ALL OVER THE PIPES, THE MIRROR AND FRAME IS FILTHY, THE FAUCETS ARE NEVER WASHED OFF THEY'RE LEFT WITH SOAP AND AJAX AND DRIED UP TOOTHPASTE STAINS, THE SOAP DISH IS NEVER WASHED OFF, WHERE THE TOOTH BRUSHES HANG IS FILTHY AND SO IS THE CUP, THE TUB IS LEFT WITH AJAX IN THE BOTTOM AND THE TOILET IS NEVER CLEANED THOROUGHLY.

CLEANING THE BATHROOM INCLUDES CLEANING ALL THE THINGS MENTIONED. AND YOU ARE TO DO THEM ALL ROUTINELY.

8) ALSO—FROM NOW ON YOU ARE TO SCRUB THE KITCHEN FLOOR—EVERY SATURDAY—IN ADDITION ["to the bathroom" crossed out] TO THE BATHROOM FLOOR

9) ALSO, ON SATURDAYS 9 AM IS THE LATEST <u>ANYONE</u> STAYS IN BED. YOU GET UP AND GET TO YOUR ASSIGNED CHORES—THERE WILL BE NO EXCEPTIONS—EXCEPT FOR ILLNESS. <u>CHORES</u> FIRST EVERYTHING ELSE SECOND.

TEKO YOU BE ESPECIALLY REMINDED OF THAT. BY 12 NOON EVERYTHING SHOULD BE COMPLETED!

THESE ARE YOUR REGULAR ASSIGNED CHORES—BUT THIS IS NOT TO SAY THAT AT TIMES YOU MAY NOT ["not" inserted] BE REQUIRED TO DO OTHER THINGS, —GO DOWNTOWN TO PICK UP SOMETHING FOR

There was a page missing from the spiral notebook in which Ieshea had written. The page that follows is written in script. It seems that Ieshea is talking about Sunday morning:

get the paper and go back to bed but I want the paper here—in the morning. And sleeping late means 12 noon—no later.

12) TEKO—AFTER 10:30 I want that stereo turned·down.

Also you may continue to keep your room door closed but that practice you have of making people stand knocking at your door or talking to you through your door is to stop. If I send Danny or Hakim back here to tell you something or if they want you then all they have to do is open the door. I don't know what makes you think you're entitled to so much more privacy than anyone else around here.

13) <u>Telephone bill</u>—Teko Don't give out my # You may use my phone for brief messages—no long, drawn out conversations Because of your attitude and the message units you don't have a phone in your room and until I can get an outlet put in Danny & Hakim's room you both will just be without the phone.

Memory-aids writing (Table 4–9). We collected many examples of the ways in which the Shay Avenue families used writing as a memory aid. Calendars in kitchens were marked with reminders of day-to-day events, and notes to jog the memory of a family member were sometimes placed on the refrigerator. Telephone numbers and brief reminders were written on odd scraps of paper and on the back of envelopes. Lists of groceries were similarly written on any paper that was available. Some lists served multiple purposes. One such list that Jemma wrote was found on the corner of an early sketch of a painting that Jerry was working on. The list began with the words, "For clean colon," and underneath was written "Pycillium seeds." This was followed by a list of foods.

> Leafy Veg,
> Fruits
> fish chicken
> Lemon Juice
> Sour Milk
> Whole Grain Breads

It is interesting to note that it was on the back of this particular piece of oak tag that Tasmika had written, "Drugs are bad for your health so! Please do not! take!"

In Ieshea's box were many lists. Ieshea's lists were organized under the headings of "Dairy," "Frozen Foods," "Canned Foods," and so forth. Ieshea explained, "Because I used to shop in this one supermarket and I knew where everything was and I would try to put down, you know—" Ieshea hesitated, and we queried, "In order?" Ieshea nodded, "In order. And so in the way that I would go in, like, there would be the dairy. . . . I knew where everything was in the aisles so I put my list that way and it would make it easier to shop." One of Ieshea's shopping lists is shown in Figure 4–7.

Another list that Ieshea gave us was written one Thanksgiving. (See Figure 4–8.) It is not so much a shopping list as a list of all the products that she would have liked to have bought for the holidays. Ieshea then selected her purchases from items on the list and she bought as many as she could afford.

Table 4–9 • Memory-Aids Types and Uses of Writing

Group Studied	Types and Uses of Writing	Examples
Townspeople (*Ways With Words*, S. B. Heath)	Writing to serve as a memory aid for both the writer and others.	Grocery lists; notes in photo albums; list of things to do; recipes; reminder notes of dues, meetings, chores; lists of telephone numbers.
Roadville (*Ways With Words*, S. B. Heath)	Writing to serve as a memory aid for both the writer and others.	Grocery lists; labels in baby books; outlines of sequence and content of circle meetings; frequently called telephone numbers jotted in front of phone book.
Trackton (*Ways With Words*, S. B. Heath)—used primarily by women	Writing to serve as a reminder for the writer and only occasionally others.	Telephone numbers; notes on calendar.
Suburban families (*Family Literacy*, D. Taylor)	Writing to serve as a memory aid for both the writer and others.	Lists; schedules; appointments; reminders; telephone numbers and addresses; calendars and monthly planners.
Shay Avenue neighborhood (*Growing Up Literate*, D. Taylor and C. Dorsey-Gaines)—used by both men and women	Writing to serve as a memory aid for both the writer and others.	Writing of college schedules; bathroom schedule for potty-training a young child; recipes; monthly planner, listing appointments and information to be remembered; list of postnatal exercises; list of friends to attend baby shower; presents lists; menu for Thanksgiving dinner; lists of food for a party; notes on refrigerator; notes on dates of menstrual cycle; lists of books read and books to read.

Schedules were sometimes committed to paper and later discarded when they were no longer relevant. One schedule that we managed to save was written by Pauline at the time when she was studying computer programming at a community college. (See Figure 4–9.) It is a list of instructors and assignments and contains personal notations that are not easily read by anyone but the writer. For instance, the two asterisks must have been significant to Pauline but they are difficult for us to interpret. The schedule provides us

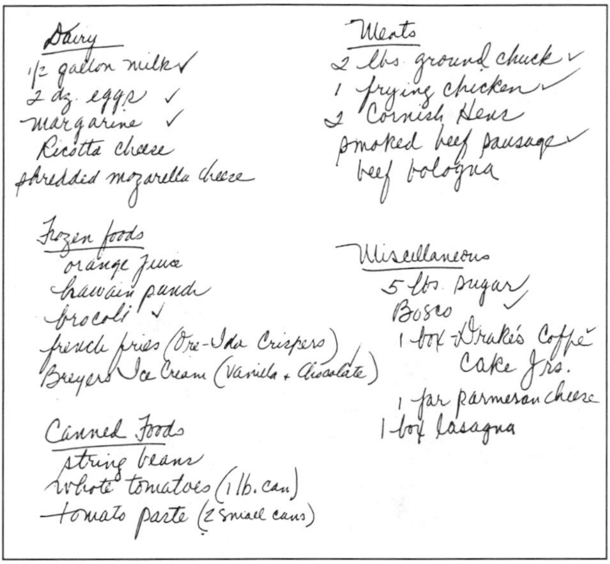

Figure 4–7 • One of Ieshea's Shopping Lists

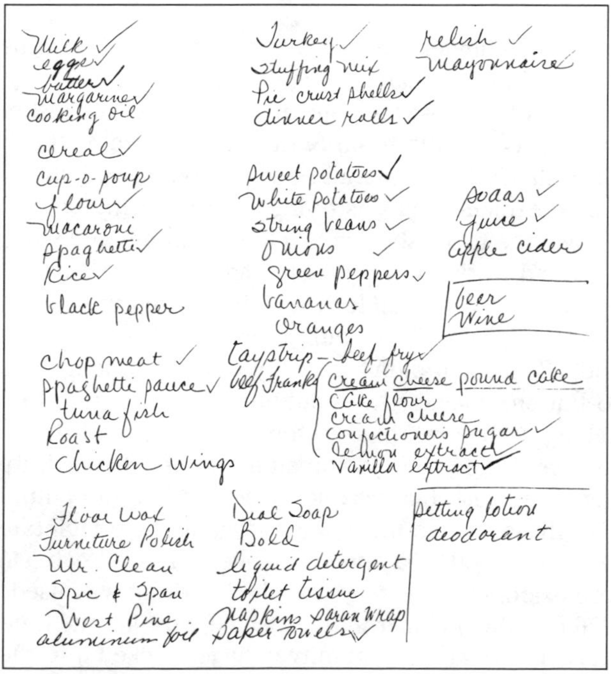

Dairy
1/2 gallon milk ✓
2 dz. eggs ✓
margarine ✓
Ricotta cheese
shredded mozarella cheese

Frozen foods
orange juice
hawaiin punch
brocoli ✓
french fries (Ore-Ida Crispers)
Breyers Ice Cream (Vanilla + Chocolate)

Canned Foods
string beans
whole tomatoes (1 lb. can)
tomato paste (2 small cans)

Meats
2 lbs ground chuck ✓
1 frying chicken ✓
2 Cornish Hens
smoked beef sausage ✓
beef bologna

Miscellaneous
5 lbs sugar ✓
Bosco
1 box Drake's Coffee
      Cake Jrs.
1 jar parmesan cheese
1 box lasagna

Figure 4–8 • Ieshea's Thanksgiving List

Milk ✓
eggs ✓
butter
margarine ✓
cooking oil
cereal ✓
cup-o-soup
flour ✓
macaroni ✓
spaghetti ✓
Rice ✓
black pepper
chop meat ✓
spaghetti sauce ✓
tuna fish
Roast
Chicken wings

Turkey ✓
stuffing mix
Pie crust shells
dinner rolls ✓
Sweet potatoes ✓
White potatoes ✓
string beans ✓
onions ✓
green peppers ✓
bananas
oranges
Taystrip - beef fry ✓
beef Franks

relish ✓
mayonnaise ✓

sodas ✓
juice ✓
apple cider

beer
wine

Cream cheese pound cake
Cake flour
cream cheese
confectioners sugar ✓
lemon extract
vanilla extract ✓

floor wax
furniture polish
Mr. Clean
Spic & Span
West Pine
aluminum foil

Dial Soap
Bold
liquid detergent
toilet tissue
napkins saran wrap
paper towels ✓

petting lotion
deodorant

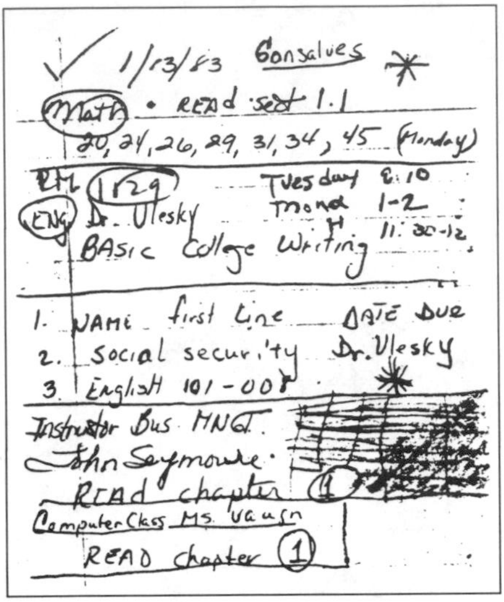

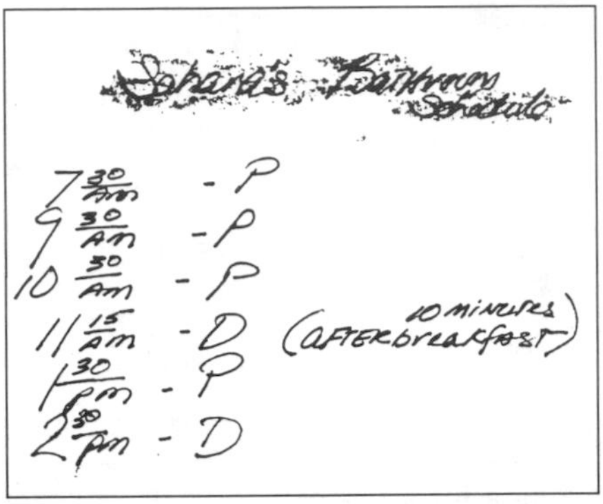

Figure 4–9 • Pauline's College Schedule

Figure 4–10 • Ieshea's Schedule for Sarita's Potty Training

with an important reminder that not all writing is written to be understood by others. Personal memos can be original in notation.

Another schedule that we were given was the one that Ieshea had written when she was trying to potty-train Sarita. (See Figure 4–10.) It was among the papers in Ieshea's telephone and address book, and she laughed when she found it. She explained, "I was trying to train Sarita, potty-train her, so I was putting down the times she went to the bathroom and what she did, you know, so to try and work out a schedule I figured if she did it the same time every day, you know." We asked Ieshea if she needed the piece of paper, and she smiled and said, "No." Then with a giggle and in a small, high, falsetto voice she said, "Because it didn't work!" We began to laugh, and Ieshea was laughing too but she managed to continue, "I didn't stick to it!" When we stopped laughing, Ieshea returned to the original idea of the schedule. "But I figured, like, every time she did something in her diaper if I put down the time and everything, like, that was her schedule, then I could, like, take her to the potty at these certain times, then it would help facilitate it." We told Ieshea that it was a good idea and she replied wryly, "Yeah. On paper."

One more example of the ways in which writing was used as a memory aid is the 1976 monthly planner that Ieshea kept during the time that she was working as a secretary at a community college. Tucked into the pages of the planner are her attendance record from the college and an interoffice memo on which Danny had drawn a picture of Superman. The planner tells us much about Ieshea's life in 1976. In April she took Danny to the dentist on the fifth and thirtieth of the month. On the second she had noted that the rent was due, and on the sixth she filled in her income tax forms. In May she had noted a doctor's appointment and an appointment with the principal of the elementary school. Throughout the early months of the year she noted the beginning and end of her menstrual cycle and in June, on Friday the twenty-fifth, she had written "conception." This was followed on the twenty-ninth by a notation marking her birthday: "30 YEARS OLD WOW!" and underneath she had written "Sat. 29 June 1946 11:05 pm." On July 13 Ieshea had made a note to remind herself to call the doctor to make an appointment "in ten days." On a Wednesday she had written variations on the name of the father of her unborn child. On August 5 she had written the name of the doctor and "A-Okay." Underneath she had written:

> no cigarettes
> no coffee
> no tea

On August 6, Ieshea had noted the rent and listed the bills she had to pay. The next day was Teko's birthday. Two weeks later, on August 20, she had another list of bills to be paid. Birthdays, bills, and the months of her pregnancy, together with school occasions and the children's visits to the dentist and the doctor, were the mainstay of her planner; however, Ieshea also used the book to mark the course of her relationship with the father of her child. She had written notes to herself about his coming and going and about her feelings for him. The dates were marked and, although we are sure that she did not need the planner to remember what happened to her during the months of her pregnancy, the notations she made then have special memories attached to them as tangible artifacts of a time when she experienced such intense joys and sorrows.

Financial writing (Table 4–10).   Living below the poverty level makes managing money an important aspect of everyday life for the families living in the Shay Avenue neighborhood. Making ends meet took considerable time and effort. Jerry made financial plans when he was due to be released from prison, and Ieshea recorded in her monthly planner the due dates and amounts of bills to be paid. Other pieces of scrap paper were found in Ieshea's box with similar lists that included utility bills and loan payments that were due. One list was of the prices of the particular toys that she wanted to buy her children for Christmas. Later in the study, Ieshea talked of another Christmas and of the way in which she had budgeted her money so that the children could have at least one of the presents that they had told her they would like. Danny only wanted one present, a "bomber" jacket, and Ieshea was concerned because she could not afford to buy one for him. She talked of how difficult his life had been that year and of how much she wanted him to have this

Table 4–10 • Financial Types and Uses of Writing

Group Studied	Types and Uses of Writing	Examples
Townspeople (*Ways With Words*, S. B. Heath)	Writing to record numerals and amounts and purposes of expenditures, and for signatures.	Checks; signing bills and writing check numbers on them; filling out tithe envelopes for church; ordering from mail-order catalogues.
Roadville (*Ways With Words*, S. B. Heath)	Writing to record numerals and amounts and purposes of expenditures, and for signatures.	Checks; signing forms; filling out church, school, and mail-order forms.
Trackton (*Ways With Words*, S. B. Heath)	Writing to record numerals, amounts, and accompanying notes.	Signatures on checks and public forms; figures and notes for income tax preparation.
Suburban families (*Family Literacy*, D. Taylor)	Writing to record numerals and amounts and purposes of expenditures, and for signatures.	Checks; bill signing; keeping financial records of expenditures; preparing financial statements for accountants and IRS; filling in order forms and magazine subscription forms; paying (filling in amounts and signing) for extracurricular activities of children.
Shay Avenue neighborhood (*Growing Up Literate*, D. Taylor and C. Dorsey-Gaines)	Writing to record numerals and amounts and purposes of expenditures, and for signatures.	Writing weekly and monthly budgets; working out financial payments in specific situations and for specific items; filling out forms that require statements on financial status; signatures on checks.

special present, but to buy it would have meant that there was no money left to buy presents for her other children. It was at this time that we gave the families the second stipend from the Elva Knight research fund. We placed the money inside cards and wrote "With love from Elva Knight." Ieshea opened the card and counted the $120 that we had tucked inside. Smiling, she told us that this was exactly the price of the jacket that Danny wanted for Christmas, and she said that she was going to buy it for him. Juggling money and hoping for the best was the way the families lived. Calculating, weighing priorities, and, when necessary, doing without helped them manage on the little money that was available to them.

Another example of financial writing was the many forms that the families were required to fill in to obtain the assistance that they needed. When Tanya visited the Urban League she was given forms to fill in that focused upon her financial situation. (See Figure 4–11, pp. 168–70.) Many of these forms were irrelevant, but there were sections for which she was asked to give numerical information.

Filling in forms, budgeting, and planning made life possible but not easy. When Public Service demanded payment from Ieshea in April for winter heat, the bill had to be settled; and if that meant doing without some other necessity, the price had to be paid. For Ieshea this meant going without food.

Public-records writing (Table 4–11). We did not find any examples of individuals in the Shay Avenue families writing to create public records. It would seem that this category pertains mostly to the writing of announcements of church services and forthcoming events. The family members sometimes talked about their religious beliefs, but none of the families that we visited attended a church or a temple on a regular basis.

Expository writing (Table 4–12). Evidence of the writing of expository texts was found in various situations during the years of the Shay Avenue study. School papers were occasionally written, but we did not observe any work-related uses of descriptive and explanatory writings. Personal uses of such texts were easily discernible, however, and can be found in the descriptions of categories already presented. It is important to emphasize here that the purpose of writing was not usually to create an expository text, but to communicate through connected prose. It is for this reason that this is perhaps the most diffuse of the categories. It may tell us something of the individual

Table 4–11 ● Public-Records Types and Uses of Writing		
Group Studied	Types and Uses of Writing	Examples
Trackton (*Ways With Words*, S. B. Heath)	Writing to announce the order of the church services and forthcoming events and to record financial and policy decisions.	Church bulletins; reports of the church building fund committee.
Roadville (*Ways With Words*, S. B. Heath)	—	—
Townspeople (*Ways With Words*, S. B. Heath)	—	—
Suburban families (*Family Literacy*, D. Taylor)	Writing to record financial and policy decisions.	Association committee reports.
Shay Avenue neighborhood (*Growing Up Literate*, D. Taylor and C. Dorsey-Gaines)	(Not a significant category; no examples have been found.)	—

APPLICATION FOR COUNSELING

POLICY OF THE URBAN LEAGUE OF   COUNTY

The information supplied by clients of the Urban League of   County on this application is to be used only for the purpose of determining the housing services required by the client, and is to be kept in the strictest confidence. This information will not be given to other agencies without receipt of written consent of the applicant.

COUNSELING AGREEMENT

I agree to participate in the comprehensive housing counseling program recommended to me by the Urban League of   County,   . a counseling agency approved by the U.S. Department of Housing and Urban Development.

I agree to participate in counseling for a period of not less than one' (1) session or more than three (3) years, from the date of this agreement. I further agree to provide to, the counseling agency whatever financial records and family information the agency needs to provide the counseling which they deem necessary.

I agree that, as a part of my counseling program, the mortgagee holding my HUD insured mortgage obtained or to be obtained by me, may inform the counseling agency of any delinquency in mortgage payments, if delinquency should occur.

Signature_____Date_____

Signature_____Date_____

SERVICES RENDERED

Apartment Listing

Homeownership Counseling

Pre-Purchase Counseling

Consumer Education

Tenant Counseling

Social Services

Legal Assistance

Emergency Assistance

Referral Services

Employment

Miscellanous

Tenant(s)	Housing Type:
Property Address	Housing Condition:
	1. Standard
	2. Substandard
	3. Heavy Deterioration
Owner	
Owners Address	
Phone#	

Tenants	Rent	Utilities	Total

Figure 4–11 • Tanya's Urban League Form

```
DATE:_____

NAME_____PHONE NUMBER_____

ADDRESS_____

MARITAL STATUS: _____SINGLE_____MARRIED_____SEPARATED_____DIVORCED_____WIDOW(ER)

FAMILY COMPOSITION:

NAME_____AGE_____RELATIONSHIP_____

NAME_____AGE_____RELATIONSHIP_____

NAME_____AGE_____RELATIONSHIP_____

NAME_____AGE_____RELATIONSHIP_____

NAME_____AGE_____RELATIONSHIP_____

EMPLOYMENT:

EMPLOYER_____GROSS MONTHLY SALARY $_____

ADDRESS_____NET MONTHLY SALARY    $_____

TELEPHONE NUMBER_____S.S.#_____YEARS EMPLOYED_____

                POSITION_____

EMPLOYER_____GROSS MONTHLY SALARY $_____

ADDRESS_____NET MONTHLY SALARY    $_____

TELEPHONE NUMBER_____S.S.#_____YEARS EMPLOYED_____

                POSITION_____

OTHER INCOME:

RENTAL INCOME MONTHLY_____

NAME AND TELEPHONE NUMBER OF TENANTS:_____

                                     _____

                                     _____

PUBLIC ASSISTANCE_____CASEWORKER_____

CASE NUMBER_____FIELD OFFICE_____

S.S.I._____G.I. ALLOTMENT_____PENSION_____

SOCIAL SECURITY_____INSURANCE_____UNEMPLOYMENT_____

DEATH BENEFITS_____REAL ESTATE_____OTHERS:_____

AMOUNT:_____PER WEEK:_____PER MONTH_____

                ALIMONY/SUPPORT_____

BANK ACCOUNTS:

SAVINGS_____AMOUNT IN ACCOUNT $_____

CHECKING_____AMOUNT IN ACCOUNT $_____
```

Figure 4–11 continued

Continued

NATURE OF THE PROBLEM:

_____
_____
_____
_____
_____
_____
_____
_____

RECOMMENDED COUNSELING PLAN:

_____
_____
_____
_____
_____
_____
_____

MORTGAGEE INFORMATION:

MORTGAGEE'S NAME_____
ADDRESS_____
TELEPHONE NUMBER_____MORTGAGE #_____
                        FHA#_____
HOW LONG HAVE YOU OWNED YOUR HOME_____HOW LONG HAVE YOU LIVED IN APT_____
LAST PAYMENT MADE TO MORTGAGEE_____LAST RENT PAID TO OWNER_____

MORTGAGEE VERIFICATION:

DATE_____SPOKE TO_____

MORTGAGEE COMMENTS:

_____
_____
_____
_____

HOUSING INSPECTION:

_____WILL REMAIN IN POSSESSION AT THE TIME THAT THE DEED IS CONVEYED TO HUD.

_____WILL NOT REMAIN IN POSSESSION AT THE TIME THAT THE DEED IS CONVEYED TO HUD.

CHECK ONE OF THE FOLLOWING:_____ARREARS_____FORECLOSURE STARTED____SHERRIF SALE_____

HUD COMMENTS:

HOUSING INSPECTION:_____

Figure 4–11 continued

Table 4–12 • Expository Types and Uses of Writing		
Group Studied	Types and Uses of Writing	Examples
Townspeople (*Ways With Words*, S. B. Heath)	Occasional tasks brought home from the job, or church and civic duties; writing in connected prose to summarize generalizations and back-up specifics for other people; writer envisions or knows audience and attempts to include only those definitions and facts believed not to be known to the addressee; often includes numerals.	Quarterly or annual reports of business operations; summaries of group and individual past actions (accident or quality-control reports, church nominating committee summary).
Roadville (*Ways With Words*, S. B. Heath)	—	—
Trackton (*Ways With Words*, S. B. Heath)	—	—
Suburban families (*Family Literacy*, D. Taylor)	Tasks brought home from work or educational institution; writing in connected prose to summarize generalizations and back-up specifics for other people; writer envisions or knows audience and writes to the addressee.	Work-related papers; college and school papers; pieces for members of specific associations.
Shay Avenue neighborhood (*Growing Up Literate*, D. Taylor and C. Dorsey-Gaines)	Tasks rarely brought home from work, occasionally from educational institution, often completed for personal purposes; writing in connected prose to summarize generalizations and back-up specifics for other people; writer envisions or knows audience and writes to the addressee.	College and school papers; writings on criminal law; letters to school regarding status of children's health and schoolwork; autobiographical writings.

family members' facility for the development of a literary form that is considered to be important within academic and some work-related settings. However, we cannot presume that individual family members focused upon the form of what they were writing when they used expository texts as a means of communication. Thus, the category reflects neither the real world nor the contextual tying that takes place in everyday life. The autobiography that was written by Tanya's mother (see the following section) and the letters that Ieshea wrote to Teko's teacher and the school nurse are all examples of the ways in which some family members wrote in connected prose. The drafts of Ieshea's letters show us that she is aware of form, even though her main purpose was to communicate. Her awareness of form emerged in other ways. For instance, on one occasion when we looked through the box of papers that Ieshea had kept, we came across a piece of paper with the word "odious" written at the top. We asked her if she had written the word. She answered, "Yeah," and then explained, "Because I used to write nasty letters and different things," her eyes opened wide, "and I would try and find hateful words, you know." Ieshea began to laugh mischievously. "I like to write intellectual letters that make people have to go to their dictionary to understand what I was saying to them." Thus we can say that Ieshea researched the language of her texts, just as we can say that Jerry researched the factual content of the texts that he wrote as he worked to develop information regarding the legal situations of his fellow prisoners. They were both adept at using expository texts for the purposes of communication.

Further Examples of the Types and Uses of Literacy: Reading

Sociohistorical reading (Table 4–13).   Other types and uses of literacy emerged from the Shay Avenue study that were not specifically addressed in the two studies that we have used to form a comparative frame. One of these categories is sociohistorical reading. Reading was one of the ways in which family members explored their personal identities and the social, political, and economic circumstances of their everyday lives. Ieshea had books on Afro-American culture, and Jerry's lists of books contain a number of books by Black scholars. Magazine articles, such as the ones that were featured in *Ebony* that we have mentioned, and newspaper accounts of national and local events all added further dimension to individual family members' understanding of themselves. But there is another and equally important aspect to the sociohistorical types and uses of literacy that we found within these family settings. Writings were kept, to be read, reread, and cherished through the years. Learning more about one's personal life history and the history of one's race through scholarly and popular texts was complemented by the personal writings that were saved. Together these works formed social histories of the families' lives.

Several months after we began to visit Tanya she gave us some handwritten notebook pages that she thought might be helpful to us in our study. She explained that this was the story of her mother's life. She told us that her mother had written it sometime during the last year of her life. Tanya told us that her mother had given it to her so that she would understand the circumstances of her mother's life, and from the way in which Tanya spoke we knew implicitly that it was an act of love that had led Tanya's mother to write her life story for her child. Here is what she wrote:

To be lonley is a very sad thing I wish their were know lonley people in the world.

Group Studied	Types and Uses of Reading	Examples
Shay Avenue neighborhood	Reading to explore one's personal identity and the social, political, and economic circumstances of one'e everyday life; reading and rereading cherished writings that create a permanent record of the family's life history.	Reading literature that has personal significance to one's everyday life; reading autobiographical writings; reading names of family members in the family Bible; saving the first writings of one's children, poems they have written, pictures they have drawn; saving birthday cards and love letters.

Table 4–13 • Sociohistorical Types and Uses of Reading

I know of a child who was very very lonley and even more so as a women,
Oh she had a few so called friends and a mother that didn't seem to care for her at all. Her father pasted away when she was very young, so she didn't know very much about him, in fact she didn't know much more than his name.
She was not a pretty girl and very shy and did not make friends very easyley, so she spent most of her time along, dreaming and wishing that some day she would be happy someday ["someday" crossed out], but dreams just don't come true for some people I guess.
She was big for her age so she tryed to be with the older girls and boys but that didn't work eather, because she was not good at anything The ["The" crossed out] The other kids liked to do. So that was that.
She didn't even do w ["w" crossed out] very good in school, not because she was slow or anything, but she was so afried that people would make fun of ehr if she mack a mistake in class that even if she knew the right answer she would not try, so fanley she hust droped out of school altogeather, and that made things even worse.
She didn't have any boyfriends even though she was sixteen, the only boys that talked to her where boys that only wanted her body, and that was know good as far as she was consered.
Her maine trouble was that she had know one she could talke to she kept her feelings inside
So one day she said to herself, what I ["I" crossed out] am I living for, so she tried to take o ["o" crossed out] own life, and later was sent away for treatment for 6 months.
When she came home she felt a better ["better" crossed out] little better but not much
One Sunday after church she met a young boy and they talked and soon they began to date
She was hap ["hap" crossed out] happer a ["a" crossed out] than she had ever been before. She liked her ["her" crossed out] him very much and she thought that he felt the same way, Anyway they dated for about a year, and then her big happy bubble broke, because she was going to have a baby, and when she told him, he just left town leaving her all alone again She did not know what to do and had no

one to talk too, She knew that she could not get rid of the baby or give it away, but how could she keep it when she was still so young herself.

She tried to talk to her mother but again that was a lost cause Now she thought to herself what am I going to do, pretty soon she would start to show.

She had talked to God from the very begaining, but she knew that she herself had to do something, but what.

So fa ["fa" crossed out] she went to a lady that she had once lived with and asked her to help her and after awhile the lady did. She helped her to get into a home for unwed mothers and thats where the baby was born.

She was still afriad and still very much alone, but a least she knew that she was not the only girl in the world that had made a mistake.

After the baby was born she at least had something to live for, but their were ["were" crossed out] was still a very rough road to go ["to go" crossed out; "ahead" written above]. She had now ["now" crossed out] no place for her and her son to live or how would she support them and lots of other things she had to work out

So the first thing she had to do was try to find someone to take care of her son untill she was able to do so herself and that was not easey at all. but after a few months she did, and with some very nice people that grew to love him almost as much as she did.

They let her see him as often as she liked and that made her very very happy but now she had to try to find work to support her son and herself, and that was not going to be easy because she did not finish high school but she tryed very hard, doing anything she could find but what she made was not enough to take care of two people.

Then after a long hard year she was put on the welfare and soon had her baby with her

You know the welfare don't give you very much to lil ["lil" crossed out] live on and she had a very hard time ["trying" inserted here at a 45-degree angle to the text] makeings ends meet, but some how they made it.

Then about a year later she met a man that was very nice to her and her child, he would buy them food and toys for the baby and take them many places they had never been before. he was a lot older than she was and as time went by he wanted to be more then just friends, but she was afraid of what mite happen if she did what he [something after "he" is crossed out with a spiral of scribbles] wanted her to do. So soon after that he just stop going to see her, and again she was alone.

For a long time she wouldn't go out with anyone. She loved her baby very much, but he did not take the place of a ["a" crossed out] male companionship. She didn't go out very often so their for it wasn't very easy for her to meet people. but after a few months she did meet another man through some friends and this time she did go all the way and got caught once more, but a least this time the man did not run away at least not at first. After she had told him he did keep on helping her and the be ["the be" crossed out] her son, but after her daughter was born he started to slow down about going to see her and then later he stoped altogether, and thats when she made up her mind not to have anymore children a least not for a very long time if ever

So she made up in her mind just to try and raise her two very young children the best that she knew how and she did very well for a long while and the three of them were very happy, she got a job at night so that she could be with her kids during the day when they were awake, and it worked out very well for about three years or maybe a litter ["litter" crossed out] little longer. And then she started to meet new people and go out more and more often and then she started to date more. Andd a little later she started to drink not very much at firs ["firs" crossed out] first and that was a big miostake in her life also.

She found that when she was drinking she made friends easley, and she also found it easy to talk to anybody know matter who they were, and that made her feel big in some strange way and she liked it. But don't get me wrong she still took very good care of her two children. She tried to give them all the thing that she allways wanted when she was a child herself, such as lots of love, care happyness and everything that goes with being a mother. But she still had that hangup about drinking.

After a few months of this drinking she began to notice a differance in her childres behaivor, they weren't really bad but were not the same, at first t ["t" crossed out] she tryed to say that it was because they had no father and were now old enough to really need one. So she made up in her mind that so was going to try to give them one. Don't get me wrong she did not go around throwing herself at men but she did look around. After awhile she did run into an old friend of hers that had always like her, but she did not like him at least for a boyfriend. But later they did get togeather.

He was u [line is crossed out]

He was a very lonley man oh he had a very nice family but he always felt out of place because he was born with an ear defect and had trouble speaking, so he stayed to himself a lot. But after they got togeather he seemed very happy. He loved the children very much, and they loved him just as much. In fact he wanted to marry her and give the children his name while they were still young.

But she was so used to being misused and being unhappy that when someone good and someone that loved her came along t ["t" crossed out] she was to blind to see it But he still stuck by her for three years still hoping that she would change her mind and marry him, but as you can proubley guess she did not instead she treated very badley and soon he left, And she just kept on drinking more and more and knowing at the time that she was only hurting herself and her young children. Soon she became very ill and that when she found out that her so called friends only wanted to be around her becaus would keep them supplied with drinks. The whole time she was sick, witch was over three month, none ofher friends came to see her or even offered to help take care of her children, so there she was once again alone with no one but god to turn to. And with the help of god and the doctors she again back home with her little familey.

She had promised herself that she would make a lot of changes in her life as of that day and she did for a very long time. But again things started going bad for her so she went

The autobiography ended here, the last page lost or perhaps never written. Tanya's mother died soon after. She was thirty-eight years of age, and Tanya was eighteen.

We collected other autobiographical stories written by members of the Shay Avenue families; examples of these are presented in the section "Autobiographical Writing," below. Tanya's mother's autobiography is included here because it was written for Tanya to read.

Saving the writings of other family members as part of one's social history is an important aspect of the sociohistorical uses of literacy. Among the writings that Ieshea had saved was her eighth-grade graduation book. She showed it to us one day when Jemma was visiting her. Ieshea and Jemma talked about their graduations, and Jemma said that she had a similar book to the one that Ieshea cherished. At the front of Ieshea's book were the following words: "Go all my friends I hold so dear and I ask them all to write a page that I may read in my old age." Ieshea turned the pages and said, "I glance though that because a lot of people die," and then she frowned. "Some people in there are dead, you know."

Some of the sociohistorical pieces that were collected were written by others but nonetheless had relevance to a family member's social history. Certainly some of the examples that we placed in the category of confirmational reading could be included here. Certain pieces that we collected from Jerry are of particular importance to our understanding of this use of literacy. While Jerry was showing us one of the notebooks that he had kept during the time that he was in prison, he read some of the poems that he had collected. One of these poems was entitled "The Little White Girl and the Colored Ebony Boy." Jerry told us that he didn't know who had written the poem. He explained, "I picked up a lot of stuff down there, from, you know, old-timers and this and that because we were people. We lived together. We ate together. We showered together and everything like that, and I learned a lot." Jerry began to read the poem. The following version of the poem is a transcription of what Jerry read, so we have not tried to maintain the poetic form, presenting the piece instead as a continuous text.

Once upon a happy time when all the world knew joy, there lived a little white girl and a colored ebony boy. They both lived in a fairy world.... Two different colors of clay, but they loved each other dearly. One day while playing in the sand an old man passed them by. He said, "I'll be damned. It makes you want to cry." He bowed his head and spoke, "I sure would like to play. I don't know your names, so I'll call you Night and Day." The little girl looked up into the old man's face and tears were in her eyes. He knew he had fallen from her grace and this caused him to be surprised. "What have I done, my child? I know I've hurt you deeply, and I'll do anything to make amends." And the little girl spoke sweetly. "I know you called us Night and Day because we are different colors. Our fathers and and our mothers told us to stay away from each other. Please, kind sir, don't tell our fathers and our mothers." The little boy, who once felt joy, stood tall on his ebony legs. He said, "Please, kind sir, there's only one request that I beg. Tell on me, not her." He stamped his toe in the sand, "We ain't no night and day. My name is Billy, and I live in a shack; her name is Polly May. See that house up on the hill, painted gold and blue? Why, I love her better than God loves prayers, but I'm of a different hue." The old man bowed his head, and his blood was running wild, for never in his born years had he heard such from a child. "Hasty words are only spoken. Dreams are put to bed. But when two kind young hearts are broken, I'm sorry my child for what I've said. True: White is white and black is black as any child can see. You sometimes put them a little different when you get as old as me." So Polly and Billy went back to playing as the old man said, "Goodbye," and they knew that he would not tell on them from the teardrops in his eye. They weren't the tears of sorrow, but more the tears of shame; and the one lesson that he had learned was to ask strange kids their names. And he should live for tens more years the philosophy he'd employ, the lesson he'd learned from the little white girl and the colored ebony boy.

Jerry flipped through the pages and it was then that he said, "You know, it's so much stuff. That, er, it's stuff I love. Like, this is my money," he said, holding his notebook up. "Right here. You may want money, I could sit back and read some of this." Jerry paused and then began to read again:

Fellowship •

When a feller hasn't got a cent
And is feeling kind of blue,
And the clouds hang thick and dark
And won't let the sunshine through,
It's a great thing, oh my brethren,
For a feller just to lay
His hand upon your shoulder in a friendly sort of way.

It makes a man feel queerish,
It makes the teardrops start.
And you kinda feel a flutter
In the region of your heart.
You can't look up and meet his eye,
You don't know what to say
When a hand is on your shoulder in a friendly sort of way.

Oh this world's a curious compound
With its honey and its gall;
Its cares and bitter crosses,
But a good world after all.
And a good God must have made it,
Leastwise that's what I say,
When a hand is on your shoulder in a friendly sort of way.

Jerry was silent for a moment, as if connecting the poem he read with the life he had lived. "And these things, man, they really meant a lot to me and I made a lot of friends in there. I taught people how to read and write. Some people, they even went to school with me and I couldn't believe that they couldn't read and write. . . . And I'm still the same way right around here. I put that sidewalk in there. I had the guys help me. I put signs up on the stores. . . . But I'm still right here in this poor-ass area, and I should have had me a home somewhere, you know, this is what I feel, but maybe I'm just destined to be one of those types of people that will stay here."

Financial reading (Table 4–14). Reading to consider and sometimes make changes in the economic circumstances of one's everyday life was an important category in the types and uses of literacy that we found during the course of the study. The families that we visited in the Shay Avenue neighborhood lived far below the poverty level, and their financial situation greatly affected the ways in which they could live their lives. Bills were received and had to be paid, and threats by the public utilities to cut off service had to be countered and somehow delayed. Food stamps had to be rationed so that the families could eat, and coupons were collected to help in some small way.

Table 4–14 • Financial Types and Uses of Reading		
Group Studied	Types and Uses of Reading	Examples
Shay Avenue neighborhood	Reading to consider (and sometimes to make changes to) the economic circumstances of one's everyday life; reading to fulfill practical (financial) needs of everyday life.	"Keeping an eye on the economy" (with the view to establishing a small silk-screening business); reading stock market reports; reading prices of cars and appliances; reading apartment ads (paying particular attention to prices); reading forms, including statements about one's financial status; reading "money-off" coupons; reading prices in supermarkets and on other products.

Buying clothes for children had to be thought about and prices considered. Making ends meet took time and effort. "Extras" had to be obtained through the sacrifice of some necessity. When Tasmika began to take ballet lessons, Jemma and Jerry had to find the money to pay for the tuition; then they had to buy the ballet shoes that Tasmika was supposed to wear. Jemma went shopping, comparing prices and eventually bargaining for the shoes that she wanted to buy. When we visited Jemma just after she had bought the ballet shoes, she showed them to us. We admired them with her and laughed because they were so tiny. Jemma told us how much she had paid for them and then told us how much they were in the other stores. Jemma said that the man who sold them to her had given her an extra $2 off the shoes, so they had really been a good buy.

Housing created an overwhelming financial dilemma for the families. In each of the homes that we visited, there was talk of the price of apartments and of the difficulties the families faced as they looked for places to live. Pauline sometimes talked of having her own apartment when she started work, and on one occasion she talked of her dream of owning a $60,000 condo. Once when the state lottery was at a record high, Cora told us that her children had bought a ticket and that they had said the first thing they were going to do if they won was to buy her a house.

Reading advertisements for apartments in the local papers was a weekly ritual for Tanya during the first few months that we visited her, and later, when she prepared to leave Cathé's home, she once again studied the rentals advertised in the local paper as she searched for a place to live. Jerry also read the ads and talked of the relative prices of apartments in neighboring towns. Ieshea was placed in a similar position when she moved out of the apartment that she had occupied in her parents' home. During the last two years of the study, she moved several times as she tried to find a place to live that she could afford on the benefits that she received.

The extent to which literacy can become a financial process is well il-lustrated by another of the items in the notebook that Jerry showed to us. "I have a list," Jerry said, "of everything I needed when I come home. . . . I came home," Jerry turned his notebook so that we could see the page. "This is what clothes I bought. What I needed. My budget I figured out. And everything else. . . . This is before I even came home. . . . And I keep my word." Jerry laughed. "I keep my word on everything important," he said. In Jerry's note-book there was a clothing list. It stated, "Figuring that I will want a three room apartment with heat, the rent must be equal to the salary I will be receiving per week. Giving a rough estimate with a bring home pay of $150 I should be able to make it very nicely without using any money made from art. I would like to pay at least three months rent in advance where I could have the first month to get myself straight." This entry was followed by a weekly budget, a monthly budget, and a quarterly budget. Then Jerry had written, "Therefore an estimate of $960 would pull me through three months without working. Considering that I will need to buy my own furniture and that the apartment will only be temporary I should be able to pick out some pretty good stuff. . . ."

Obtaining funds for educational purposes was also important, and al-though funding was not always obtained, many attempts were made. When Trisha tried to enter a degree program that would eventually enable her to apply for law school, she was given financial aid forms to read. She supplied the information that was requested but was then told that she could only receive financial support if she was a full-time student. The money was not enough for her to go to school full-time, so she was unable to attend the college to which she had applied. Jemma told us a similar story. Jerry had applied to a local community college when he lost his job, but he was told that his unemployment benefits made him ineligible for financial aid. Jemma said he was receiving $145 a week, and she asked how that could be too much money. Iehsea had been in a similar predicament when she had tried to return to school in 1985. She had completed all the necessary paperwork but her forms were misplaced at the college, and the financial aid arrived too late for her to attend college that semester.

In each of the families there was talk of the ways in which family members would change the circumstances of their everyday lives if the opportunity ever arose. Tanya talked of going to college and having her own business so that she could afford a better place to live. Ieshea spoke of finishing her associate degree and finding a good job so that she could help her children. Pauline talked of the kind of job she would like, first as a computer programmer and then later as a realtor. Imagining life-styles that were not immediately obtainable seemed to be one of the ways in which individual family members coped with the economic realities of their day-to-day lives. Thus, Pauline read the stock market reports in the hope that one day she would be working and have money to invest, and Jerry "kept an eye on the economy" with the view to establishing a small silk-screening business. On one occasion Jerry told us that he and Jemma had sat down and planned their finances for the new business that Jerry hoped to start. He told us that Jemma was going to be his secretary and that they had worked out how many hours she would work each week and how much money she would get paid. The plans that Jerry and Jemma had made were written and saved to be read.

Environmental reading (Table 4–15).   Environmental print is perhaps the most visible type of print in any urban neighborhood, and certainly we found a plethora of such writings in the vicinity of Shay Avenue. However, it was not easy to gain a clear understanding of the impact of such print upon the day-to-day lives of the families. When we walked with Tasmika through the streets one afternoon, she read the signs on the fronts of the few local stores and, from a chalkboard, she read the list of produce that was on sale at the fruit and vegetable stand. Jemma talked of Jamaine going grocery shopping with her and of his knowing the names of some of the products that she bought. Words on T-shirts (such as Jarasad's, which had "Growing Up" written in bands to form a pattern, and the ones that Jerry printed, including one that stated "It's a dog eat dog world"), together with fast-food packaging and television commercials, were all a part of the environmental print that we found in the neighborhood.

Other kinds of environmental print were written on walls, and we were especially interested in this, since it was written locally to be read by those who lived in the community. There was the extermination notice on the wall in the hallway opposite the door to Jerry's apartment, and the graffiti written on the walls of the school. On the side of the school away from the main entrance, the door was covered with a large sheet of metal. There was wire over all the windows, and some of them were encased in wood. The door was not used by the students, and there was no reason for the teachers to go out that way, as the playgrounds and parking lot were on the other side of the building. Perhaps it was for this reason that the large expanse of gray painted bricks were covered in print, for only the children and young people rounded the corner and played in the street. To us, it seemed that what was written

Table 4–15 ● Environmental Types and Uses of Reading		
Group Studied	Types and Uses of Reading	Examples
Shay Avenue neighborhood	Reading the print in the environment.	Signs on storefronts and businesses; road signs; billboards; graffiti; T-shirts and gum wrappers.

was also read. Signs of friendship, notes of bravado, and salutations filled the space:

> Bambi was here
> but now she's
> Gone she left her name
> to carry on those who
> new her new her well
> Those who didn't
> Can go to *Hell*

> My name is
> Bambi I now
> I'm bad you
> [crossed out] with me
> I kick you
> [crossed out]

> My name is candy and I will rock your soul
> all night and day my love is so strong that
> you will feel like so very
> special and once you have a little
> Loving you will be back for more
> I am a sweet and loving home girl

> I was born in a Jungle
> Raised in a cave
> And chicken I crave

> I was born and raised in a barrel of butter knives

> fat ass Brown
> he's the clown

> Rosan
> -N-
> Rosas
> friends
> for ever

> RAHEIM
> GOT
> THIS
> AND
> YOU
> KNOW
> THAT!

> Jennifer
> was
> here in
> "1982"
> The Best than
> all the rest

Table 4–16 • Instrumental Types and Uses of Writing		
Group Studied	Types and Uses of Writing	Examples
Shay Avenue neighborhood	Writing to meet practical needs and manage/organize everyday life; writing to gain access to social institution or helping agency.	Writing out schedules; keeping calendars and appointments; planning a Thanksgiving dinner; keeping telephone and address books; signing name on visitors' pass to gain access to school (stating classroom to be visited, teacher's name, time of arrival; and, later, writing time of departure); filling out application for day care; school forms; forms for summer programs, health check-up forms, hospital forms, forms for social agencies, form for "Existing Housing Assistance Payments Program: Preliminary Application for Tenant Eligibility," and applications for counseling by Urban League.

DO NOT
FORGET
MOOKIE
[a heart drawn here]
JAMES

I am going to tell you
What I am going to do I'm
going to BURN MONDAY, kill tuesday, put
wednesday in the Hospital, then I'm going
to call tHURSDAY to tell FRIDAY, to tell
SATURDAY, not to kill SUNDAY, ON "MON"

We showed Tanya the graffiti that we had copied down, and she told us that the kids often wrote on the walls of the school. When she read the last piece she said, "Just out of the blue. Said it to his friends and they loved it. Probably the dummy in school. Have all his friends doin' his homework for him. Flunkin' all his tests."

Further Examples of the Types and Uses of Literacy: Writing

Instrumental writing (Table 4–16).   Instrumental writing—writing to meet practical needs and to manage or organize everyday life—was of primary importance to the families of Shay Avenue. It includes writing to gain access to social institutions or helping agencies. Again, instrumental uses are embedded in the categories that we have already presented. The forms that Tanya read when she visited the Urban League (shown in Figure 4–11) and the forms she was given when she applied for Home Energy Assistance (Figure 4–1) required her to write; another example of these forms, this one for housing assistance, is presented in Figure 4–12.

DIVISION OF HOUSING
BUREAU OF RENTAL ASSISTANCE

SECTION 8 EXISTING HOUSING ASSISTANCE PAYMENTS PROGRAM

PRELIMINARY APPLICATION FOR TENANT ELIGIBILITY

PLEASE PRINT

APPLICANT NAME				TELEPHONE			SPONSORING AGENCY (IF APPLICABLE)
ADDRESS				COUNTY			INDIVIDUAL CONTACT
CITY	STATE	ZIP CODE		SOCIAL SEC. NO. — —			ADDRESS

FAMILY COMPOSITION

CITY   STATE   ZIP

FAMILY MEMBER NO	NAME LIST EACH FAMILY MEMBER WHO WILL LIVE IN DWELLING - IDENTIFY FULL TIME STUDENTS	RELATIONSHIP TO FAMILY HEAD	AGE	SEX
1		HEAD OF HOUSEHOLD		
2				
3				
4				
5				
6				
7				
8				

FAMILY MEMBER NO	INCOME SOURCE	CURRENT ANNUAL RATE	FAMILY MEMBER NO	INCOME SOURCE	CURRENT ANNUAL RATE
	WAGES			SSI	
	SOC. SEC.			PENSION	
	AFDC(WELFARE)			OTHER WELFARE	
	UNEMPLOYMENT			OTHER	
	TOTAL GROSS ANNUAL INCOME				

FAMILY MEMBER NO	ASSETS SAVINGS, STOCKS, CERTIFICATES, REAL ESTATE, TRUSTS	AMOUNT
	TOTAL ASSETS	

FOR OFFICE USE ONLY
BEDROOM SIZE ☐
DATE RECEIVED
PRELIMINARY DETERMINATION
☐ ELIGIBLE ☐ INELIGIBLE

SIGNATURE

WARNING. SECTION 1001 OF TITLE 18 OF THE U.S. CODE MAKES IT A CRIMINAL OFFENSE TO MAKE WILLFUL FALSE STATEMENTS OR MISREPRESENTATION TO ANY DEPARTMENT OR AGENCY OF THE U.S. AS TO ANY MATTER WITHIN ITS JURISDICTION.

I hereby declare that the above information is true to the best of my knowledge and authorize release of information concerning my earnings received from any source.

DATE   SIGNATURE OF APPLICANT

APPLICANT WISHES TO:
☐ Remain in Present County
☐ Relocate to _____ County
APPLICANT WISHES TO:
☐ Remain in Present Unit
☐ Relocate to New Unit

FOR STATISTICAL PURPOSES ONLY:

MINORITY CODE (check one)
1. White ☐
2. Black ☐
3. American Indian or Alaskan Native ☐
4. Asian or Pacific Islander ☐

ETHNIC CODE (check one)
0. Non Hispanic ☐
1. Hispanic ☐

PRESENT HOUSING (check one)
1. Substandard ☐
2. Without housing or about to be without housing ☐
3. Standard ☐
4. Leasing in Place ☐

DISPLACEMENT STATUS (check one)
1. Government Action ☐
2. Natural Disaster ☐
3. Private Action ☐
4. Not Displaced ☐

PRESENT HOUSING COST
$_____ Monthly Rent

FAMILY STATUS (check as many as applicable)
1. Head/Spouse 62 or Over ☐
2. Head/Spouse Disabled ☐
3. Head/Spouse Handicapped ☐

LANDLORD'S NAME & ADDRESS
_____
_____
_____

PHONE NUMBER: _____

Figure 4–12 • Tanya's Form for Housing Assistance (Excerpt)

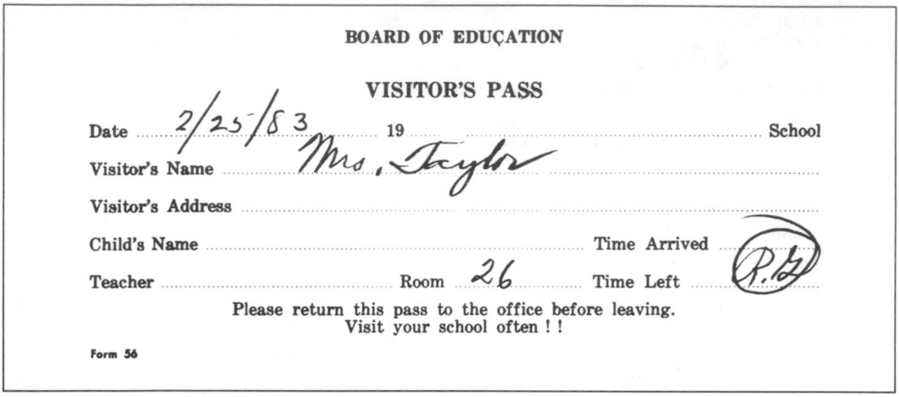

BOARD OF EDUCATION

VISITOR'S PASS

Date *2/25/83* 19 .... School

Visitor's Name *Mrs. Taylor*

Visitor's Address ....

Child's Name .... Time Arrived ....

Teacher .... Room *26* .... Time Left ....

Please return this pass to the office before leaving.
Visit your school often ! !

Form 56

Figure 4–13 ● A School Visitor's Pass

Other forms included applications for day care, forms pertaining to the schooling of children, applications for summer programs (when such programs were available), health care forms, hospital forms, and forms filled in for other social agencies.

Then, too, writing schedules, keeping a monthly planner, noting dates on calendars, and keeping telephone and address books are also instrumental uses of writing. Sign-in and sign-out forms were others. The doors to the elementary school that the children attended were kept locked, and visitors were required to sign the register when they arrived. Times of arrival were noted; further entries were made at times of departure. Classrooms to be visited and the names of teachers were also written into the book. Then the visitors (usually parents) were given passes before they made their way into the school from the entranceway that was watched by the guard. (A typical visitor's pass is shown in Figure 4–13.)

In the day-care center, children were signed in. Jemma said that when Jamaine went to day care Tasmika often signed the attendance book; in Ieshea's family, Danny sometimes signed for his sisters.

Autobiographical writing (Table 4–17).   The autobiographical writings that the families shared with us make up the most sensitive and revealing of categories. Occasionally, such writings can be thought of as a celebration of family, such as when family members play with the configurations of family names or try out names on paper for a new baby. At other times it takes courage and sometimes desperation to write of oneself, especially when the writing is to be shared with others. The life history that Tanya's mother wrote

Table 4–17 • Autobiographical Types and Uses of Writing		
Group Studied	Types and Uses of Writing	Examples
Shay Avenue neighborhood	Writing to understand oneself; to record one's life history; to share life with others.	Letters written to oneself in difficult times; writing prose to oneself; writing a journal; writing names of family members; writing names of new babies, trying different names and writing in different forms of script; when new babies are born, writing names, weight, dates of birth, and times of delivery.

and gave to Tanya to read belongs in this category of writing, and so does the following letter, which Ieshea wrote to herself in 1976.

Sometimes I feel that everything I try to do is useless. That no one really cares about me. That it's just me, all alone, and it doesn't matter to anyone whether I live or die. Sure I know that if I die someone will shed a tear for me; my children, my family, my friends (one or two) but no one will wish me back alive because they love me so much that life without me may seem unbearable. I want to be loved so bad. I'm so lonely. I want someone to hold me and tell me they love me, they miss me and that they're happy just being with me. I can't seem to find my way out of this rut. My bills are all overdue, my children need medical and dental care that I can't provide for them, I can't even afford carfare back and forth to work, the little I make can't get to all the places it has to reach. My children need a man to love and care for them. To take them places, teach them things and just to be around when they need a Father. And I need a good man. I'd do anything for "my man" if he loved me and my children—and showed us that he did! Where am I going? Not back to the bottom, that's for damn sure! I'll get my shit inorder.

Recreational writing (Table 4–18). Writing was used during times of relaxation in the families in the Shay Avenue neighborhood. Crossword puzzles and conundrums were occasional leisure-time activities that included the use of print, and doodling was a frequent pastime. Tracing over letters in words,

Table 4–18 • Recreational Types and Uses of Writing		
Group Studied	Types and Uses of Writing	Examples
Shay Avenue neighborhood	Writing during leisure time for the enjoyment of the activity.	Crossword puzzles; conundrums; doodling; letters.

drawing stars, and making faces filled odd moments. (See Figure 4–14.) Occasionally doodles appeared as patches of shading, as on a piece of paper that Pauline used when writing out a college schedule. Corners of papers were sometimes decorated with motifs; for Jerry, these small sketches were sometimes developed into larger works of art. The children also doodled. Ieshea's papers were filled with the scribbles of her young children.

Creative writing (Table 4–19).   There were a few times when writing became an art form, as the doodling of names became a means of self-expression. Experimenting with different types of script, making "bubble" letters, and playing with patterns were all ways in which members of the families wrote the names of one another. Again, for Jerry this form of writing became the basis of the signs that he made. His experimentation with the shape, size, and configuration of letters was one aspect of his work and of his artistic ability.

It was not only the patterns of individual words that became a creative form, for writing became art when poems were written. Teko wrote poems, and he sometimes shared them with his mother. Two of Teko's poems, probably written in the late seventies, were given to us by Ieshea and are included here.

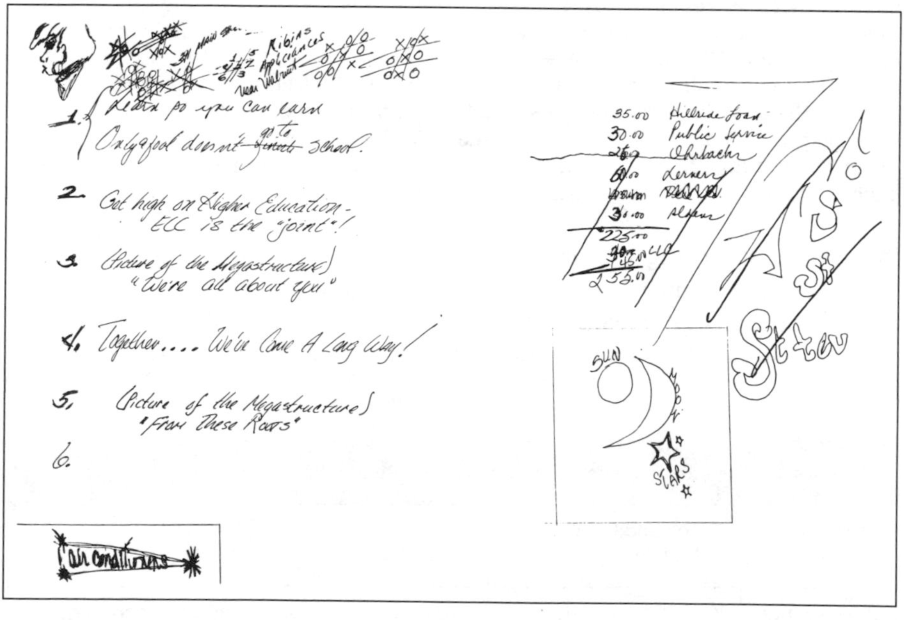

Figure 4–14 • Doodles

Table 4–19 ● Creative Types and Uses of Writing		
Group Studied	Types and Uses of Writing	Examples
Shay Avenue neighborhood	Writing as a means of self-expression.	Writing poetry; painting with children, experimenting with the size, shape, and color of letters and the configuration of letters in words; writing names of family members in different forms of script; playing with the configurations of letters in the names.

Paradise ●

For all I have been fooled many times
for thinking I have had paradise
to only come to a false conclusion
I found my paradise was only an
illusion. Now I think I really know
what it will mean to me
and I will put it on this paper
just for you to see.
Paradise is having a girl
and not a worry in the world
Paradise is living in style,
and having money in big piles

Love ●

Love is what you see
when you think of you and
me; Love is what you find
when you have us in mind
With you and I together
our love could last forever
With our love as bright as
the stars; I could bend Iron bars

Educational writing (Table 4–20). The educational types and uses of writing that we found in the Shay Avenue study are scattered through this text. Of primary importance are the ways in which family members wrote as they worked to educate themselves. Jerry's notebooks were filled with poems, wise sayings, and notes on criminal law. Some of the notes that he made were by hand, but most were made on a typewriter. "I had a typewriter," Jerry said. "I can type faster than the average typist, and I only use three fingers." Jerry moved his fingers rapidly pressing imaginary keys and making the noise of the machine with his tongue and lips. He laughed, "And begone, Jack! I be on the way!" Trisha also used a typewriter. She practiced speed typing on a second-hand electric typewriter that she bought for herself when she was studying to be a paralegal secretary. Ieshea also worked to educate herself. She prided herself upon her ability to write articulate letters. She used a dictionary and wrote multiple drafts to ensure that her letters were well written.

Writing to fulfill school and college assignments took place on a daily basis during the school year. For the children this meant that they brought home an endless array of faded dittos and workbook pages. For the parents of the children it meant studying for courses at a community college. During the time that we were visiting the families, many of the parents enrolled in college courses that they hoped would lead to future employment. Tanya took a course in paralegal studies, Pauline in computer programming. Trisha also studied paralegal courses, and Ieshea returned to college to try to complete her associate degree. (She had taken some basic college courses towards her degree.) Jerry, who had previously taken courses in psychology and sociology, applied to a nearby community college, and Jemma also talked about going back to school. In each of the families was what we could call a general orientation towards studying.

Work-related writing (Table 4–21).   Work-related uses of writing were not a prominent feature of the lives of the families in the Shay Avenue neighborhood. This, of course, is hardly surprising, as jobs were scarce and difficult

Table 4–20 • Educational Types and Uses of Writing		
Group Studied	Types and Uses of Writing	Examples
Shay Avenue neighborhood	Writing to educate oneself; writing to fulfill college assignments.	Practicing shorthand; typing to increase speed and accuracy; writing drafts and final copies of term papers and other assignments; writing out notes pertaining to criminal law; writing out lines and poems from books read; writing down poetry that someone has recited.

Table 4–21 • Work-Related Types and Uses of Writing		
Group Studied	Types and Uses of Writing	Examples
Shay Avenue neighborhood	Writing pertaining to employment or self-employment.	Filling in job applications and writing résumés; preparing lettering for silk-screening; sign making.

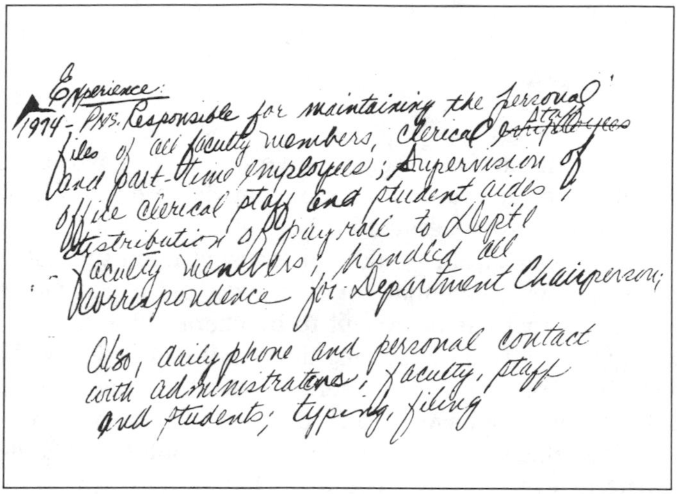
Experience:
1974-Pres. Responsible for maintaining the personal
files of all faculty members, clerical employees
and part-time employees; Supervision of
office clerical staff and student aides;
distribution of payroll to Dept'l
faculty members; handled all
correspondence for Department Chairperson;

Also, daily phone and personal contact
with administrators; faculty, staff
and students; typing, filing

Figure 4–15 • A Draft of Ieshea's Résumé (Excerpt)

to obtain. We did find examples of job applications and résumé writing. At one time Pauline was thinking of enlisting in the armed services. She studied the application forms and began to fill them in, but as far as we know they were never sent. Similarly, in 1979 Ieshea filled in an application that was printed in a civil service job opportunities newspaper. But the application was never sent, as she was at home taking care of Hakim, who was then a baby. At about the same time Ieshea also made drafts of her résumé. (See Figure 4–15.)

Environmental writing (Table 4–22). Finally we have included the category of environmental types and uses of writing, as they were of such importance to Jerry in the last years of his life. He painted signs on storefronts and businesses, and he painted logos on the sides of tractor-trailers. He was

Table 4–22 • Environmental Types and Uses of Writing

Group Studied	Types and Uses of Writing	Examples
Shay Avenue neighborhood	Writing in public places for others to read.	Designing and painting signs for storefronts and businesses.

sincerely interested in the visual enhancement of the inner-city neighborhood in which he lived.

Commentary

In this section on literacy in a comparative frame we have presented the examples of the types and uses of literacy that Heath defined in *Ways With Words*, and we have also suggested further categories that emerged during the course of the Shay Avenue study. In focusing upon the categories, an openness of meaning is essential, for any given piece can fall into many categories. A poem that has been kept to be cherished and read was once written to be given. Thus, in presenting the newer categories we have given a few specific examples and then referred back to earlier descriptions of categories. In so doing we have attempted to create a measure of contextual tying that reflects, albeit superficially, the plurality of literacy configurations that are a part of everyday life. The data that we have presented in this comparative frame is considered in depth when we ask, in our next and final chapter, "What have the families taught us about literacy?"

Five
Families, Literacy, and Educational Policy

The real potential of anthropology for policy makers is that it makes possible, following established methodological and disciplined procedures, the
examination of the particular cases as tests of the need for and efficacy of
policies made at other levels, and that it does so through direct observation of and involvement with those most affected by the policies themselves.

Charles Harrington

Slowly, through these pages, we have been moving from ethnographic description, through increasingly abstract and tentative arrangements of data,
towards the interpretive explanations (see Bateson 1958, p. 281; Geertz 1983,
p. 21) that we have been developing during the course of the study. What
have we learned from the Shay Avenue families? How have they helped us
understand the social, political, and economic forces that shape their lives?
What have they taught us about literacy? And finally, how can we, as researchers, educators, and policymakers, use the information to enhance the
learning opportunities of young children so that they can develop the literacy
behaviors they will need to survive, prosper, and become productive members
of American society?

What Have We Learned from the Shay Avenue Families?

The images of the families that have been generated through ethnographic
descriptions and interpretive explanations do not match the findings of the
more traditional, large-scale studies reported in the social science literature.
We found that the families' spent time together, that there was a rhythm to
their lives, and that they enjoyed each other's company. Friends visited. Children played. People helped one another. Sometimes there was sadness and
grief, at other times there was anger and resentment, but there was always

a quiet determination in the way in which they approached the difficulties that confronted them. Their optimism about the future and their ability to imagine what life would be like if conditions were better seemed to keep them going, struggling and surviving, albeit precariously, against the odds and without the support of the society to which they belong.

In *Black Children: Their Roots, Culture, and Learning Styles*, Janice Hale (1982) argues persuasively that "the orientation of American social scientists has been to define Black home environments as pathological and Black parents as deficient in preparing their children for school" (see also McAdoo, 1981). We agree with Hale and would add that the stereotypic images perpetuated in the mass media only serve to exacerbate the difficulties faced by the families themselves, the communities in which they live, and the society to which they belong. In the newspapers, sensational stories about people who are poor vie for space with articles that focus upon poverty and the "system." Some stories are informative and sensitively written, but most are written to entertain. They make us draw in our breath, tut, shake our heads in agreement or disbelief, and feel anger, sadness, and perhaps shame.

All of these reactions are possible when one reads articles such as the one published in the *Atlantic* entitled "Poor Mom" (Ehrenreich 1986). In this piece the writer reviews a book that explores the feminization of poverty, but she begins by tracing images of the poor since the Kennedy administration in the early sixties. The author writes, "By the time Ronald Reagan arrived to lead the right's war on 'welfarism,' the poor had been virtually condensed into a single, thoroughly repellent image: a young black male, apprenticing as a mugger, who had figured out how to buy vodka with food stamps." In the next paragraph the writer adds to her earlier image by stating, "Poverty was becoming female territory ... and for anyone willing to listen a new stereotype of the poor was obviously in order—not the menacing young black male or even the multiparous black matriarch annually fattening her brood. A better representative, given the fact, would be a white woman (although the poor are disproportionately black and Hispanic, the majority are still white), with one or two children (70 percent of the women on welfare have no more than two), who has seen better times." It is clear from this piece that the author is reporting upon stereotypic images that she herself did not create, but whatever her stance, the descriptors that she chose help to both re-create and perpetuate these destructive representations that are then passed back and forth between the print and visual media.

One of television's most blatant and disturbing examples of the re-creation and perpetuation of these harmful images was aired on January 25, 1986, when CBS broadcast "The Vanishing Family—Crisis in Black America," a documentary that has since become known as "The Moyers Report." In May *The Boston Globe* responded to the program with an article entitled "Teen-age Pregnancy and the Black Family." Anita Diamant, the author, writes that the report "was filled with grim statistics and all-too-familiar impressions of ghetto life: noise, crowding, poverty, danger," and that "the young parents interviewed seemed cavalier, resigned, or unrealistic about their own futures and the needs of their children." That we have learned to accept these images is made clear by the response to the film. Again we quote Anita Diamant in *The Boston Globe*: "A flurry of newspaper editorials greeted the documentary, many of them applauding the program's apparent conclusion that welfare is a primary cause of adolescent pregnancy." A final statement from Diamant underscores the ways in which such superficial reporting finds only what it is seeking and ignores the possibility that there are alternative perspectives and explanations. Diamant writes:

The objections to the CBS special center on the lack of context it provided in terms of the whole spectrum of black family life that exists, even in the blighted neighborhoods of Newark, New Jersey, which was the focus of the documentary. Nor did it allow the possibility that some teen-agers do overcome the odds and become productive adults and excellent parents. The multiform causes for the "epidemic" of black teen-age pregnancy were reduced, in the Moyers Report, to two dramatic stereotypes that are embedded in many white Americans' deepest beliefs about black people: the notions that welfare encourages antisocial behavior and that black men are irresponsible and, at least, potentially threatening. (p. 19)

We wonder how the lives of the families that we visited would have been represented on such a show. Would the reporters have listened if Jerry had shared with them some of the poems that he loved to read? Would Tanya have seemed irresponsible as she made a home for her children in an abandoned building after her mother died? Would they have watched as Shauna sat next to her mother doing her homework with Pauline looking over her shoulder to make sure that she understood the questions and was getting the problems right? And would they have gone to court with Ieshea and Danny and watched as Danny played with his young sister while he waited for his case to be heard? Our impressions of the families with whom we spent our time, the people with whom we talked in the Shay Avenue neighborhood, and the young men that we met as we walked through the streets cannot be reconciled with the images that the media have helped to both create and perpetuate. Their lives do not fit any of these preconceived notions or rigid conceptions of Black families or families who are poor and living on welfare. The experience and reason of the families themselves create more fragile and sensitive images.

As we contemplate the families with whom we have worked, any preconceived or rigid conceptions of family life fade away. Each is an original, and each serves to emphasize the variety of patterns of cooperation and domestic organization in the institution that we call family. Morris (1981) speaks of such flexible household arrangements as "an adaptive response to an uncertain social and economic environment" (p. 123). We agree with her interpretation and would add that the variety of social support systems and coping strategies that we have observed underscores the resilience of families faced with the enormous pressure of societal uncertainty. Undoubtedly what makes these families so determined in their resolve is the ethos of a people, a racial minority, "struggling to survive under the tragic conditions of economic inequality" (Davis 1981). But we would also argue that there are characteristics of these families that have enabled them to survive that are typical of "functioning" families (see Schlesinger 1982) irrespective of their race or social circumstances. Focusing specifically upon the Shay Avenue families, we would describe these family characteristics as follows:

1. The parents shared a sense of conviction in their own abilities and they were determined to raise healthy children.
2. The parents provided loving environments in which children were cared for with tenderness and affection.
3. The parents created structured home environments in which there were family expectations of cooperation and participation within a framework of rules that were understood by the children and reinforced by the parents.
4. The parents were concerned for the safety and well-being of the children at home, as they played in the neighborhood, and as they walked to and from school.
5. The parents valued the growing sense of competence and independence that the children experienced as they participated in the social life of their own family and in the social life that they shared with their friends and neighbors in the community in which they lived.

The descriptions that we have constructed throughout the text of the resilience of the families (what works and how it works) emphasize that if we wish to create healthly environments in which families can live productive lives, we must provide opportunities for parents and children to become actively involved in the research that will eventually help shape the social policies that enable them to survive and prosper. Our task is to build alternative paradigms and broad-based theories that will provide explanations of the ways in which families participate in the construction of their own environments (see Taylor 1987; in press a,b). Thus our explanations should be imaginative and intuitive as well as analytic and well trained. We can begin by questioning our practices for collecting data, the framework of our interpretations, and the underlying assumptions on which our research is based. What do we count as evidence—small strips of behavior? Surface features? Responses to the questions on some questionnaire? Is such data the basis for far-reaching social policies? We have learned from the lives of the Shay Avenue families that it is not. They have taught us that if our social policies are to be effective, we must involve the families themselves. When researchers work with families, stereotypic images fade. Fieldwork becomes the mode of inquiry (see Appendices A and B).

In our own experience, families welcome the opportunity to take part in research projects in which the researchers are willing to participate in the lives of the families. Thus a balance can be created as people work together. When we spend time with families, a better understanding can be gained of how social policies shape their lives. Studying with families can change our perceptions of racial minorities, teenage mothers, and those students who have dropped out of school. Societal pejoratives no longer have any meaning. New sensitivities replace old stereotypes. And eventually the socially constructed accounts of the research can be used as the basis for more humane, family-centered policies that provide opportunities for all parents and children to become active members of the society to which they belong.

How Have the Families Helped Us Understand the Social, Political, and Economic Forces That Shape Their Lives?

We have learned from the families that the difficulties that confound their lives are shaped into personal configurations of poverty. However, inadequate housing, the lack of essential services, poor schools, limited access to higher education, and restricted job opportunities all have an impact on their daily lives. Society has placed them on a collision course which, despite the odds, they survived. Then, instead of recognizing their efforts we blame them for the "inadequacies" of their survival. We say, "It is your fault that you are poor. You should work harder. Take care of your children. Stop taking advantage of the welfare system." We do not hear when Jerry says, "I'm a producer. I can produce," or when Tanya says, "People tell me all I can do is hope for the best. I think if I gave it my go I think that my kids will turn out fine. I'm hopeful. Hopefully ... there's no reason why my child should be standing out there on the corner. I'm not going to have it."

The families that we visited in the Shay Avenue neighborhood bring the verification of personal circumstance to the reports that are published nationally on the difficulties that are faced by many Black families and families who are poor. We can move between the families and the reports, making the connections so that we can "see" the lives of parents and children in the reports that are made. The connections are made particularly apparent when we think of the families within the context of *A Children's Defense Budget: An Analysis of the FY 1987 Federal Budget and Children*, the 1986 report of The Children's Defense Fund.

When we think of Tanya, Queenie, and Gary, we remember their struggle to live in an abandoned building as they tried to find an apartment to rent.

Many of the nation's poorest families are not only finding it difficult to locate and pay for decent housing but impossible to afford any housing at all. Lingering unemployment, falling incomes among poor and near-poor, and continued cutbacks in a range of government income supports and other programs have greatly reduced the amount of money many poor families have available to spend on rent or mortgage payments.

A 1983 report by the Congressional Research Service found that more than 60 percent of very low-income households (households with 50 percent or less of the national median income) had serious housing problems. They live in housing that is physically inadequate, overcrowded, or imposing too heavy a cost on their meager financial resources....

At the same time that fewer affordable new units are being built, the ones in existence are suffering steady attrition due to demolition, arson, abandonment, condominium conversion, or conversion to nonresidential use. According to the U. S. Department of Housing and Urban Development's Annual Housing Survey, these combined causes removed some 2.8 million rental units between 1970 and 1977. The government estimates that 2.5 million families are displaced by private or government action each year....

Those families in the worst situations are being squeezed out of the housing market altogether. This has created a crisis of homelessness among families with children. There are more homeless people in the United States now than at any time since the Great Depression. (Children's Defense Fund 1986, pp. 194, 196)

When we think of Pauline and Shauna, we remember Pauline attending school and then dropping out when she could not find a job near enough to her home for to use her newly gained skills.

In 1983, more than half a million persons (508,000) younger than twenty-two were heads of households with young children. Of that group of young family heads, more than one in four (130,000) was unable to find work for all or part of the year. (Children's Defense Fund 1986, p. 89)

Teens, especially minority teens, face difficult odds in the job market. Teen unemployment is lingering at an all-time high. Young workers who are employed are disproportionately in low-paying jobs. In 1979, 37.3 percent of sixteen- to nineteen-year-old workers and 13.7 percent of twenty- to twenty-four-year-old workers paid on an hourly basis earned wages of $2.90 an hour or less. If the job was full time, $2.90 an hour would support a family of three at the poverty line.

In 1984, 65.3 percent of sixteen- to nineteen-year-old workers and 28.5 percent of twenty- to twenty-four-year-old workers were earning less than $4.00 an hour, a wage that, if the worker could get a full-time job, would leave a family of three just below the poverty line. In other words 65 percent of teen workers and 29 percent of workers in their early twenties—essentially twice the rates of 1979—could not earn wages in 1984 sufficient to bring an intact, one-income family with a child out of poverty. (Children's Defense Fund 1986, pp. 212–13).

When we think of Jerry and Jemma, we remember them as they tried to stay together with their two children, Tasmika and Jamaine. We remember Jerry losing his job, sick with worry, hurt, overwhelmed, and dying.

Most families headed by a worker who has just lost a job expect to rely on the unemployment insurance (UI) system to cushion the impact of the loss of income. Set up during the 1930s, the UI program is financed through federal and state payroll taxes on employers and covers 86 percent of all employed persons (the remaining workers are primarily self-employed or engaged in certain types of agricultural or domestic work). Those whose jobs were covered by this system and who have worked relatively steadily during the previous year can receive up to twenty-six weeks of benefits after losing a job, with the weekly amount based on a percentage of their prior wages....

Until the early 1980s, the UI system provided an effective buffer for most unemployed workers in America, particularly during periods of recession. For example, in May 1975 more than two-thirds of all unemployed persons received UI benefits. Even as recently as 1980, nearly half of all unemployed workers obtained help through the UI system.

In the past five years, however, the financial protection this system provides for workers and their families has been eroded seriously by the combination of persistently high and lengthened unemployment, federal and state budget cuts, and structural changes in the economy....

Because eligibility for unemployment benefits is based on work experience and wage levels during the previous year, the UI system is particularly ineffective in reaching many of the most vulnerable jobless Americans, who are disproportionately young parents, women, and minorities. (Children's Defense Fund 1986, pp. 132, 133, 134)

When we think of Ieshea, we remember the time when she went without food so her children could eat.

Families that do not have enough income to meet their needs must, as a last resort, rely on income support provided by the government. But the chief government income support program for poor children, Aid to Families with Dependent Children (AFDC), has many problems that prevent it from doing this job as effectively as an income maintenance program should. AFDC does not help all poor families, provides less help than it should to those who do qualify, in some cases acts as a disincentive for two-parent families to form or to stay together, and provides little help to families trying to move toward self-sufficiency....

Because payments vary from state to state, the amount of money an AFDC family gets varies considerably, depending on the place of residence. But because standards of need are so low and payment levels are even lower, AFDC families almost invariably live on incomes far below the poverty level....

Thus, virtually every family on AFDC faces a daily struggle to meet its children's basic needs for food, clothing, and shelter with minimal government support. Families survive day-to-day, often falling behind on rent or utility payments, turning to charity providers for food at the end of the month, rarely buying even used clothing, and trying to get small school fees waived. Surviving on AFDC is itself virtually a full-time job.

These families have no margin to cope with crises or emergencies. (Children's Defense Fund 1986, pp. 137, 140, 142)

We remember how Ieshea tried to help her sons Teko and Danny as they grew older, and we remember her sadness as she realized that she could not help them.

Children from poor and minority families are often channeled into general, vocational, or special education programs, sometimes regardless of their potential, while more advantaged students are steered into college preparatory courses....

Regardless of race, students from poor families are three to four times more likely to drop out than those from more affluent households. In large public school districts in our major cities, where the great majority of students come from poor families, dropout rates frequently exceed 40 percent. (Children's Defense Fund 1986, pp. 222, 223)

Only 42.6 percent of black and 52.8 percent of white eighteen- to twenty-one-year-olds from impoverished families in 1983 had earned high school diplomas.

Only 22 percent of all black sixteen- to nineteen-year-olds and 29 percent of all Hispanic youths in this age group were employed as of November 1985—half the employment rate of their white peers. (Children's Defense Fund 1986, p. 88)

On November 12, 1986, in *USA Today*, reported to be the most widely read newspaper in America, the lead article focuses upon "a Louis Harris survey which found that teachers and legislators think parents should play a big role in their kids' education but aren't." In the article, the Secretary of Education, William Bennett, is quoted as saying, "The decline of the American family constitutes perhaps the greatest long-term threat to our children's well-being." We would reply, based upon the present research and upon years of working with families, that it is *the decline of social, political, and economic support for families that constitutes the greatest long-term threat to our children's well-being*. There is a line in William Golding's *Free Fall* that reads, "You cannot blame the boat if it breaks loose at last and goes where the water carries it." Families have been set adrift; we cannot blame them when their boats founder, or take credit when, through their own endeavors, they manage to stay afloat. We have lost sight of the interrelationships that exist between the family, the school, and the workplace. Our programs to support and enhance the day-to-day lives of families with young children are fractured, disconnected, and totally inadequate. Schools in low-income areas and inner-city neighborhoods receive inadequate funding (for New Jersey, the Children's Defense Fund quotes a low of $2,616 per student per year in less affluent areas and a high of $5,375 in more well-off communities), and the children are often penalized because of the lack of resources and the limitations of the programs. The social and economic programs that are provided are often targeted at isolated problems. Too often they are irrational, incoherent, and conceived without consideration of the connections that exist between healthy families, schools that educate, and productive workplaces. And yet families and schools are blamed for sending young people into the workplace without the education that they will need to obtain jobs.

What Have the Families Taught Us About Literacy?

There was a time early in the study that we found it hard to justify our literacy research. With these families struggling to provide food and shelter for their children, why were we studying their reading and writing? What was the point? How could a study of literacy help them? It was difficult for us to think that our work had any relevance at all. For several months we continued, numbed by the experience of visiting the families, unable to think it through. We talked between ourselves and with other researchers about the interrelationships between advocacy and research. One researcher commented seriously that he kept his "good works" separate from his research projects. Stung, we continued, feeling neither charitable nor benevolent. We encouraged each other and hoped that eventually we would understand our own participation in the struggles of the families. It was Tanya who helped us begin to see the importance of literacy. Her name on the hospital bracelet became a symbol of her plight. Reading the newspapers, even if she did not find an apartment to rent, provided her with an opportunity to struggle for her own survival. Through the life that Tanya shared with us, we began to gain some understanding of the ways in which literacy is used in everyday life (see Szwed, 1977; Taylor 1982b), and through our study of literacy we began to understand, although in a somewhat muddled way, the complex and involved societal contexts in which print gets written and read. Ours is a literate society, and at some level, by studying the manner in which print is used by ordinary people in both ordinary and critical situations it is possible gain a view of the workings of a social system and of the ways in which it can impede, constrain, or enhance our everyday lives.

During the past five years, as we have discussed the uses of literacy in the families in the Shay Avenue neighborhood, our attention has been frequently drawn to the many ways in which the economic circumstances of their lives affect the uses of literacy that we have begun to describe. Contrary to the seemingly popular belief, we would argue that you have to be bright to be poor—and survive. In writing of hunger in America, Lelyveld (1985) asks in *The New York Times Magazine*:

Is it possible that significant numbers of poor people are turning away from the welfare system to private charity because they find the hours of waiting, the cold indifference and occasional rudeness more than they can take? (p. 68)

In answering the question that he poses, Lelyveld states:

It's possible, but I didn't happen to meet any in talking to families across the country.... Instead, I kept running into people who had tumbled out of the system because they had failed to comprehend or comply promptly with one of its many demands for documentation. (p. 68)

Applications for food stamps, AFDC, WICS, reminders of obligations to report changes of circumstances to the Welfare Board, notices on assignment of support rights, and "What to Bring with You When You Apply for Home Energy Assistance" are all examples of the instrumental uses of reading and writing that are a part of the everyday lives of the families with whom we worked. Their economic circumstances create a social climate in which print in various forms is used to intrude upon the ways in which they live—private becomes public when you are poor. On one occasion Tanya told us of the questions that she was asked when she was pregnant with Queenie and she applied for food stamps. As she filled in the forms, which created a permanent written record of her personal life and financial situation, she was asked how many times had she had sexual intercourse and where it had taken place. "They've gotten everything," Tanya said. "They know everything about you."

In studying the Shay Avenue families within the comparative framework that we have presented, it is perhaps the uses of reading and writing to obtain assistance that catch the eye. Clearly, obtaining food and shelter can depend upon one's ability to read and write. Skeptics may suggest that such paperwork is often completed by others. In our experience, such help from social agencies is difficult to obtain; besides, it is evident that the families with whom we were working are more than the fillers in of forms—*they are active members in a print community in which literacy is used for a wide variety of social, technical, and aesthetic purposes, for a wide variety of audiences, and in a wide variety of situations.* Indeed, in examining the data presented in the tables in chapter 4, the similarities between Heath's townspeople, Taylor's suburban families, and the families in the Shay Avenue neighborhood are far more striking than the differences. Thus, in focusing upon the children, we cannot emphasize enough that *they are active participants and interpreters in a social world in which texts are written and read.*

The paradoxical dichotomy between these findings and those that have come to be accepted (and expected) are cause for serious concern. For example, in *High School: A Report on Secondary Education in America*, Boyer (1983) states:

Dropouts tend to come from poor families. They have more siblings, more broken homes, higher levels of parental punitiveness and lower self-esteem. Their parents also have less schooling. Simply put, many students who leave school come from stressful homes. (pp. 244–45)

True, some of the parents with whom we worked did not finish high school, and some of the older children did drop out of school during the four years that we visited the families. In addition, some might argue that many of the children came from "broken homes." But no one can deny that these were *literate homes*. One of the explanations for this apparent paradox lies in the persistent use of obsolete definitions of literacy as a series of dispassionate skills that can be counted, measured, and weighed. Even when we speak of literacy as a social process, we rarely look beyond the literacy event and the linguistic transactions that take place. So much of the process remains buried in the multiple layers of communication that are a part of our contextual worlds.

We forget that to be literate is a uniquely human experience, a creative process that enables us to deal with ourselves and to better understand one another. The autobiography that was written by Tanya's mother speaks directly to this issue. The writer, who died when she was thirty-eight, never finished high school, and yet she was able to write fourteen pages of connected prose, which she gave to her daughter. It is a vivid example of one of the ways in which families create one another as parents and children "bring each other into being by being part of the matrix in which the other exists" (Bateson 1984). Tanya's mother "failed" in the usual societal sense of the word; however, if one takes a theory-of-use perspective using an insider's view of language (see Harste, Woodward, and Burke 1984) she was successful, for she succeeded in tying together texts and generations as she created new understandings of her life and the world in which her children and grand-children live.

This autobiography; the law work that Jerry did and the poetry that he read; the letters that leshea wrote and the pieces she tore from the local newspapers; the other creative and expressive types and uses of literacy that we have found in the Shay Avenue neighborhood; and the data presented by Heath (1983) and Taylor (1983) provide us with the opportunity to raise questions about the ways in which we conceptualize literacy, the theoretical frames of our research, and the practical application of the outcomes of these frames in the teaching of young children to read and write in school. In *Words and Values*, Rosenthal (1984) writes, "Words lead complex lives and lead us along with them in complex ways." The structures that we create are not the structures of the world (Goodman 1982). The descriptions and categories that we fashion quiet the chatter—a legitimate enterprise that becomes a fragile endeavor when we replace the world with the constructions that we make. Literacy is not a discrete event, nor is it a package of predetermined skills. The complex, yet oversimplified, boundaries that we have established so that we can count, weigh, and measure literacy do not exist. They are of our own making.

Thus, in the context of our interpretations, problems arise when we ignore the social processes of (con)textual tying and we take our traditional ways of thinking about literacy—the rigid hierarchies and taxonomies and pre-determined sets of skills that we create—and place them in classrooms for children to learn. Again, literacy is not some list of dispassionate skills that we invent in the isolation of our experimentation, nor is it a series of events to be teased out of ethnographic data. Literacy cannot be quantified in num-bers, nor is it directly related to the frequency of use. It cannot be taught through a decoding process, nor through a series of disconnected (if well-ordered) exercises. *We can pull language apart, but we cannot expect children to do the same* (Taylor and Strickland 1986). Children need to be able to create public and private text worlds with continual opportunities to use their expressive abilities to generate new meanings and maintain personal and shared interpretations of the social, technical, and aesthetic types and uses of literacy. It would be hard to dispute the assertion that, in most of our schools, few such opportunities currently exist.

Stated more formally, we would argue that:

1. To be literate is a uniquely human experience, one that enables us to deal with ourselves and to better understand one another. It is never a mechanical process that is solely dependent upon skills that are taught.
2. Sex, race, economic status, and setting cannot be used as significant

correlates of literacy. The myths and stereotypes that create images of specific groups (families who are poor, inner-city families, teenage mothers and their children) have no relevance when we stop counting and start observing and working with people.

Focusing specifically upon the Shay Avenue families, we would argue that:

1. The families use literacy for a wide variety of purposes (social, technical, and *aesthetic* puposes), for a wide variety of audiences, and in a wide variety of situations.
2. Literacy is not always liberating. The economic circumstances in which the families live create a social (political?) climate in which print in various forms is used to intrude upon their everyday lives.
3. Education and literacy cannot be used interchangeably. We found family members who were highly literate, and yet they were not educated in the traditional sense of the word.

How Can We Use the Information We Have Gained from the Shay Avenue Families to Enhance the Learning Opportunities of Young Children So That They Can Develop the Literacy Behaviors They Will Need to Survive, Prosper, and Become Productive Members of American Society?

Martin Luther King once said, "Education must enable one to sift and weigh the evidence, to discern the true from the false, the real from the unreal, and the facts from the fiction" (1983, p. 41). *Growing Up Literate* was written in the spirit of this ideal. The text that we have created is neither fact nor fiction, for we cannot tell the story as the families would tell it themselves. What we have written is a series of ethnographic descriptions and interpretive explanations, versions of what is real and unreal (myths and stereotypes), that we have constructed during the five years that we have worked on the study. At the time of writing this section, some of what we have written has been read by family members, and by the the time we go to press it will have been read by all of the families who participated in the study. Through the sounding of ideas and exchanging of thoughts, changes may have been made to the descriptions, and new information may have been included. The text is fluid, a social construction that enables us to "sift and weigh" as we try to come a little closer to lives of the families and the children who participated in the study.

This is the way in which it has worked. But there are other ways in which the study worked, for in trying to understand the families we were also trying to understand ourselves, true and false, personal perceptions and deceptions, the ethnocentrism of our own mental baggage. It is here that we, as researchers, educators, and policymakers who wish to enhance the learning opportunities of young children, must begin. If we believe that the family is the primary institution that endows meaning and value to human life, we must support the family and help parents to raise and educate their children. We must "sift and weigh the evidence, . . . discern the true from the false, the real from the unreal, and the facts from the fiction." We can begin by examining critically our own assumptions about people. Spivak and Albert (1985) speak to this issue when they responded in a letter to *The New York Times* to a letter that had been published following the article on hunger in America that we quoted from earlier in this chapter. In response to the article, a person had written that ignorance of basic nutrition and unwise shopping help keep people hungry. Spivak and Albert replied:

In a two-year nutrition survey of 400 low income Boston families, we found that the causes of hunger are varied and complex, involving factors beyond the control of individuals. For instance, low-income neighborhoods often lack supermarkets that sell items needed to prepare food from scratch, and transportation to other areas is often costly and difficult. Kitchens may be overcrowded and may have no working refrigerator or stove. As in many middle-class families, heads of households are often too exhausted to bake and cook after working all day.

Unfortunately, insensitive assumptions about the causes of hunger can become the basis upon which food policies are made. (p. 78)

Spivak and Albert exposed the senselessness of a popular belief. Perhaps we too would have been able to recognize the asininity of the idea that ignorance of basic nutrition and unwise shopping help keep people hungry. But other harmful suppositions are more subtle and difficult to discern. In the 1986 New York Regents/Commissioner's regional conferences report, "Education Success for All: Better Beginnings—Stronger Completions," there is much to be applauded, but there are also underlying assumptions that need to be given serious consideration. On page 13, the last paragraph begins, "Dennis, age 17, is enrolled as a sophomore at his inner city high school with an enrollment of 4,000 mostly minority, mostly poor students." It is not difficult to see how easily the reader of the report can move from "mostly minority, mostly poor students" to "minority students *are* poor students." Isn't that the assumption? If this is the way we think of inner-city students, how can we help them?

If we are to teach, we must first examine our own assumptions about families and children and we must be alert to the negative images in the literature ("dropouts come from stressful homes"). Instead of responding to "pathologies" we must recognize that what we see may actually be healthy adaptations to an uncertain and stressful world. As teachers, researchers, and policymakers, we need to think about the children themselves and try to imagine the contextual worlds of their day-to-day lives. We can best illustrate this through our observations of the children in the Shay Avenue neighborhood. The literate lives of these children, as presented in chapter 2, leave us with the lasting impression of some of the universals of childhood. Richard Coe (1984) writes, "For the very small child the supreme experience is of a very small place, complete in itself, and perfect in its completeness" (p. 206). Through their drawings and writings, the Shay Avenue children remind us of the importance of *their* homes and families. If we draw a visual representation (interpretation) of the contextual worlds (see Taylor 1987) of the lives of these children, it would look like the illustration in Figure 5–1.

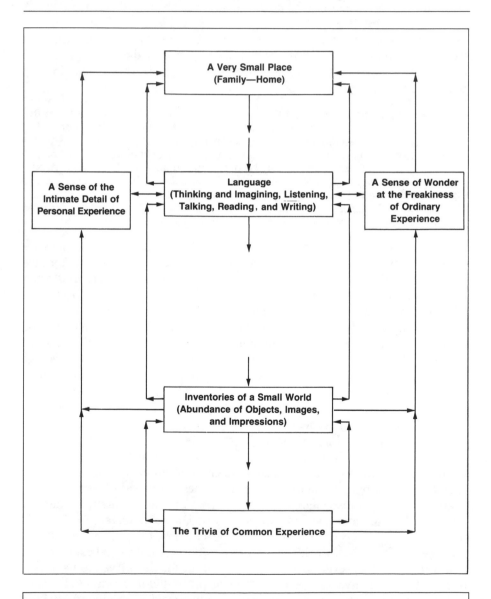

Figure 5–1 • The (Con)textual Worlds of Childhood

We would begin with a very small place (see Hart and Chawla 1980): the children's homes and families, reflected in the houses that they drew and the "I love you" notes that they wrote. Within these homes, where the children live with their families, they learn to think about the world, experience living and imagine life, listen to others, talk, read, and write.

We are lucky, for through the children's use of language we can become privy to their sense of the intimate detail of their own personal lives, and we can begin to appreciate their sense of wonder at the freakiness of ordinary experience. One day during the summer of 1984 we asked Tasmika, then age nine, to draw a map of her neighborhood. (See Figure 5–2.) Tasmika began by drawing the apartment building in which she lived. Tasmika talked as she drew. "This is the porch," she said. "This is the steps." "This is the chimney." She talked about the shape of the chimney and showed us in her drawing how it appeared to her. She put the number of the building on the wall and wrote the name of the street underneath. Then she drew another building. "This Burger King," she said. "This is the inside of Burger King. These are the people—I mean the chairs. And these are the people taking the customers."

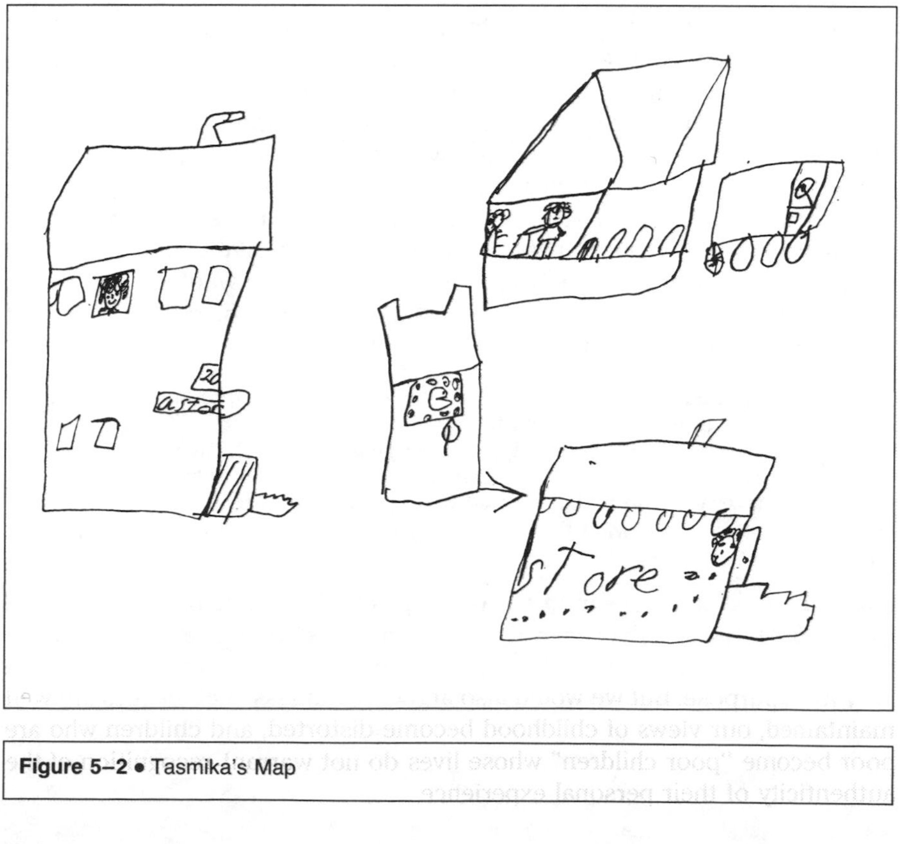

Figure 5–2 • Tasmika's Map

Tasmika continued to talk. "And this is a customer. He's diggin' in his pocket to get out his money." Tasmika drew the customer's legs. "Puttin' on pants," she said. "And this is a truck." Tasmika paused in her explanation and continued to draw. "And this is his truck." She drew the wheels, "One, two, three, four." Jamaine was watching her. "Where's the door?" he said. Tasmika drew. "Here's the door," she said, "and the handle." Then she drew the steering wheel. "Here's the horn," she told us. "You go, 'BEEP BEEP BEEP Beep-beep BEEP.' " One of Tasmika's friends arrived while she was drawing, and we asked Tasmika where the friend lived. Tasmika said that she lived "upstairs." She returned to her drawing and drew her friend looking out of an upstairs window in her apartment building. We asked Tasmika where she went to buy candy. She said, "To the store." Tasmika drew the store and told us that it was "around the corner." "Here's somebody going in," she said. "Somebody just went in. Here they are. Peekin' through the door." Tasmika drew the candy in the store and told us that Pac-Man was also inside. She drew the video game in a space between her buildings and an arrow to indicate that the machine was inside the store.

It is not difficult for us to "see" in Tasmika's talking and drawing her sense of the intimate detail of her everyday life. Tasmika has spent time looking up at the chimney that sits high on the top of her apartment building. She has watched as customers "dig" in their pockets to find money for the hamburgers that they order. She has observed people as they enter the store and can talk about their movements as they are "peekin' through the door." From her drawing and the way she talks as she works, we can gain some understanding of the abundance of objects, images, and impressions that are a part of her small world. The intimate detail of Tasmika's personal experience and her sense of wonder at the freakiness (whimsical/quixotic nature) of ordinary experience is uniquely fashioned; however, we would argue that, in similar ways, all children help to create the worlds in which they live. Colin Turnbull puts this better than we can when he says:

In all cultures, at all times known to us, the children are a source of wonderment for they are the supreme example of the human potential for creation. They are themselves filled with wonder during their first years, as the strange world around them slowly reveals itself. Their wonderment is one of the major tools that will shape their destiny, for in looking at the world around them they have to discover not just what things are, what they can do to or with them, but what things *mean* for children. (1983, p. 25)

For some this may appear to be a romanticized portrait of childhood; we would agree that if such images of the lives of young children are not balanced with more realistic pictures of their day-to-day lives, such images can serve very little purpose. But we would also argue that unless such images are well maintained, our views of childhood become distorted, and children who are poor become "poor children" whose lives do not warrant recognition of the authenticity of their personal experience.

Again we return to the children of the Shay Avenue neighborhood, this time to a map that was drawn by Hakim when he was in first grade. Ieshea gave us many of the pictures that Hakim drew, and we can see in them the same sense of wonder and intimate detail that was contained in the other children's drawings. However, when we asked him to draw a map of his neighborhood he interpreted the request in a different way from Tasmika. What Hakim did was to draw a series of intersecting and interconnecting lines to represent the streets in his neighborhood. When he had finished we asked him to show us where his house was on the map. Hakim pointed to the middle of his map and, as he did not wish to write, one of us wrote for him. We asked him to show us where his friend lived and where he went to school. Hakim pointed off the map in answer to each of our questions, and we wrote the names of the places we had asked him about on the roads that led in the direction of where he was pointing. (See Figure 5–3.)

Hakim's map reminded us of our conversation with Pauline and Trisha about the location of essential services, and of our conversations with Jerry about the buses he had to take and the time it took for him to get to the factory where he worked. The map came to symbolize for us the societal

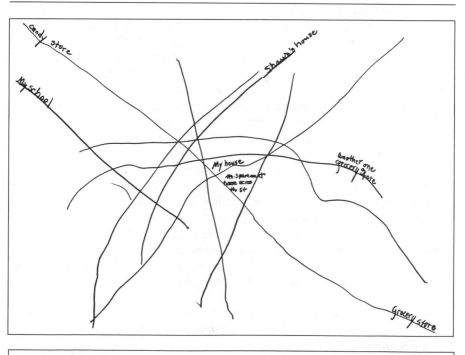

Figure 5–3 ● Hakim's Map

dislocation of the families that we visited, and the *acquired* deprivation of
the children. Their opportunities were limited by the lack of services in the
neighborhood in which they lived and the lack of resources in the schools
that they attended. Thus, as they grew, they became increasingly isolated
from the outside world. There were times when we visited the families that
the situation seemed hopeless, desperate, beyond our (educators', researchers', and policymakers') ability to change. But then we would think about
Tasmika's map and all the drawings and "I love you" notes written by the
children in the Shay Avenue neighborhood, and we would remember that like
all children they shared the sense of wonder of which Turnbull spoke, and
we would realize that their situation is not hopeless at all.

While we wait for the governmental support for families that is so urgently
needed, we can make changes in their schools that will begin to make a
difference. We can start by recognizing that the "negative" aspects of the lives
of inner-city children (this applies to all children but especially those placed
at risk by society) are significant factors in the development of their creative
potential. We cannot ignore what John Dewey (1938) referred to as "the
intimate and necessary relation between processes of actual experience and
education." Queenie's descriptions of the journeys that she made with her
mother and brother to get buckets of cold water from the tap in the basement
of the abandoned building in which she lived were rich in detail and vividly
told, but in her classroom there was no opportunity for her to tell the tale
or to write about her experience. The abundance of objects, images, and
impressions that filled her day-to-day world did not fit on the "dittos" that
she copied from the board. In our visits to the school that Queenie attended
we remember, as we do for Shauna, the rows of orderly desks, the board
work, and the lines for the bathroom. We have no doubt that most of the
teachers that we met cared for the children in their classrooms; yet few of
the teachers knew much about the children's everyday lives. The doors of
the school were locked when the children went inside. The teachers focused,
as they were expected to do, upon the curriculum that was set and the
preparation for the tests that were to be given. The impact upon teachers of
the administrative requirements for children to do well on the tests left no
time for them to learn about the lives of the children that they taught.

What a difference it would make if curriculum practices and procedures
enabled teachers to create classroom environments in which they are given
the opportunity to legitimize the literacy learning of their students by encouraging them through reading and writing to:

1. Help them appreciate their own configurations of reading and writing.
2. Develop/maintain/expand upon personal images of themselves as literate learners.
3. Think about the ways in which they can use reading and writing in
   their everyday lives and in job-related situations.

Unfortunately, our schools are not easily arranged to provide opportunities for teachers to share such experiences with their students. In an article in *Phi Delta Kappan*, Larry Cuban (1986) made this point when he wrote, "State mandates aimed at getting teachers to teach more and better may serve instead to freeze into place a practical pedagogy that is ill-suited to stretch students' minds." In the drive to raise standards (as measured through tests of achievement) there is little room for teachers and children to think, develop, maintain, expand, or appreciate the literate lives of one another. Literacy becomes a series of disconnected skills or a set of comprehension exercises that some learn and others do not.

In the families that we visited, most of the children were able to maintain the shift between home and school and sustain both worlds. At home, their parents provided literate environments plus support for their children in school and balanced these aspects of family life with their strong desire for their children to become independent survivors in a sometimes hostile world. In school, the children learned that their survival demanded different skills, and that they were dependent upon their teachers. Their daily lives and their complex social and cognitive communicative abilities were not relevant to the definitions of school learning, which were limited by the exercises that were given and the tests that were set. Is it possible that Danny knew that when he dropped out of school before he had completed eighth grade? How many children are there like Danny who have learned to survive, who are productive members of their social world, but who cannot translate this productivity into the ways in which their schools expect them to learn? Danny could read and write. He was articulate and bright. Would he have made it if his teachers had been able to recognize his creative potential for learning and legitimize his literate life? From our conversations with Danny, and from observations of him when he was with his family, we are convinced that he could have done well.

In building the position that we have presented for your consideration, we are left asking ourselves some important questions:

1. What if teachers and policymakers reject the mythical thinking of test givers and technocrats and opt instead for the scientific thought of the many researchers and scholars who seek local knowledge through their observations and work with teachers and children in classrooms and community settings?
2. What if teachers take that local knowledge and build a vision with their children of a participatory democratic society in which everyone has the opportunity to contribute and prosper?

Jerry Harste's work (1986) provides at least one answer to these questions:

The activities we plan are not sacrosanct. They are neither inherently good or inherently bad. There is always more from where they came from. If educators understand the relationship between the *paper curriculum* and the *real curriculum* then it should be clear why children must be our curricular informants. We've let tests and materials be our curricular informants, but this was wrong. Instruction, in the final analysis, is the theory of meaning that gets played out in transactions between learners of all sizes in classrooms. To understand instruction is to understand practical theory. (pp. 64–65)

We would add to this statement that not only have we let tests and materials be our curricular informants, but we have also used them to grade and sort the students who pass through our educational institutions. Thus it was possible for Ieshea and Jerry to grow up literate and yet fail in school. We expect students to excel on narrowly defined tasks, yet give no credit for the complex communicative skills that are so essential to everyday life. If we accept this position, another question follows: How can we justify or formally sanction approaches to the teaching of reading and writing in schools that rely so heavily upon outmoded and rigidly predetermined curricular practices?

Literacy cannot be treated as a neutral technology. In our construction of literate environments for children in school we need to begin by:

1. Considering the ways in which children can grow in the imagination of their own social experiences.
2. Recognizing the complex communicative abilities that are a part of children's everyday lives, so that every child is given the opportunity to experience a private sense of challenge and a public sense of achievement.

Again, we are not suggesting a parody of uses but using literacy for genuine purposes—social, technical, and aesthetic. The Shay Avenue families can help us in this endeavor. Their determined survival and the ways in which they provide for their children create for us the opportunity to learn of the many ways in which we can help families with young children who are surviving under such stress that they cannot always support the education of their children. At a time of changing social realities, when more and more children come from families who are homeless, single-parent families in which the parent is working for minimum wage or is unemployed, or families in which both parents are struggling to maintain a home together, our concern must be for the social welfare of their children. School policies should enable teachers to create classroom environments in which the nurturing of young children is not separated from their academic instruction. Teachers should be encouraged to establish with their students expectations of cooperation and participation within supportive frameworks of rules that do not necessitate the imposition of unrealistic organizational structures and unreasonable controls. Finally, every attempt should be made to create an atmosphere that places value on the children's growing sense of competence and independence so that their lives are not separated from the outside world. Such policies, if promoted by our schools, would depend upon close contact between teachers and parents. Family and community involvement in school programs would be essential, and our children would surely benefit from the connections that were being made in their everyday lives. We must love them, engage their imaginations, laugh with them, and sometimes cry. The vividness of children's experiences should not be dulled by the pedantry of programs that lack respect for their everyday lives.

Afterword
Apprenticeship in Ethnography

Catherine Dorsey-Gaines

> Then, if you are doing ethnography or natural history, you record carefully what your attention has allowed you to see. Knowing that you will not see everything and that others will see differently, but recording whatever you can so it will be part of the cumulative record.
>
> Mary Catherine Bateson

Let me go back. Denny came to the college to interview for a position in the Early Childhood and Family Studies department. She came well prepared, with a background in family studies, reading, and curriculum development. Her enthusiasm for teaching was such that all who spoke with her caught the fire. Yes, she would definitely complement the other personalities in the department—she was just as concerned and excited about thinking and learning as the other members of the faculty. The department had made an excellent choice.

One day as we sat in my office, Denny talked about the work she had done on her dissertation, which was about to be published. She talked about the families and the children she had studied. Her zeal for the subject was electrifying. I began to think of my classroom experiences and the families of children I knew who were successful in school. These children came from very different economic situations from the suburban families that Denny had studied, but their families' interest in learning and wanting their children to be successful was just as great.

Denny seemed interested in what I was saying. She seemed almost excited. Her question was "Can you introduce me to such a family?" I was floored by her question, because of course I knew many such families, but to produce one right then was a startling idea. I had not taught a class of children on a consistent basis in several years. At that time I was working as a supervisor twice a week and a demonstration teacher once a week in three urban parochial kindergarten classrooms. However, I was certain that I could easily find such families. All the children in the kindergarten classes were potential candidates. Denny queried further, and as she spoke, a particular family came into my mind.

I knew of a family, a nontraditional family that was low on the economic scale, one that problems seemed to follow like a gray cloud ready to burst with rain at any given moment. What were the characteristics of this family that correlated or were similar to those of the families Denny had studied? Maybe there were none. But the criteria Denny had set were clear; and this family did have a six-year-old who was perceived by her mother as successfully learning to read and write. This criterion, at least, had been met. And if there was one such family, surely there would be others—I was certain of it.

The first problem—identifying a suitable family—was solved. The next was getting in touch with them. I knew that this family lived in another town. I had not seen them in quite some time, and they did not have a telephone. Further, I did not know the address, though I could remember the general location of the street and the house. However, since I had lost contact with them after the young woman's mother had passed away, I was not certain she would be where I had last seen her. I began to worry; the problems were mounting. Why had I mentioned to Denny with such conviction that these children did indeed exist? The existence of the children was not the problem, but finding them certainly was.

Help, however, was on the way. My son Jeff was on school break, and I presented the problem to him. His immediate response was, "Mom, let's go! We'll find them." We met Denny and set off to find the family. Jeff's determination to help us succeed marked the beginning of our research.

Now, as I look back, finding the families was actually the easy part. Delving through the literature in a new area while keeping up with my own field of study was and continues to be the most difficult part of this project.

Webster's defines an apprentice as "one who is learning by practical experience under skilled workers a trade, art, or calling; an inexperienced person." This definition seemed appropriate. Even though I had been an educator for over twenty-five years, an educator involved with quantitative research and other academic areas of seeking and exploring, I was a beginner at ethnography. After one has taught for many years, one begins to see patterns forming and pieces of puzzles fitting together. However, it is almost impossible to see the many phases of literacy that are within the complex structure of children's learning.

I had successfully taught children reading, but I had been more concerned about the curricular area of reading and not so much the foundations of literacy. I had wanted to develop or reinforce skills and prepare activities that developed along a skills continuum. Individual and group learning was important to me, though, and I was especially curious about the individual differences of children. I was interested in designing a diagnostic tool to answer such questions as: What skills do children have? What concepts have they mastered? Can they think critically? Can they make generalizations? I was also concerned with how I could examine the level of functioning of a child for any given skill or concept. I wanted to know how children learned concepts, and thus how reading was experienced. Of course, my concern was based upon the patterns of children's development and the importance of parents in this developmental process, but I did not consider the impact of the family on literacy an important aspect of learning.

Because I was bringing to our team a curriculum background, the issues that concerned me were whether the learning experiences were similar for all of the children we would be studying. Should there be a common offering of experience, a common curriculum that would ensure success and eradicate individual differences? How would looking at families and the effect of the learning style on the child be different from the way curricula were traditionally developed? Were societal forces and educational trends making changes in the kinds of pressure families felt? The question that concerned me most was whether ethnographic research was a legitimate and useful tool for education or just a fad.

It took very few words and very little time before I became convinced of the usefulness of ethnographic research.

Over the months, Denny introduced me to ethnographers, wrote proposals so that we would become conference participants, and introduced me to ethnographic conferences, where we presented our research in symposiums, talks, and workshops. Through all this I listened, I wrote, and most of all, I observed.

My constant questions at the beginning were "Are we getting any data?" "Are we wasting our time?" "Is this really ethnographic research?" "How do I define it to others?" "Are the families participating in a manner so that we will be able to get information that can be considered worthwhile?" "Are we just making friends and not engaging in a study?" "Are we being helpful?" "Do they really like us?" "Are we disrupting their lives?" "Are we intruders?" "What will happen to these families after our research is over?"

Questions, questions—I had millions of them! Step by step, as we began the research and methodically moved into the lives of these families, my questions were answered. Some were answered immediately; others, in our weekly meetings; and still others, as we neared the end of the study. To all my questions, Denny consistently replied, "Write it down, Cathé. Whatever you observe, write it down." She cautioned, "Be descriptive. Quote dialogues. Give a setting, look around, and note specifics. Jot down the time. Write critically, and state things event by event. Time is important; so is who was present and how things were stated. Be thorough."

Sometimes I thought I was being too specific; then, as Denny and I wrote to each other and talked, I found I was not being specific at all. I prayed for her not to lose her patience and for me not to lose mine. At times I felt Denny was making mountains out of molehills, yet who was I to make the assessment? As it turned out, she was always correct in her judgment.

A shared enthusiasm for the work characterized our visits to the families.

This neophyte researcher was on a constant high and wrote everything down. Afterwards, it was a revelation to discuss the logs we kept and exchanged with one another. We would observe the same scene but see different things, although there was never an occasion on which we disagreed about what we saw. Thus, we were able to build complementary and supportive perspectives, with the writing of one informing the commentary of the other.

Gaining access to the families each week was not easy. They welcomed us and made us feel at home once we entered their dwellings, but I could not get over the feeling that maybe we were intruding. In the beginning, we were strangers in a foreign land. Picture, if you can, this multiracial team, one in a suit, pocketbook, gloves, and hat, the other in sports attire; we didn't look part of the environment. We were variously thought to be social workers, people from the welfare office, or just someone coming to give the families "grief" (this last notion was stated by one of the mothers).

Soon, however, we became friends of the neighborhood people. They queried us about our whereabouts if we had been absent the previous week, appearing to have sincerely missed us. Members of the staff of the neighborhood school were friendly, cooperative, and concerned. They were interested in our work and questioned us. (However, when we asked them for Queenie's address and whether she was in school that day, they were extremely protective and refused to give us her address. Although we were frustrated in our attempt to locate Queenie and Tanya that day, we knew that the school authorities were only doing their jobs.)

Denny constantly reviewed the literature as we worked. Everything we did was for a purpose and could be supported by some expert in literature, philosophy, architecture, language development, anthropology, psychology, or education. This I probably enjoyed most. As I broadened my scope, I could incorporate my new learning with my classroom experience in child development and curriculum and multicultural understanding.

As we continued the research, I realized that Denny was allowing us to develop a model for fieldwork procedures. However, she would be the first to assert that there is no such thing as a standard way of doing fieldwork. Because of the individuality of each study, one should only use a model to understand or learn the craft. One should not use it as a single path on which to proceed.

Through this study, I learned that every part of a child's environment is a place of learning. Allowing children to draw from their environment, to photograph their environment, encouraged the children to "become," and literacy would spring forth. I learned to use my ears, develop my sight, and recognize their worth. Memories were revived. I remembered things I had pushed aside for years. I also relinquished baggage that had attached itself to my thinking. Looking at the children, I felt them, heard them, smelled them, and tasted their lives. I became a part of the families; I held them and tasted their language. I listened, I learned. I participated, I grew. I remembered, I understood.

About ethnographic research, Turnbull asserts:

We are likely to discover more about ourselves than about others, and in so doing discover unknown riches in our own lives. (1983, p. 16)

Through this study, and with the guidance of an experienced ethnographer, I acquired riches to add to a lifetime of academic experiences. Living with the Shay Avenue families enriched my life and added to my knowledge in an impressive way. It is an experience I will remember forever.

Appendices

Appendices

Appendix A

Fieldwork as a Mode of Inquiry

Denny Taylor

The researcher working with informants/participants:

1. Brings an anthropological perspective to the philosophical and theoretical framework of the research endeavor.
2. Is interested in some aspect of the life situations of a particular group of people (family/community/school).
3. Has little knowledge of the particular group to be studied (but has extensive knowledge of more general literature, from novels through social science literature to history and biographies).
4. Is interested in generating interpretations (fine-grained analyses) of the status quo.
5. Studies aspects of life situations in context.
6. Begins with the question "How do my informants/participants construct the life situations in which I am interested [sharing stories/playing games/going to school]?"
7. Devises ways of collecting data with the informants/participants (note taking/audio recording/taking photographs).
8. Employs theoretical sampling procedures (may begin with a single informant/participant).
9. Allows data collection to evolve as the study proceeds.
10. Begins data collection on the first day of meeting with the informants/participants.
11. Generates hypotheses as the study develops.
12. Holds hypotheses in readiness to be accepted or rejected as further data is obtained.
13. Moves constantly between data collection and data analysis.
14. Discusses the inferences/hypotheses generated in the research with the informants/participants. (It is their construction of everyday life that the researcher tries to reconstruct.)
15. Presents the findings in a form that is readable by a general audience.

16. Presents sufficient data for alternative interpretations to be generated.
17. Provides the informants/participants with the opportunity to read the account of the research and includes their interpretations and comments in the final text.

Appendix B

Methodological Notes: A Plan of the Research

Denny Taylor

The plan of the research presented here was part of an attempt to clearly articulate the conceptual framework of the Shay Avenue study. It emerged out of the early phases of the research and was intended to give direction to the several years of research that followed. The plan was submitted to the National Institute of Education (Taylor and Dorsey-Gaines, 1983b), but was not funded. However, the reviews were encouraging and supportive. The research continued, and although we did not receive financial support, the writing of the NIE proposal had provided us with an opportunity to create a framework for the research to guide us through the subsequent years.

The Conceptual Framework for the Empirical Study

While our first concern is to develop research techniques that are sensitive to the unique complexities of the family, our main concern is in developing ways of studying literacy in a family context. Thus the study will be firmly grounded in the wealth of information gleaned from existing literacy research; in the findings of anthropological research, which has particular significance to family studies; and in research that focuses specifically upon Black family life. It is within this context that the work of such researchers as Anderson, Teale, and Estrada (1980), Billingsley (1968), Cremin (1976), Hill (1971), Leichter (1973, 1974, 1978), McDermott (1976a, 1976b), Scribner and Cole (1981), and Sulzby (1981) is significant both in the formulation of the conceptual frame and methods to be employed in the proposed study.

Discussing the consequences of literacy, Akinnaso (1981) speaks of the importance of using the learner's social, cultural, and linguistic background for the structuring of school instruction. It is within this context that he notes the promise of such researchers as Heath and Szwed. In a paper entitled "The Ethnography of Literacy," Szwed (1977) states,

There is in this sort of study a need to keep literacy within the logic of the everyday lives of people; to avoid cutting these skills off from the conditions which affect

223

them in direct and indirect ways; to shun needless abstraction and reductionist models; in short to stay as close as possible to real cases, individual examples, in order to gain the strength of evidence that comes with being able to examine specific cases in great depth and complexity. (p. 15)

Szwed succinctly describes the broad conceptual frame that we feel is essential for the exploration of the family contexts in which young children learn to read and write. Such a conceptual framework can adequately accommodate the inevitable complexities of a study that recognizes the multiple everyday contexts in which a diversity of literacies are a part of a child's world; and the employment of this ethnographic approach provides the data collection procedures that are essential if we are to capture that world.

The Major Organizing Questions Explored in the Study

The organizing questions have evolved from the early family literacy research of Taylor (1981, 1983) and Taylor and Dorsey-Gaines (1982) and from the concurrent synthesis of the literature (see Szwed 1977):

1. Literacy in the neighborhood:
   a) What positions do reading and writing hold in the local environment, and what is the range of their social, cultural, and political functions and uses?
   b) What are the constraints limiting the functions and uses of literacy within the local environment?
2. Family literacy:
   a) How do the personal biographies and educative styles of the families shape the literate experiences of the children?
   b) How do the children initiate, absorb, and synthesize the educational influences in their lives?
   c) Why and under what circumstances do family members read and write?
   d) How are reading and writing used socially by family members and by children?
   e) How do the children represent knowledge of their world in and out of print?
3. Family literacy and literacy in school:
   a) What is the relationship between the teaching of reading and writing in school and the families' needs and wishes for literacy?
   b) What is the relationship between the teaching of reading and writing in school and the families' styles and values of literacy?
   c) What are the interrelationships between the ways in which the children are taught to read and write in school and the ways in which they learn to read and write at home?
   d) How do the children's experiences of everyday literacy help or hinder them as they learn to read and write in school?

4. Literacy in a broad societal context:
   How can schools build relational contexts in which Black children living in poor urban environments can be taught the functions and uses of print so that they will be able to move effectively into the larger societal context while still maintaining their own culture?

The Participating Families

Beattie (1964) stresses that it is more useful to make comparisons between institutions (in this instance, the family) that have similar backgrounds and contexts than it is to compare institutions that have very different backgrounds and contexts. He emphasizes that there may be great differences in the social significance of that which is described, adding that "to compare things implies that in at least some respect they are different as well as that they are similar, and differences are only meaningful against comparable backgrounds" (p. 48). With these thoughts in mind, rather than pursue any notion of sociological representation, we believe it is important to select families who live in the same neighborhood. Thus the notion of comparability will be established for variations to be explored.

Data Collection

The qualitative field research procedures to be employed in the proposed study are similar to those used by Taylor (1981) and Taylor and Dorsey-Gaines (1982) in their prior studies of family literacy. The procedures, which are firmly grounded in the ethnographic tradition of Frake (1962), Hymes (1974, 1980), and McDermott (1978), are synthesized for the reading field by Green and Bloome (1983) in their comprehensive description of adequate criteria for ethnographic research in educational settings.

A variety of data collection procedures will be employed, including ethnographic techniques as described by Pelto and Pelto (1978), and Spradley (1979). Any aspect of the lives of the families will be of interest in the early stages of the research, and it is hoped that, by the setting of such broad boundaries, any preconceived notions that we have of family literacy will be less restricting. New approaches to data collection will be constantly sought (Mead and Metreaux, 1953), and the families will be encouraged to participate in this endeavor.

Participant observation. Fundamental to the success of the field research is the special role that the researchers develop and maintain as participant-observers. Pelto and Pelto (1978) speak of the need to legitimize "a kind of information-getting behavior that was not previously a part of social expectation within the community" (p. 182). Such a sensitive position takes time to establish and must be constantly renegotiated as the research proceeds.

Within the present context, the research of Taylor and Dorsey-Gaines (1982) has enabled them to establish the legitimacy of their presence within the local community in which the proposed study will take place. New families will be sought as the researchers network within the community. Fieldnotes will be kept from the first meeting with each prospective family, and detailed accounts will be kept of all subsequent meetings. Everyday activities, such as talking with friends, going shopping, and visiting social service agencies, will become a part of the research agenda as an attempt is made to describe the margins of awareness and moment-to-moment literate activities of the individual families, as well as more explicit literacy tasks such as reading newspapers and doing homework.

Recorded conversations. Many open-ended conversations will be audio-recorded with individual family members in which questions pertaining to literacy will be embedded within the more general discussion of everyday family life. Such conversations will be audio-recorded with grandparents, aunts, uncles and other relatives as well as with parents as an attempt is made to construct a multigenerational perspective of the personal biographies and educative styles of family members. The data will add another dimension to the analysis of the multiple contexts in which the children experience print on a daily basis and will add to our notion of family literacy.

Photographic observation. In a paper published in *Studies in Visual Communication*, Worth (1980) argues that "the photo is an aide-memoire to the scientist equal to his pencil, notebook or typewriter" (p. 17). This is undoubtedly true but, like Worth, who writes of the photographic studies of Mead, Bateson, and Birdwhistell, we would also argue that the photographs themselves do not have any intrinsic merit. For it is the pictorial images as structured representations that can be analyzed that are important. The recent experience of Taylor and Dorsey-Gaines (1983a) in the use of still photography suggests that it will provide the researchers with the opportunity to record the everyday social and cultural circumstances of literacy use. Photographs will be taken of the family members as they go about their daily lives, and special attention will be given to the task of capturing family literacy occasions as they occur within the ongoing events of everyday life. Thus, photographs will be taken of family life that include such events as the filling in of forms for a school fund-raising candy sale and the doing of crossword puzzles (both literacy activities observed within the community of the proposed study); and these photographs will then be used in discussions about literacy with family members.

Observations of the children at home and at school. Every attempt will be made to observe the children as they go about their everyday lives. Observations will be made of the children as they interact with their families and with their friends. The children will also be observed at school. Each child will be observed as he or she moves through one entire school day (see Barker and Wright, 1966). These observations are particularly important for the questions focusing on family literacy and literacy in school (see above). The observation will begin when the child gets up in the morning and will continue as the transition is made from home to school. Detailed notes will be made throughout the day and will continue as the child returns home after school.

Children as ethnographers.   Wagner (1979) states that "we simply have not seen enough of what people do and the physical contexts in which it is done." He continues, "We know too little about how people themselves see the settings and their activities" (p. 286). Hart (1979) in his everyday study of children's experience of place, addresses this issue and urges researchers to hold in abeyance "reflective abstraction and to engage the landscape along with the children." In the proposed study, the children themselves will play a vital part in sharing their world. One of the ways in which children will be encouraged to participate is through the use of still photography. The children will be given cameras to take pictures of the important places in the neighborhood and of the print in their everyday environment. The photographs will then be used as the basis for conversations about the multiple uses of reading and writing in their everyday world. The discussions will be audio-recorded. It is in this way that we hope to gain access to what Erickson (1982) has called "the crucial sites in everyday life, situations of time, place, and action where learning is most likely to be occurring" (p. 163).

Collection of artifacts.   Levine (1982) stresses that "we cannot afford to ignore the content and functions of written materials" and argues that "the information that they contain is a strategic social resource" (p. 263). In the proposed study, detailed accounts will be made of the content and functions of the print in each home, and every attempt will be made to gain an in-depth understanding of the ways in which the families themselves use print in their daily lives. Attention will be paid to their needs and wishes for, and styles and values of, print to determine the positions reading and writing hold within the family setting. To accomplish this task, individual family members will be asked to show us the print in their home (see Taylor 1981). Thus, rather than the collection of inert lists, the data will contain not only the items of print but also information pertaining to the ways in which each item is (or is not) used as a social resource by individual family members. Collections will be made of the children's writing endeavors, and these will be discussed with the children themselves as well as with the parents.

Data Analysis

The purpose of the data analysis will be to develop a narrative account that minimizes the levels of reconstruction and provides a description of experience within a clearly stated theoretical frame. Data analysis will begin on the first day and will continue throughout the study as the researchers move through the multiple levels of data, seeking recurring themes that can be explored in greater depth in the field through the collaborative process and through the concurrent synthesis of the literature. This will lead to the articulation and refinement of emerging patterns as a continual attempt is made to expand the process of conceptualization. Thus, in a very real sense, data collection and analysis become interrelated phases of a single process, and verification changes in complexity as it becomes part of the process of discovery (Diesing 1971, p. 230).

A separate file will be maintained for each family as an attempt is made to capture the richness and originality of their individual lives. This will enable us to build an in-depth description of the educative styles and personal biographies of the families, which will provide, in great detail, a structured version of the ways in which the children themselves initiate, absorb, and synthesize the educational influences in their lives. The data will also be filed according to the analytic themes and categories that emerge as the multiple levels of data are obtained. It is in this way that we will develop an account of the study that will enlarge our understanding of the learning styles, coping strategies, and social support systems of young children living in poverty who are successfully learning to read and write. At the same time, we will develop an account that will directly address the question of how schools can build relational contexts in which Black children living in poor urban environments can be taught the functions and uses of print so that they can move effectively into the larger societal context while maintaining their own culture.

Methodological Issues

Research as a collaborative venture. The proposed study is a collaborative venture with the participants, but it is also a collaborative venture between researchers. The two principal investigators represent a multiracial team and as such they have worked together for the past two years. It has been a time of sounding ideas and exchanging thoughts as sensitive issues have been explored; as Merton (1972), in his seminal paper on the sociology of knowledge, writes, "Insiders and outsiders in the domain of knowledge unite. . . . You have a world of understanding to win" (p. 44). It is within this context that a critical measure of understanding will be gained of the social, cultural, and political contexts of literacy acquisition.

Access without intrusion. We have already emphasized the important role of the participants in such field research. Their cooperation and support is essential for the success of the venture. But how much of their lives can a researcher reasonably ask a family to share? Where are the boundaries, and how are they to be established? The question of access without intrusion (Taylor 1979) will be addressed early in the study and will be resolved on a day-to-day basis in the ongoing dialogue between researchers and participants. We believe that it is through our willingness to involve the families in the research process that we will be able to establish boundaries in an atmosphere of mutual trust and cooperation.

References

Akinnaso, F. N. 1981. The consequences of literacy in pragmatic and theoretical perspectives. *Anthropology and Education* 12 (3): 163–200.

Anderson, A. B., W. B. Teale, and E. Estrada. 1980. Low income children's preschool literacy experiences: Some naturalistic observations. *The Quarterly Newsletter of the Laboratory for Human Cognition* 2–3: 59–65.

Barker, R. G., and H. F. Wright. [1951] 1966. *One boy's day: A specimen record of behavior.* Hamden, CT: Archon Books.

Bateson, G. 1958. *Naven.* Stanford, CA: Stanford University Press.

Bateson, M. C. 1984. *With a daughter's eye: A memoir of Margaret Mead and Gregory Bateson.* New York: William Morrow.

Beattie, J. 1964. *Other cultures.* New York: The Free Press.

Billingsley, A. 1968. *Black families in white America.* Englewood Cliffs, NJ: Prentice-Hall.

Bloome, D. 1983. Reading as a social process. In B. Hutson (ed.), *Advances in reading—Language research.* Vol. 2. Greenwich, CT: JAI Press.

Bloome, D., and E. Theodorou. In press. Multiple layers of classroom discourse: Where teachers and students stand. In J. L. Green, J. O. Harker, and C. Wallet (eds.), *Multiple perspective analysis of classroom discourse.* Norwood, NJ: Ablex.

Boyer, E. L. 1983. *High school: A report on secondary education in America.* New York: Harper & Row.

Children's Defense Fund. 1986. *A children's defense budget: An analysis of the FY1987 federal budget and children.* Washington, DC: Children's Defense Fund.

Coe, R. N. 1984. *When the grass was taller: Autobiography and the experience of childhood.* New Haven: Yale University Press.

Comer, J. P. 1980. *School power: Implications of an intervention project.* New York: The Free Press.

Cremin, L. A. 1976. *Public education.* New York: Basic Books.

Cuban, L. 1986. Persistent instruction: Another look at constancy in the classroom. *Phi Delta Kappan* 68 (1): 7–11.

Davis, F. G. 1981. Economics and mobility: A theoretical rationale for urban Black family well-being. In H. P. McAdoo (ed.), *Black families.* Beverly Hills: Sage Publications.

Dewey, J. 1938. *Experience and education.* Kappa Delta Pi Lecture Series. New York: Collier Books Edition, 1963.

Diamant, A. 1986. Teen-age pregnancy and the Black family. *The Boston Globe Magazine*, May 18. pp. 19, 20, 22, 24, 26, 28, 30, 32, 34, 36, 38, 43, 45, 47.

Diesing, P. 1971. *Patterns of discovery in the social sciences.* Chicago: Aldine-Atherton.

Ehrenreich, B. 1986. Poor mom. A review of *Woman and children last: The plight of poor women in affluent America. The Atlantic* (April): 125–30.

Erickson, F. 1982. Taught cognitive learning in its immediate environments: A neglected topic in the anthropology of education. *Anthropology of Education* 13 (2): 149–80.

Florio, S., and J. Shultz. 1979. Social competence at home and at school. *Theory into Practice* 18 (4): 234–43.

Frake, C. O. 1962. Cultural ecology and ethnography. *American Anthropologist* 64: 53–59. Reprinted in A. S. Dil (ed.), *Language and cultural description: Essays of Charles O. Frake.* Stanford, CA: Stanford University Press, 1980.

Gardner, H. 1980. *Artful scribbles: The significance of children's drawings.* New York: Basic Books.

Geertz, C. 1983. *Local knowledge: Further essays in interpretive anthropology.* New York: Basic Books.

Georges, R. A., and M. O. Jones. 1980. *People studying people: The human element in fieldwork.* Berkeley: University of California Press.

Gilmore, P., and A. Glatthorn. 1982. *Children in and out of school.* Washington, DC: Center for Applied Linguistics.

Goodman, N. 1982. The way the world is. In E. Bredo and W. Feinberg (eds.), *Knowledge and values in social and educational research.* Philadelphia: Temple University Press.

Goodman, Y. 1986. Children coming to know literacy. In W. H. Teale and E. Sulzby (eds.), *Emergent literacy: Writing and reading.* Norwood, NJ: Ablex.

Goodman, Y. M., and B. Altwerger. 1981. *Print awareness in preschool children: A study of the development of literacy in preschool children.* Occasional Paper No. 4. Tucson: Program in Language and Literacy, University of Arizona.

Green, J. L. 1983. Research on teaching as a linguistic process: A state of the art. In E. Gordon (ed.), *Review of Research in Education.* Washington, DC: American Educational Research Association.

Green, J. L., and D. Bloome. 1983. Ethnography and reading: Issues, directions, and findings. In J. Niles (ed.), *Thirty-second yearbook of the National Reading Conference.* Rochester, NY: National Reading Conference.

Hale, J. E. 1982. *Black children: Their roots, culture, and learning styles.* Provo, Utah: Brigham Young University Press.

Hale-Benson, J. E. 1986. *Black children: Their roots, culture, and learning styles.* Rev. ed. Baltimore: The Johns Hopkins University Press.

Hansen, C. 1981. Living with normal families. *Family Process* 20 (1): 58–75.

Harrington, C. 1982. Anthropology and education: Issues from the issues. *Anthropology and Education Quarterly* 13 (4): 323–35.

Harste, J. C. 1986. Composition and composition instruction as projected code: Understanding semiotic universals and practical theory. Paper presented at New Directions in Composition Scholarship Conference, University of New Hampshire, Durham, New Hampshire.

Harste, J. C., V. A. Woodward, and C. L. Burke. 1984. *Language stories and literacy lessons.* Portsmouth, NH: Heinemann.

Hart, R. A. 1979. *Children's experience of place.* New York: Irvington Publishers.

Hart, R., and L. Chawla. 1980. The development of children's concern for the environment. Prepared for The International Institute for Environment and Society, Berlin, Federal Republic of Germany. Published in J. Wolwill and N. Watts (eds.), special issue of *Zeitschrift fur Umweltpolitik* on Environmental Psychology (Fall 1980).

Heap, J. L. 1986. Sociality and cognition in collaborative computer writing. A paper presented at the University of Michigan School of Education Conference on Literacy and Culture in Educational Settings, Ann Arbor, MI.

Heath, S. B. 1983. *Ways with words: Language, life, and work in communities and classrooms.* Cambridge, MA: Cambridge University Press.

Hill, R. B. 1971. *The strengths of Black families.* New York: Emerson Hall.

Hughes, L. 1951. What happens to a dream deferred? *The panther and the lash.* New York: Alfred A. Knopf.

Hymes, D. 1974. *Foundations in sociolinguistics: An ethnographic approach.* Philadelphia: University of Pennsylvania Press.

———. 1980. *Language in education: Ethnolinguistic essays.* Washington, DC: Center for Applied Linguistics.

Kellogg, R. 1970. *Analyzing children's art.* Palo Alto: Mayfield Publishing Company.

King, M. L. 1983. *The words of Martin Luther King, Jr.* Selected by C. S. King. New York: Newmarket Press.

Leichter, H. J. 1973. The concept of educative style. *Teachers College Record* 75: 239–50.

———. 1974. The family as educator. *Teachers College Record* 76: 175–217.

———. 1978. Families and communities as educators: Some concepts of relationship. *Teachers College Record* 79: 567–658.

Lelyveld, J. 1985. Hunger in America. *The New York Times Magazine.* June 16. 20–23, 51–53, 59, 68, 69.

Levine, K. 1982. Functional literacy: Fond illusions and false economies. *Harvard Educational Review* 52: 249–66.

Marklein, M. B. 1986. Parents: Help teachers teach your kids. *USA Today.* November 12. 1A.

McAdoo, H. P. 1981. *Black families.* Beverly Hills: Sage Publications.

McDermott, R. P. 1976a. Kids make sense: An ethnographic account of interactional management of success and failure in one first-grade classroom. Unpublished doctoral dissertation, Stanford University, Stanford, CA.

———. 1976b. Achieving school failure: An anthropological approach to illiteracy and social stratification. In H. Singer and R. Ruddel (eds.), *Theoretical models and processes in reading.* Newark, DE: International Reading Association.

———. 1978. Criteria for an ethnographically adequate description of concerted activities and their contexts. *Semiotica* 24 (3–4): 245–75.

Mead, M., and R. Metreaux. 1953. *The study of culture at a distance.* Chicago: University of Chicago Press.

Merton, R. K. 1972. Insiders and outsiders: A chapter in the sociology of knowledge. *American Journal of Sociology* 78: 9–47.

Morris, L. 1981. Women in poverty: Domestic organization among the poor of Mexico City. *Anthropology Quarterly* 54 (3): 117–24.

New York Regents'/Commissioner's Regional Conferences, The University of the State of New York and The State Education Department. 1986. *Education success for all: Better beginnings—Stronger completions.*

New York Times. 1986. Now you see him. *Business Magazine.* December 7. 78.

Pelto, P. J., and G. H. Pelto. 1978. *Anthropological research: The structure of inquiry.* New York: Cambridge University Press.

Rosenthal, P. 1984. *Words and values: Some leading words and where they lead us.* New York: Oxford University Press.

Schlesinger, B. 1982. Functioning families: Focus of the 1980's. *Family Perspectives* 16 (3): 111–16.

Scribner, S., and M. Cole. 1981. *The psychology of literacy.* Cambridge: Harvard University Press.

Spivak, H., and J. Albert. (1985). Causes of hunger. Letters to the Editor, *New York Times Magazine.* August 18. 78.

Spradley, J. P. 1979. *The ethnographic interview.* New York: Holt, Rinehart & Winston.

Stoppard, T. 1983. *The real thing.* (Reprinted with revisions.) London: Faber and Faber.

Sulzby, E. 1981. *Kindergarteners begin to read their own compositions: Beginning readers' developing knowledge about written language project.* Final report to the Research Foundation of the National Council of Teachers of English.

———. 1986. Writing and reading: Signs of oral and written language organization in the young child. In W. H. Teale and E. Sulzby (eds.), *Emergent literacy: Writing and reading.* Norwood, NJ: Ablex.

Szwed, J. F. 1977. The ethnography of literacy. Paper presented at the National Institute of Education Conference on Writing, Los Angeles.

Taylor, D. 1979. An ethnographic study of the family's role in the development of reading skills and values. Paper presented at the American Educational Research Association, San Francisco.

———. 1981. Family literacy: The social context of learning to read and write. Unpublished doctoral dissertation, Teachers College, Columbia University, New York.

———. 1982a. Cathé and the beginning of the project. Working paper.

———. 1982b. Translating children's everyday uses of print into classroom practice. *Language Arts* 59 (2): 546–49.

———. 1983. *Family literacy: Young children learning to read and write.* Portsmouth, NH: Heinemann.

———. 1987. The (con)textual worlds of childhood: An interpretive approach to alternative dimensions of experience. In B. Fillion, C. Hedley, and E. DiMartino (eds.), *Home and school: Early language and reading.* Norwood, NJ: Ablex.

———. In press a. Conversations on family talk. In *The power of talk.* Urbana, IL: National Council of Teachers of English.

———. In press b. Ethnographic educational evaluation: For children, families and schools. *Theory into Practice.*

Taylor, D., and C. Dorsey-Gaines. 1982. The cultural contexts of family literacy. Paper presented at the National Reading Conference, Clearwater, FL.

———. 1983a. *Family literacy: A descriptive study of Black children living in poverty who are successfully learning to read and write.* Report submitted to the Elva Knight Research Committee of the International Reading Association.

———. 1983b. *Family literacy: A study of Black inner-city children successfully learning to read and write.* Research proposal submitted to the National Institute of Education.

———. In press. Growing up literate: Learning from inner-city families. *The Journal of Negro Education.*

Taylor, D., and D. S. Strickland. 1986. Family literacy: Myths and magic. In M. R. Sampson (ed.), *The pursuit of literacy: Early reading and writing.* Dubuque, Iowa: Kendall/Hunt Publishing Company.

Teale, W. H. 1986. The beginnings of reading and writing: Written language development during the preschool and kindergarten years. In M. R. Sampson (ed.), *The pursuit of literacy: Early reading and writing.* Dubuque, Iowa: Kendall/Hunt Publishing Company.

Turnbull, C. M. 1983. *The human cycle.* A Touchstone Book. New York: Simon & Schuster.

Wagner, J, ed. 1979. *Images of information: Still photography in the social sciences.* Beverly Hills: Sage Publications.

Worth, S. 1980. Margaret Mead and the shift from "visual anthropology" to the "anthropology of visual communication." *Studies in Visual Communication* 6 (1): 15–22.